"Margaret Gibson's evocation of urban southern society in the 1950s is so on target it's scary. This is a brilliant book."

—Shannon Ravenel, cofounder of Algonquin Books

"With the fine line drawing of an acute novelist, Margaret Gibson has given us not only an enthralling memoir of family portraits but also a powerful evocation of history. The world of her story is the genteel white South on the cusp of the great change of civil rights—a story too little told from this vantage point and with such unguarded candor. She tells it with integrity and heart, but always with fierce clarity. I laughed, I sighed, I was there. A remarkable achievement."

—Patricia Hampl, author of *I Could Tell You Stories: Sojourns in the Land of Memory*

"Margaret Gibson's *The Prodigal Daughter* is a lovely memoir, rich with family history, vivid details, and a lively sense of storytelling. It is a moving story of self-discovery and awareness within a complex family portrait."

—Jill McCorkle, author of *The Cheer Leader*

"Amid Margaret Gibson's descriptions of the song of a mockingbird, the hard ways of sisters with each other, schooldays in Richmond, and her own growing into knowledge, difference, and indeed love, lie the stuff of all people's lives, thus transforming a bookish evening into an experience shimmering with light, enjoyment, and above all happiness."

—Sam Pickering, author of *Indian Summer: Musings on the Gift of Life*

D1373950

# The Prodigal Daughter

# The Prodigal Daughter

## Reclaiming an Unfinished Childhood

Margaret Gibson

University of Missouri Press
Columbia and London

Library of Congress Cataloging-in-Publication Data

Gibson, Margaret, 1944–
    The prodigal daughter : reclaiming an unfinished childhood / Margaret
Gibson.
          p. cm.
    Summary: "Gibson recounts her childhood in conservative Richmond,
Virginia, and her growing estrangement from her sister and parents.
Returning home years later to meet the needs of her stroke-crippled sister
and her incapacitated parents, Gibson offers a deeply moving recounting of
her reconciliation with the family she left behind"—Provided by publisher.
    ISBN 978-0-8262-1783-7 (alk. paper)
    1. Gibson, Margaret, 1944– —Childhood and youth.   2. Gibson, Margaret,
1944– —Family.   3. Women poets, American—Family relationships.   4. Adult
children of aging parents—Family relationships.   5. Sisters—Family
relationships. I. Title.
    PS3557.I1916Z46 2008
    811'.54—dc22
    [B]

                                                            2007035578

Designer: Jennifer Cropp
Typesetter: BookComp, Inc.
Printer and binder: Thomson-Shore, Inc.
Typefaces: Palatino, Cochin, New Berolina

This book is dedicated to
the memory of my parents and my sister.

---

Love bade me welcome: yet my soul drew back. . . .
"You must sit down," said Love, "and taste my meat."
So I did sit and eat

—George Herbert

# Contents

The author gratefully acknowledges the editors of the following publications in which the chapters listed first appeared, sometimes in different forms: *Blackbird:* "The Queen of Hearts" and "South-bound," Spring 2007 and Fall 2007, respectively; *Creative Non-Fiction,* "Thou Shalt Not Kill," 1992; *Image,* "Faith, Hope, and Charity," Fall 2007; *Southern Review,* "Catechism," Fall 2007.

I would like to thank early readers of this manuscript, especially Joanne Barkan, who read chapter by chapter as the book evolved and whose comments and encouragement were essential. Grateful thanks also to Mary Flinn, Louis D. Rubin Jr., Shannon Ravenel, and especially to my husband, David McKain. And praise be for Beverly Jarrett at the University of Missouri Press! I am also grateful to my fine editor, Jane Lago, for her comments and insights.

Whenever I was in Richmond over the last decade, I would have had no "home place" without my good friends Ellen Williams, Tina Lewis, and Mary Flinn; my cousin Anne Simmons; and my cousin Leigh Doyle—all of whom opened their homes and their hearts, told me their stories, and made the long journey home one we shared together. I would also like to thank the staff of The Chesterfield at Brandermill Woods for their care of my parents and my sister: especially Holly DeJarnette, Tracy Daniels, Kim Able, Cindy M., Cindy D., Bonna, James and Helen Thompson, Susie West, Tara, Katedra, Linda, Florence, Barnsy, Carolyn, Irene, and Patsina. Thanks also to Linda Call and Vic Harper for their invaluable help to my family over the years. I would also like to acknowledge with love and gratitude my favorite aunts, Louise Doyle Fultz and Billie Ferguson Poag, who told me family stories and showed me photographs.

None of the characters in this memoir are fictional; however, some names have been changed.

Above all, he thought of his childhood, and the more calmly he recalled it, the more unfinished it seemed. . . . To take the past upon him once more, and this time really, was the reason why, from the midst of his estrangement, he returned home. We don't know whether he stayed there; we only know that he came back.

—Rainer Maria Rilke

# The Prodigal Daughter

1

## *Southbound*

---

## June 2002

Southbound, the train leaves New London station in bright morning light. I've stowed my suitcase and taken a seat by the east window to watch the river, its surface so silken that the pilings of an
abandoned pier reflect, refract, and plunge like roots through the
flowing mirror that carries an ash-blue streak of cloud, a shining
sky. At the mouth of the broad river, out where the saltwater of the
Sound absorbs the fresh water of the river, a small red house flashes
in a shimmer of sun, a lighthouse in every sense of the word.

The wind has risen and now ruffles the water, and in the change
of light I remember the small red brick house, far south in Virginia,
where I spent a shy childhood anchored to my mother. The *little red
hen house* she had called our home in Richmond. The affectionate
nickname not only revealed her deeper roots in the farm fields of
Dinwiddie and Amelia Counties, it also showed how she deflected
disappointment—she turned a phrase, she put on a good face. From
her, from my withdrawn father, from my difficult sister, and from
conventional west-end Richmond—"the center of social rest" as I've
heard it called on a nationally televised newscast—I had been running away most of my life—because, as I used to tell myself, *I was
different.*

With a shriek of its whistle, the train gets under way.

I keep three black-and-white family snapshots in my wallet, and,
as the train car rattles south, I take them out. They are not gems of
wholeness, harmony, and radiance, but they seem decisive. Here I
am standing alone, dressed for church, in a full skirt and small hat
that tells me it's the 1950s. I am eleven, posed in the front yard, sun
full in my face. The sun shines white on the grass of the well-cut

1

yard, onto which a shadow falls. The photographer's shadow spreads onto the grass between me and him, inky black. It is a silhouette of head and shoulders, and although I recognize the silhouette taking the picture as my father's, it now also seems to be the shadow of death. I hear my parents reciting in unison the Twenty-third Psalm. This is the Valley of the Shadow of Death. Death is taking my picture, the same Shadow of Death I confused as a child with God. Death the Maker of Things Invisible was also God the Father, Creator of All Things, Author and Lord of the Visible, Judge and Justifier. To see God, I remember thinking, you had to die.

And here is my mother. There is something in her eyes and the set of her smile as she looks through the camera, through even my father, who is most likely holding the camera, an ensnaring beyond flirtation, a possession that has leaped over desire and its obstacles, over the finite and the uncertain. She has won. She is unsurpassable. Whoever you are, within this gaze she has you. In glory, she will enter the Kingdom, a triumphant mother, a child of God to the end of time.

The third photograph gives me, at first glance, my cousin Jane and me. Jane, a slim and lovely young woman, holds me in her lap. I am four, dressed in a dotted-swiss dress I remember was pink and which I wore for church or for company coming. Between Jane's body and mine, there is a darkness out of which an arm strains into the light beneath only part of a face. It's hard to see my sister—Betsy, as we called her then—but there she is, squirming her way into the picture, struggling to be seen. Although I appear innocent, even demure, looking down at my patent-leather shoes, I lean back at an uncomfortable slant, using my body to block my sister from Jane's lap and evidently from my mind. For the years I didn't want see my sister, she wasn't there. I turn over the snapshot and find in my childish handwriting these words—*Jane and me.*

I shuffle through the three photographs again, ending with the one of me on the grass of the front yard. I inhale a scent of cut grass and lilac in our yard and the too sweet, nearly rotten scent of daffodils cut for the vase. I inhale again, and I smell summer heat on the sticky tar of Lexington Road, thunderclouds, the swell of rain, clean laundry on the line in the backyard, my mother's skin.

Aside from the years of World War II, my parents have lived in Virginia within a radius of seventy miles most of their lives, intimate with the look of things around them there—with the James River, mimosa, old fields of scotch broom and red clay; with red brick houses and magnolia trees and the sedate respectability of west-end Richmond. To see one magnolia tree anywhere might summon for them the avenue of magnolias in front of my aunt's stately house, Alandale, near Bon Air, where Dad grew up; to see an old barn with a slumped roof might remind them of the farm in Mom's Amelia County; one spreading oak might bring back with it the small red house where I lived with them, and with my sister, rubbing elbows and ideas, striking sparks from the friction.

Or are the oaks and magnolias, the barns and front porches, the cry of the backyard mockingbird for my parents only single sensations, lit for a moment, flying and flown, single notes in a passing moment? My parents are in their nineties, in residence in a nursing home. So much has slipped away. Emptiness in the mind: they must feel it spread and deepen, much as shadow takes a field into dusk and nightfall. To what we see, to what we think, to what we are, remembering offers an odd mix of distance *and* immediacy—an apparent contradiction resolved only by greater intimacy and depth, not by any easy harmony. Returning home, I realize, I'm now looking for memories we can hold in common; I'm looking for common ground.

And my sister, Liz, how does she see things, now that, bedridden or in a wheelchair, she looks out onto a field from a single window, the porch railing beyond it like prison bars. Aside from her honeymoon in Bermuda, my sister has lived all of her life in or near Richmond. If she was happy, or sad, I never knew for sure, and I didn't ask. In earlier years, she would have considered such questions—asked by me—absurd.

Now, from farther down the train car, a woman's voice rises and swells. She's talking on a cell phone without any idea of how far her voice carries. "I want to go home already," says the woman, now only five or ten minutes out of the station. "I want to go home," she says again, adding, "but I need to get away."

*I want to go home, I need to get away.* The train's refrain, heard at root level in the mind.

I remember how, having left home and my first marriage, I sent a card to my mother, signing it "The Prodigal," in my twenties focused on departure only, perpetual departure beyond anyone's reach. Back then, I thought that a change of location would be enough to confirm who I was. Living in Richmond was not for me. I could no longer, not without an angry struggle, talk to my family or my friends about politics—the war in Vietnam, the continuing Civil Rights movement. I was fed up with manners, with the politeness Thomas Jefferson called "artificial good humor." Manners my mother called *breeding*. In the eyes of most of the people I grew up with, manners were equivalent to virtue, and it was hard to convince Richmonders that manners and custom offered poor substitutes for right thought and right action. Nor could I talk to anyone, least of all myself, about religion. Raised a fundamentalist Presbyterian, in college educated as an agnostic, I threw up my hands, abandoned the field, and ran away full tilt into what I called my own life—that is, into the unacknowledged and unlived lives of my parents, my mother's in particular. She hid in the blind spot of my eye, in an inner room of my psyche for too many years. I might make my own choices, live my own life, but in the shadows she stamped her foot or offered whispered judgments. If anger is a variant of self-love, in those years I loved myself, did as I pleased, and was willing to live with the consequences and with the debts my willfulness ran up. I was *different*—by which I meant that I also had no reason to keep in touch with my conservative, materialistic sister. Let her have cars and clothes, the big boats, the house by the golf course. I had my books. Let her have the luxury of extra calories; I had the economy of poetry.

Out the train window, the phragmites sway like a wheat field, and I look out on hummocks of mud, low-tide mud, a bird in the marsh light. After a tunnel of trees, the world widens out into a clearing of light at Deep River's salt marshes. As I always do, I watch for the glint of the distant lighthouse, a compass needle at the horizon where the Sound and the sky meet. Once across the Connecticut River, I know where I'm heading. I feel it in my bones.

*Relax,* I tell myself. *It's hours and hours before you get there.*

And yet I'm in a hurry to get there. For years the far-flung daughter, I now have a new role in the family. My sister had been the daughter who stayed home, the late-favored one who gave my parents a grandchild. After her stroke, I'm the long-distanced caretaker and daughter-turned-mother—a southbound prodigal—more so now with my mother's deepening senility and loss of independence. She knows me, but she can't easily tell me how she is. She begins a sentence and breaks it off before she reaches the verb. Her startling aphasia is interrupted only now and then by the miracle of a complete sentence. She needs diapers. She needs a wheelchair. Her doctors don't think she'll recover what only months ago she took for granted. My mother had always been the boss; now she has sunk deeper into the quicksand we call second childhood. *Childhood*—a dark cloth pulled over the head. Confused by my mother's decline, my father calls me often, asking for advice. The miles and miles that had once protected me from them are now too many. Earlier in my life, I'd spent years running away; now I spend much of each year returning home. There's not much time left in the season of dying. It's time to mend, to sort through, to set to rights; it's time to heal, to recover, to get to know the strangers I call my family.

My eyes blur. I wonder if there's enough time. On my last visit, before she took her afternoon nap, my mother motioned me closer, something to tell me. The look on her face said she had a wisdom to impart. "Life is . . ." she began, and as I leaned in to listen during the long pause, ". . . something you wait for," she concluded, closing her eyes.

More than likely it will be my mother who will keep Death waiting. "I'm not leaving here until I know you'll be with me in Heaven," she once stated with implacable certitude, a few years back when she lived in the suite in Assisted Living.

"You may be here a long time, then!" I'd teased. But for my mother, then reclining with her two cats on the four-poster bed I called her throne and parliament, wearing an old bathrobe, her wig propped on the bedside table, neither my salvation nor the length of her mortal life were laughing matters. It nearly took my breath away, her unquestioned assurance of control—over God, over her own mortality, over me.

On the edge of her bed there had been her boxed Bible with the large print. In that box, carefully folded beneath the Bible, I had earlier that day found two of my mother's bras, both stretched out from carrying her womanly heft. I hadn't known whether to laugh or to cry, so I'd laughed—the Bible and her brassieres, her two principle means of support, nestled together for safekeeping. My mother was an angry woman in those years, someone who locked her door against the nurses and my father. "He comes in the middle of the night and takes my pills," she'd insisted. She took Valium for a condition she called "hot mouth."

"Dad has his own pills, Mom. He wouldn't take yours. Perhaps you're having a dream?" I was becoming used to offering both my mother and father "counsel."

"No, I see him with my own eyes. Them, too. I used to have, oh, eleven bras, and now it's a good day if I can put my hands on one."

Sorting through her things, I had found bras in coat pockets, in pillowcases, beneath towels, and in the boxed Bible whose lid, I'd noticed, was riding a little high.

"I want my family all around me," now she insisted, and I softened. Beneath the certitude was her loneliness, her fear of dying, her fear of living. Saving my soul was part of what she considered her mission in life. Saving my father's soul was also part of it, and that task had taken so much energy that she had refused to cultivate friendships or visit a library, volunteer for social activities or visit a sick relative. *I have to take care of your father,* she would say, his lack of social skills, his emotional unsteadiness the reasons she must isolate herself and him. Only once did she put aside her proffered excuses. "The truth is," she'd said, "I don't really trust people." When I asked her why, she waved her hand in a vague gesture that made her words disappear, as salt dissolves in water.

My parents are both able to move about in wheelchairs, or, on a good day, my father uses a walker. But it is my sister's fate to live the life of an old woman before her time. Liz lies in a single bed in a room she prefers darkened because the light hurts her eyes. The blinds are shut. She watches television all day in her isolation at Angel House, where her husband, unable to manage caring for her after her stroke, has taken her. Before her stroke, she led an active life. A partner with her husband in the printing company they pioneered together, she ate out every night, then raced to a marina near Norfolk each weekend to be on their yacht, embracing a life of material pleasure. After her stroke, unable to walk or use her left arm and leg, Liz has become dependent on others to move from her bed, to dress, to toilet. She can't read, although her memory is sharp. Her left hand has closed into a shape that resembles how she held her hand as a child when she wanted to cast the shadow of a snouted beast on the wall to scare her older sister.

"No matter what happens," Liz likes to remind me, "I'll always be younger than you are." Once when she said that, she winked and grinned at me. I saw her as a young girl in a rakish hat and a plaid wool coat, the coat buttoned tightly around her stout body as she squinted into the camera, mischievous. Even then, the light had hurt her eyes.

"That's because my eyes are blue, yours are brown," she likes to remind me. "I got all the bad genes."

Bad genes? My mind follows her words into a memory of lunch at the restaurant my sister had picked out. She and I were taking our parents to lunch, the first meal the four of us had had together after years of strain and misunderstanding as my parents, confusing love and money, prudence and control, took away the power of attorney from my sister—considered a prodigal spendthrift—and gave it to me. After my sister's campaign of reproachful and angry silence, they'd compromised and ordered a jointly held power of attorney, a possible way for us all to make amends. As we sat together as a family in the restaurant, the three of us watched my sister eat mud pie for dessert. In two months, Liz would have the stroke that would knock her unconscious in her kitchen, but we didn't know that as she ordered dessert. She insisted on dessert. We knew she was diabetic and seriously overweight. But we were too respectful of the artificial peace to say, *Stop this. You know you're hurting yourself. Stop.*

Forkful by forkful, Liz ate steadily, luxuriously. *This is to die for,* she said. *This is to die for.*

After her husband called to tell me that Liz had suffered a massive stroke, my body often felt heavy and numb, dumb and inattentive. I startled easily. I forgot what I was doing. I couldn't listen to ordinary conversation. Twice I wandered into the bathroom and peered into the mirror on the medicine cabinet and told my reflection, "Your sister's had a stroke."

In Richmond, when I entered her room at the rehab facility—primarily a convalescent home with a rehabilitation department and a reputation for good care—a nurse was smoothing the top sheet over Liz's body, a white mound. I couldn't see her face yet, blocked by the nurse, who was removing a lumpy plastic bundle—a soiled diaper, I suddenly realized, embarrassed for my sister. Awkwardly I balanced the large vase of roses I'd just bought for her, looking around for a place to put it down, unwilling to look at my sister until the nurse had taken away the diaper. I found an empty shelf over the television, and I put the vase of roses there, glad the flowers were colorful, the arrangement bountiful, easy for her to see from a distance.

"Look," she told me, uncovering her left leg from the sheet. She wiggled her toes. "My friend Christy came and painted them."

Her toenails, which had been coated with a lacquer clear as the white of an egg, with flecks of glitter added in, flashed like mica, like quartz in stone.

"She wanted me to have sparkly toes," she added, laughing. As she laughed, I saw how crooked her mouth was. She saw me noticing.

"I'm supposed to say *Eeeee*, so the corners of my mouth stretch out, and it's working. You should have seen me before." She repeated *Eeeee*, and the long E vowel worked the affected muscles, her face now a parody of smiling. So that I wouldn't reveal in my own face mounting shock and concern, I looked around for a chair. Finding none on the nearest side of the bed, I sat on the edge of the mattress.

I said back to her *Eeeee*, and patted her good right leg. "That's good." And we both laughed. My monkey-face response, my mirroring, which might have risked her thinking I was making fun of her, had made a bond between us. We were children together again. That we could make faces at each other and laugh—that was a good sign. I thought of what long ago our family had called her, "bouncing Betsy," and I began to tear up.

"Look, I brought you flowers," I said quickly, turning my body in the direction of the roses. "And I brought some lotion. Why don't I give you a foot rub?" I began rummaging around in my knapsack.

Liz nodded. "Don't mind me if I drift off a bit." She closed her eyes after asking me to turn on the CD player beside her bed. "That's the music we used to put on when we went to sleep on the boat," she told me, opening one eye. Her face contorted, froze into a mask of grief, then smoothed out. The overwhelming feeling passed. "I've named my left arm Lazarus," she said suddenly. "I'm going to get back to where I was. I talked to God about it."

When she closed her eyes again, I poured a puddle of lotion onto my palm. In Connecticut, I had decided on touch, not talk. In our family, no one knew the gentle art of honest conversation, of talking over our differences. Instead we tripped over our words and tumbled into silences that were constricted, not spacious, the wrong sort of tie that binds. Words might be my way of attempting repair and solace. But my sister, I'd finally realized, after years of too much mud pie needed a way to bridge distances that soothed the body first. Boldly, I began the massage on her left side, avoiding the bulk of her body, keeping my focus on her affected leg, hoping that my hands would transfer to her body an acceptance and compassion, a nurture I'd never given her.

We had been sisters for more than fifty years, but I couldn't remember ever touching her body like this. One measure of love is loss; I wondered if Liz loved her body less, or more, now that she had lost the use of her left arm and leg. As I massaged her leg, wondering what she could feel, I began to hear our mother's voice, the door to our childhood bedroom narrowed open, my mother singing into the dark where Liz and I lay unready for sleep. She was singing the lullaby that ends "all through the night." I couldn't remember the rest of the words, but I could still see her, about to withdraw, and the stroke of light that crossed the coverlet as her alto patience and intimate refrain lilted over us, like a hand stroking back damp hair from a feverish forehead.

Who knows if the body believes the words we offer it, or if it listens only to the motive below the motive, octaves down. As my hands touched my sister's immobilized flesh, we were once again side by side in the dark of our old bedroom. Once again we were children, our small bodies already ripening to the sweet danger within us.

Were anyone to ask me now if I believe in resurrection, body and mind, I'd have to hum what little I remember of the song that long ago had carried us all through a night that was deeper than we could have known. As I massaged her legs, as my body faintly rocked back and forth to increase the rhythm, all the years I forgot to remember her, all the years I scorned and disregarded part of my own heart, fell away, and it came to me in a shudder of surprise that I had, all these years, loved her without knowing that I loved. What was it in me that had concealed that love so stubbornly? How was it possible to love and not to know?

"I see you," Liz said, opening her eyes and looking to the side of herself she neglected, finding me there.

Because I didn't want to cry, I said, "I see you, too, silly," and we laughed again. Neither of us wanted to cry, not yet. Liz said *Eeeee* and gave me her new, crooked smile.

"Don't stop," she added, nodding at the bottle of lotion. "It may sound absurd, but it makes me feel almost human. Please don't stop."

All that long day, I stayed with my sister. Even in the dark, I sat by her bed until she seemed to sleep. Before I left her room in the rehabilitation facility, thinking her asleep, I said quietly, standing at the door as our mother had for a moment as her song became the silence that held us, "See you in the morning." I had only whispered the words, but Liz caught them.

"I'll be right here," she said.

Close to Richmond now, the train passes through the small town of Ashland. As it rocks past the main street of shops and old Victorian houses under big oaks and maples, I remember how, in earlier years, I would look for the man in the wheelchair, who from the front porch door of his house would wave a handkerchief as wide as a towel at the train whose windows must have reflected clouds and the branches of the oak trees. Through these reflections and the flashing of light, he must have been able to see the silhouettes of passengers, their lives in motion, passing through.

On this trip I am helping my father clear out some of my mother's things.

"You won't believe what I'm finding in Mom's little pine chest," I tell my sister when I visit her in Angel House, talking to her about all the clutter of Mom's belongings, trying to keep her part of it, if in words only. "Ten pairs of white gloves and a box of yellowed engraved calling cards with her name, Mrs. John Spears Ferguson, embossed on them."

"She must have had them printed when she and Dad got married—1939."

I nod. "And I found a linen cloth with the word *Baby* embroidered on it in blue—much too fine to have been used for any baby."

"Probably the boy Mom didn't have. The miscarriage before you."

Liz looks close to tears again—since the stroke, the slightest thing can get her stuck in a mire of melancholy—and so I rush on, telling her about the file cards I've found with Mom's favorite recipes. "One is for chocolate icing—remember licking the spoon?"

She remembers and smiles.

"And, look here, I found the angels you asked about."

Because Penny, who runs Angel House, loves angels, Liz wanted me to bring her the little figures—*a gift for my keeper* she had said wearily. Apple-cheeked, the angels are identical in their neat blonde braids, idealized faces, and choir robes. Each little mouth is a shapely zero of wordless song. Each year at Christmas, my mother would unpack them and place them on the mantel, along with holly and running cedar and candles. *My two girls,* she'd say, nodding at the look-alike angels and smiling. But I was the blonde; Betsy had dark curly hair, and hair color only began the list of differences.

Now I put the angels on Liz's bedside table in the darkened bedroom at Angel House. My sister squints at them and laughs. "I remember them in the living room, on the desk. They're supposed to be you and me." Then her face contorts. After a few minutes she says quietly, "Why did Mom love you better than me?"

For once in my life, I don't try to answer her with excuses, speculations, reasons. I let the question float in the good silence between us, and I rub her arm. "I don't know," I finally say softly. "I don't know."

It all began in love, I think, looking at the two angels. It all began in love, and then something went wrong. The old silences between my sister and me are only part of it. How many times did I take out a photograph of my mother and study it in silence when I might have more usefully talked to her, confronted her, made my peace? I remember back to the times—away from home, independent, "successful"—I'd stayed up late, drinking alone, talking to my own image in the mirror, saying the things I wouldn't admit any other way.

In the house where I grew up, to say *I give you my word* was a pledge to be truthful. *Telling a story*—that was a euphemism for lying. To keep one's word was to honor a promise, but I think now that we kept our words too often hidden, secret from each other, secret from ourselves.

I wonder suddenly if my mother is still waiting to have the talk with me we'd never had, waiting to be offered what she felt she'd never been given. I wonder if we're not, all three of us, behind our different adult masks, children in hiding, arrested in some bedrock form of desire or fear.

After a while, I open the blinds to let some of the too bright light into Angel House, and Liz and I sit side by side at the bright window—she in her wheelchair—both of us squinting. She has a sketch pad and crayons beside her. I watch as, to my surprise, Liz draws what might be a kindergarten child's classic view of home. As a girl, she had enjoyed painting with oils, and her work was skilled. Now she takes up a stout crayon and draws a house with a peaked roof and a central door, squares for windows, a chimney with smoke curling out in loops and zeros. Then a tall tree with a cloud puff of green crown. Her sun is a circle with sharp radiating blades, the yellow core of a daisy with a sharp ruff of petals. *She loves me, she loves me not.*

"It's 37 Lexington Road," Liz says, laying aside the crayons. She doesn't say *our house.* She doesn't call it *the home place, our childhood home,* or *the little red henhouse.* Without any feeling in her voice, she simply gives an address. In all the snarled and dead-end circuits of her brain, she still knows, reluctantly, her way there. When she says, "Take it to Mom and tell her it's from me," I have to swallow hard before I can trust myself to answer lightly, "Sure, I'll be glad to."

I ask Liz if she remembers Mom's singing to us before sleep, and she shakes her head.

"I just remember all the things we didn't have." She pauses. "I told one of the nurses at rehab that the one good thing the stroke had given me is that we're together," Liz says, her voice firm. "We're friends."

"It feels good, doesn't it?"

"It's the way it should have been all along," Liz says, her voice as entirely free of blaming as I hope my discovery of love for her is free of pity, tinged more by gratitude and compassion.

When it is finally time for me to return and finish sorting and packing Mom's things, Liz launches into a series of jokes, one after another, jokes she has told me on the phone over and over. Clearly she doesn't want me to leave.

"Did you hear the one about the blonde who stood for hours looking into the refrigerator?"

I shake my head, wanting to leave, wanting to go before the tenderness I feel for her dissolves into impatience.

"When they asked her why she stood there staring at the orange juice, unable to move, she says: Well, the container says *Concentrate*." She laughs and begins to reel off another dumb blonde joke—breaking it off unexpectedly.

"When are you coming back?"

"How about later today? After I've done what I can with Mom's stuff—I have to spend time with Mom and Dad, too." It is, I hope, a gentle reminder.

She nods then looks at her left hand, the fingers curled inward. Using her good hand, she shifts Lazarus to the right. When she isn't mindful of her weak side, her left hand slides over the armrest and dangles onto the wheel of her chair. She looks into her lap for a long moment. I think she is going to say, "I'll be right here," but she surprises me again.

"Don't go," she says. "Tell me a story."

## 2

## Angel in the Window

The last syllables of the lullaby dissolved into the word *night*. Outside, the night was changing from deep blue to black with stars. It was cold for March. A wind had blown all day, and I could still hear it as the word *night* died into the hum of our mother's rich contralto, her song a lingering vibration as she paused in the open doorway, her body backlit by the light in the short hallway that separated her bedroom from ours. As she stood with the light behind her body, the firm flesh I liked to press myself into thinned to shadow and silhouette. I couldn't see her face, but I hoped she was smiling into the dark room where my sister and I lay in our twin beds. Tired from sewing the white dresses with the red smocking we would in a few weeks wear for Easter, she had put us to bed earlier than usual. The wedge of light in the doorway narrowed as she pulled the door toward her, quickly and certainly, leaving no time for Betsy to call out, "Sing it again!" Nothing remained of her dark form. There was only the dark of the room.

What was left of the lullaby shimmered in the thread of light, straight and thin, beneath our door, which had shut with the finality of our mother's scissors nipping off thread when she whipped the last amazing loop into the hem of a dress. Betsy called Mom's thimble a fairy hat, and she wanted it for her thumb. She had hidden it away in the pocket of her bathrobe, from which I would retrieve it in the morning, to put back into the sewing box before mother missed it. Why was Betsy always taking things? I couldn't keep her out of trouble, as Mom asked me to, and often I didn't want to.

The dark of the room was fearful, and I inched my small body further down beneath the heavy wool blankets and cold sheets tucked tightly around me. I was in a cocoon, my mother had said when she tucked me in. My bed was near enough to Betsy's that we could reach outside the covers and touch hands, but I didn't want to. It was cold in the room. I whispered the word *night*, humming to myself what the song said, *all through the night*. The prayer Betsy and I had chanted aloud, blessing our mother and father—and each other, even if we didn't want to—contained words that haunted me when the room went dark. *If I should die before I wake, I pray the Lord my soul to take.* The soul was not a thimble, not a dress. It wasn't anything outside me that I could touch or see or smell or hear. It wasn't a lullaby or a door or a blanket. I had my blanket up to my nose. Just beyond the folded cuff of the sheet, the wool smelled like graham crackers and cold air.

To die, my mother said one morning in the kitchen, washing dishes while I pretended to be eating my oatmeal, was like going to sleep. When she was in her coffin, she wanted to wear a bathrobe, billowy and powder blue, like clouds and sky. People would say, "She's only sleeping." Right now, my body was gradually warming the cold sheets, and I wasn't as frightened as I'd been only moments before, trying to understand how the Lord could take my soul if it wasn't anything anyone could touch or see or smell or hear.

Before we said our prayers, Mom read Bible stories to us. Last night the story was about Joseph who had dreams and a coat with many colors in it. Joseph learned important things in dreams, and he was wise. Tonight the story was about Jacob and Esau, brothers who didn't like each other. Esau came home very hungry and gave up his inheritance—all the money he would ever have—for a mess of pottage, which was maybe like oatmeal. Betsy would do that, but I wouldn't. Tomorrow was Saturday—we were spared oatmeal on Saturday. If I went to sleep quickly, I would wake up in Saturday morning, it would be sunny, and the four of us would sit around the white tin-topped table in the kitchen. Betsy would try to sit in Daddy's lap, and Mom would give me her special smile and forget about making me eat. Her special smile was like sunlight.

I knew that soon after we fell asleep my mother would open the door, so that she could see us from her bed. If I needed to get up to use the potty at the foot of the bed, she would shine the flashlight on me—so that I could see, she said. The gauzy beam of light from the flashlight was a magical cord that bound me to her, and I tried to pee as slowly as I could, even though the floor beneath my feet was cold. The light was the *blest be the tie that binds*, and it bound me to her—

and only me, because Betsy was sleeping over there in the dark, safe and sound under her own heavy blanket, and out of the light.

The room was so dark I could hear my breathing. I could hear my heart beating. I checked to see if I could lift both my hands and my head out from the heavy covers into the air. One night, lost in a thick hollow, tucked in tightly on three sides, turned head down into the bottom of the bed, I'd thrashed about, certain that I'd been swallowed whole. In my panic, unable to find the way to the top of the bed and to air, I'd called out so loudly my mother came running, her comforting so urgent that I'd felt more deeply afraid, even in her arms. If it should happen again, I promised myself I wouldn't call out. Making the promise made me know I was afraid, even if I told myself I wasn't.

Why was I still awake? From underneath the blanket I asked the stars that were pasted on the ceiling over the bed. Because I couldn't see them, I pretended that I was in the crooked branch of the plum tree in the backyard. It was already a mass of blooms that were a color like no other: not red, not purple, not pink. *Mauve*, my mother said, a word that sounded like a name that belonged to an old maid. When I lay back in the Y branch of the plum tree and closed my eyes, I whirled far above our house and yard, above the oaks of Stonewall Court, beyond the city of Richmond and the state of Virginia, beyond the United States and the earth and the ocean, beyond even the wind. In the plum tree, it was no longer 1950. It was the beginning of creation. If I closed my eyes and concentrated, I could fly beyond the force of gravity, into the fields of grace and light, into the garden of the stars. And there I fell asleep.

Because the kitchen was small, we were supposed to stay in our places at the table. We couldn't leave the table without asking, "May I be excused?" Both Mom and Dad had to hear us ask, and they had to say *yes* out loud before Betsy or I could get up. *Not until you clean your plate* was the answer I got most often.

Nothing was on my plate yet, and I was free to look about the kitchen. I could look at the kitchen by closing my eyes and simply breathing in. The damp smell of dishtowels left on the edge of the sink. The frying bacon smell and the bubbly smell of coffee perking. My hands, scrubbed with Ivory soap. Even the sunlight. Coming in on a slant from the window over the sink behind me, it carried the scent of leaves and grass and made the tin top of the table into a lawn. I could also smell the early morning cold-cement smell of the back stoop.

I opened my eyes. I had left the back door open on purpose, hoping to catch a glimpse of the milkman. I'd put two empty pint bottles carefully into the wire rack the night before. The milkman came later on Saturday than on weekdays. He'd replace the empties with two bottles of milk with the cream at the top, cream my parents put in their coffee to change it from black to light brown. Carrying the milk was a white man's job, at least in this neighborhood, Mom said. I was hoping I'd see his face, and then I could tell if Betsy looked like him.

My father's side of the family said I looked like my father; on my mother's side, the family said I looked like a Doyle. My mother called herself Doyle, not Mattie Leigh, a name she shunned, even though she had been named for her mother. I was named Margaret Leigh, named for my mother—and that settled it, Mom said. I'd be just like her. She must have forgotten that I had brown eyes, not hazel, and my legs were lanky, a length of bone that promised to be more Ferguson than Doyle.

No one on either side of the family knew who Betsy resembled. She was short, with blue eyes, curly brown hair, and freckles. And she was chubby. If looks alone were the link, Mom couldn't claim her and neither could Daddy. Aunt Mimi had joked about the milkman—he brought her, and that's who she looked like. Mimi was always making Mom laugh at things Mom didn't really think were funny. That's because she was Dad's older sister, and he had been bossed all his life by her and by Nanny, his mother. "They've told him what to think all his life," Mom complained, but she told him what to think, too.

I wanted to see the milkman with my own eyes. I wanted to be the judge, even though I knew I wouldn't be allowed to contradict my elders, even if I was right.

"Cat got your tongue?" asked Dad, catching my eye. He sat opposite me, nearest the icebox, the pantry closet, and the doors. One door led to the living room, one led out to the kitchen stoop, and one led down the stairs to the fearful basement. No one could come in or go out of the kitchen without getting by Daddy. Sometimes, when Mom went to the icebox for the eggs, she stood so near him, he ran his hands up her skirt, playfully, so that Mom pretended to be shocked and pushed him away with a light laugh, almost the same laugh she'd give when she read us stories on the front porch and was happy. "I'll drop the eggs! We'll have to have scrambled!"

"Cat got your tongue," Dad repeated, his voice a little louder. Children should speak when spoken to and look the grown-up in the eye.

But I decided to risk it. I grinned at Daddy and showed him my tongue. Betsy kicked me under the table.

"That's not nice," she taunted, wanting to get me in trouble.

Dad asked if the coffee was ready, and when Mom didn't answer he stood partway up, leaned over, and took the tin percolator from the stove. "It smells ready," he said, pouring himself a cup. I tried to understand my mother's silences. There were things you kept to yourself, she always said.

"I want the money, can I have the money?" Betsy cried out, reaching toward his cup with her teaspoon. By *money* she meant the bubbles that formed on the surface of the freshly poured coffee, each bubble a coin in the bank, if you gathered them in your spoon and ate them before they popped. When they popped, your fortune went up in air. We didn't have a real fortune. We had coffee bubbles and expenses. Girls were more expensive than boys were, but expenses were also called *bills*. Wasn't that funny? Words were more fun to play with than coffee bubbles.

Mom usually said that coffee stunted our growth, and we shouldn't drink it. "Just five pennies," Betsy begged.

"Five," Mom agreed. "Five pennies, not five teaspoons."

"I'm a poor man," Dad laughed. "I need my pennies. I'm still waiting for my ship to come in."

The ship he was waiting for was sailing far away down the river on the blue-and-white china plate before me. I loved our plates because there was a story in the middle, even if none of us could agree what the story was. The plates were decorated with a blue-and-white floral border, blossoms that looked just like the winter aconite under the box bushes under Mom and Dad's bedroom window. There were also daisies and roses and tiny peonies, and these convinced me that the plate showed us the garden of Eden. There were rivers and mountains in the distance and a man and a woman in a garden looking at that ship sailing in.

"How do you know when your ship comes in it's not pirates?" Betsy asked, sucking all the money flavor from her spoon.

Just when I wasn't looking, two eggs slipped from the spatula onto my plate. Two eggs joined together sunny-side up, two strips of bacon, one piece of toast, buttery and gummy and limp. Mom hadn't put the lid over the pan to cloud the yolks, so the sun at the center shone like July. The trembling whites made my stomach turn upside down—especially the little goose pimple of white at the rim of the yolk.

Mom and Daddy were now already eating. I watched them chewing. Eating looked easy, but it wasn't. A slippery stain of yellow was on Dad's chin, and because it was Saturday he hadn't shaved yet. Mom was sitting next to me—close to the stove so I can reach things, she explained—but I thought she liked to sit next to me so she could slip little bits of more food on my plate. At the moment, she wasn't paying attention to Betsy or to me. They were talking about when to go to the Safeway and what would make the gardens in the backyard more lovely.

"Let's play forts," I suggested to Betsy, and we began to make our preparations. The white of the egg was a moat, the yellow was the fort, and the bacon strips made drawbridges over the moat and into the fort. The trick was to put down a bridge as a tease and then flip it back up before the attacking army—the fork—could get over the moat and break down the castle wall. When the egg yolk ran over everything, you lost. You didn't have to eat the egg as long as it was whole.

Betsy nibbled one strip of bacon. She was waiting for me to make the first move, I thought. But I didn't have a chance to attack.

Up came the hand she'd been holding in her lap—we were supposed to keep one hand in our lap, so as not to appear greedy. But hers already held her fork—she didn't have to reach across from right to left to pick it up. Already she was calling, "Bombs away!"

Mom, I noticed, was smiling at her.

Why was she smiling? She wanted us to eat food while it was hot. She didn't like us to play games at the table.

As Betsy's fork broke down my fort wall, I understood. Mom was smiling because, if I lost the war, I'd have to eat. That was the rule.

Mom was on Betsy's side—they were in cahoots. Betsy liked to eat, and I didn't.

"If you don't eat your egg, you'll end up just like Miss Moon," Mom warned.

Miss Moon's chauffeur picked us up on the way to Collegiate School down Monument Avenue on the days Daddy was out of town and couldn't drive us to school on his way to work. Miss Moon's house on Cary Street Road had a tower and an elevator. I thought her wheelchair was solid silver, but Mom said it was only silver color. Miss Moon had beautiful white hair, but she couldn't walk, even though she wasn't that old. She'd had polio. If you didn't eat your eggs, you got polio, Mom said; when she wanted me to eat, she'd say anything. But if I contradicted Mom, I'd risk a trip with Dad to the basement.

"Now you have to take care of the wounded," Mom crooned gently, pointing to my bleeding egg. "Better call in the Red Cross." When I said nothing, she added, "Now you eat and no fuss. After breakfast I'll read another chapter from *Poppy the Fairy*."

While Mom read, I daydreamed the story, trying to see it. I knew the words nearly by heart. *By heart* was deeper than knowing something just in your mind. If you knew it by heart you loved it word for word, the way I knew the lullaby Mom sang to us at night.

"But how did you get here?" persisted the Gentleman Giant. Listening with my eyes closed, I saw the illustration from the book, a large hand with Poppy in it, holding on for dear life to the Gentleman Giant's thumb. Poppy looked just like Betsy in a tap-dance costume. Short, chubby, dark curly hair. And always into something, making Mumsy tired or put out.

Once Mom had to chase Betsy, who was running away from a scolding, darting out the bedroom into the tiny hallway, round the corner to the living room. Close behind her, Mom slipped on the scatter rug in the hall and went down with a hard, dull slap on the wood floor. I ran over and was down on my knees next to her to see if she had skinned her knee, when she looked up, more angry than hurt, and cried out, "Look at *that*," nodding into the direction of Betsy's escape, "and look at *this*."

Her words drained away the concern I felt for her, which was replaced by an awkward feeling. I didn't think I'd done anything special. Anyone would help someone who fell down, if she saw, and

Betsy hadn't seen. All the rest of the day Mom treated me as if I was someone special, someone attached to her, her right hand. Gradually, I got used to it. Then I liked it.

*"You're not sorry you're here, are you Poppy?" asked the Gentleman Giant.*

*"Not if you like me," said Poppy. "I'd love to stay as long as you like me."*

Mom was reading those words from the book when Daddy appeared at the door to the kitchen. "Who wants to go to the Safeway?" he asked looking at Betsy, and Betsy bounded out of her chair before he finished the sentence. I put the bookmark in the book, lost in the thought that I just wanted to stay little and remain at home with Mom. But she was going to the store, too, so I got up and raced Betsy to the car.

Another morning, a Sunday, the silence at the breakfast table let me know we were in for it. Dad had come to the table late. His eyes looked blurred. If his ship had come in, it had sunk before it reached the dock. If his ship had come in, the cargo had been spoiled. Mom was annoyed at every little thing, and she was stirring the oatmeal so briskly I almost felt sorry for it. Dad had cut himself shaving and had little bits of white toilet paper stuck to the razor nicks to stop the blood. Neither of them mentioned their dinner at his boss's house the night before.

Mr. Easton was Dad's boss, although he was shorter than Dad, wore glasses, and never smiled at anyone. Another bald man, who was Mr. Easton's boss, had come into town on business. Now that I thought about it, Dad had been grouchy all week, but the dinner just might be a special occasion Mom had said with a lilt in her voice. They'd gone off to dinner gaily and woken up glum. I'd heard their voices when they came home. I'd stayed awake to eavesdrop on the babysitter, who would without a doubt give a poor report of Betsy's and my behavior. From the moment Mom and Dad had left the house, Betsy and I had been in and out of bed, asking for stories or water, pestering the babysitter, asking for favors.

"Be good little girls," Alice had warned as she put us back into bed. Alice was the Sunday school helper, but she would not suffer the little children to come unto her, not any more. She was *responsible*. She could and would tell on us, and her telling would have consequences.

Sin was not *not* getting caught, Mom's voice in my head reminded me. Sin was disobedience in the first place. Satan was a voice inside you. Satan was a snake.

"We can't, she'll tell," I protested to Betsy once the room was again dark.

"Who cares?" she said, rashly I thought, considering the consequences. She should know what the consequences were. Her bruises were only just fading.

"She'll tell on us anyway," she said.

"We've already done it," she said. "Once more won't matter."

"This is war," she said, and I fell captive to her will.

Now Dad was looking up from his coffee, his voice quiet and dark. There would be no discussion of last night, he said, until after church. Betsy sneaked a look at me and winked. But she also drew in her breath. We were indeed in for it. My stomach knotted up, and I watched Mom shoveling the oatmeal into our bowls. Would I be able to eat?

"Such an embarrassment," she said to the wooden spoon. Did she mean us? Or had something happened at dinner at the Eastons' house? Mom was still wearing a hair net to protect her perm. Without knowing why, I felt sorry for her. We were in for it, I was certain of that, and I hated suspense. But something else was wrong, too. Mom's silence rubbed it in. She didn't look in Dad's direction the whole of breakfast, not even when his spoon slipped and he got a dab of oatmeal down his front. He was an embarrassment, too, and she was punishing him with silence.

Because I was older, after church I was sent down to the basement with Daddy's belt first, barefoot, wearing only the cotton slip Mom had made and my undies. My Sunday dress was hanging neatly in the closet. I wondered if Mom was in her bedroom. She would close herself off in there and lie down on her big bed when she was overcome and wanted to get away from us. Betsy was in our bedroom, obliged to wait. For a shadow of a second, I was glad I was older. Having to go first, I didn't have as long to imagine Dad's eyes steeply fixed on me, shining in a way they never did except in the basement. Today he was angrier than usual. Usually the flare in his eyes happened when he came down the stairs to the basement, ready to give the whipping. Today at the dining room table after Sunday dinner, as he and Mom tried to get Betsy's and my stories to match, he had said, "That's enough of your lies. If we can't get a single straight story, we'll take two little liars to the basement and see what you say then." His eyes had turned a darker, dangerous brown. Then they flared. Then they went flat and dead-looking. Before that look, I trembled, afraid I'd wet my pants.

There were clean, drying sheets from Friday's washing hanging on the wires. Could I hide behind them or roll myself up in one? Could I say, "Daddy, please . . ." or "Daddy, don't you dare . . ."? Anything I tried to say would only make it worse.

When I heard his footsteps on the stairs, I tried to measure his anger from the weight of his step on the treads. When he reached me, I handed him the belt without looking at him.

*Look at me,* I heard him say, his voice hoarse.

I looked.

*Are you sorry?*

"Yes," I whispered.

*Then say so,* I heard him say. I said so, but now I couldn't hear my own voice. Dad seemed very far away. As close as he was, he was speeding away, like a car backing into a tunnel. Where was he going?

*From now on, mind your mother,* he said.

*What else?* I heard him say.

I knew that "I don't know" wouldn't satisfy him, but I *didn't* know. Then I heard myself say, from far away, as if I had followed him into the tunnel. "For lying."

These were the right words, but where had they come from? I didn't think I had lied earlier, although my story was different from Betsy's. But it was a good idea to lie now, said the tiny voice inside. Whose voice was that? That it wasn't my idea to lie, but a good idea, scared me. That I was obeying someone inside me I didn't know also scared me.

*Don't be frightened,* said my father's distant voice.

I was watching the hand that held the belt, as if the belt were a black snake. Before he strapped me with the belt, I thought I'd see it writhe or coil or twitch. But I never saw it. The fierce stinging of the belt on my legs surprised me, and I covered my mouth to muffle the crying out.

Mom took Betsy to the top of the basement stairs, then came to comfort me. I wasn't crying. I was sitting on the side of my bed nearest the wall, looking at the wall. I wanted her to comfort me, but I didn't want her to say, *This hurts me more than you.* Or, *This is for your own good.* I don't remember what she said, and I didn't say anything for a long time. But then we heard Betsy scream, and Mom jumped up from the side of my bed and ran toward the kitchen.

I always imagined that what happened to me in the basement happened to Betsy. Dad would treat us both the same, because he and Mom always said they treated us the same. When Betsy came back into the room, however, I could already see the bruises and the red welts on her legs. Did he hit her harder? Dad said he didn't. Mom said Betsy's skin bruised more easily. Betsy said he hit her harder. I wondered how he could hit her harder if he loved her more. She was his favorite, and I was Mom's.

I looked at Betsy's tear-streaked face, and I tried to feel sorry for her. Was she thinking Dad didn't love her if he hit her harder?

"Today I hit him back," she told me, once she'd stopped crying. And then I understood. Dad could hit her harder, she could be his favorite, she could even hit him back. Anger was a tie that binds, too.

Mom hadn't come into the room to comfort her, and despite my not wanting to, I felt smug. Then grim. Everything hurt too much.

The next day was Monday, and we had school. I breathed easier. Dad would go to work, driving us down Monument Avenue past the statues of the soldiers of the South, heroes on horses, each facing the direction of his death. They were commanders who had fought the good fight. They made me think of giants and "the men of old" in the Bible. In school we'd read a book, do arithmetic, sound out consonants, and my teacher Miss Nancy Leake, who was pretty, would laugh. The pain would go away. We'd arrive home in Miss Moon's limousine because Daddy was still at work, and everything would be good again.

Across the room, Betsy was digging around in her drawer. She had stopped crying, but she wasn't speaking to me—a decision that made her feel her power. Then she said, "Look at this."

She was holding a ball of twine. She tied one end of the twine to the lamp between our twin beds and unraveled the ball down the aisle until she reached the opposite wall, knotting the twine to the knob on the toy chest.

"That's your side of the room, this is mine," she announced.

"East is east, and west is west," she added.

"You can't come on my side," she warned.

Mom won't let this happen, I thought, although I wasn't sure, and I felt trapped. I kept my voice low. "That's not fair," I said. "The door's on your side."

Betsy thought. "You can use the window," she said.

Daddy was splashing water, shaving in the bathroom, up early because this weekend was the Saturday he had Army Reserves. He would be gone all day. Betsy wasn't stirring, still asleep in the bed next to mine. Quietly I turned back the covers and made my way across the hall. Mom was a mound under the covers, breathing in and out, her eyes closed.

"I see you," she said.

How could she do that? See me with her eyes closed? But her voice was as warm as I knew her body would be under the covers. "Come on under," she said.

Mom had large breasts we called pillows when they were out of her bra. I liked to lie down next to her and put my head on her pillows and snuggle. "You're up early."

I didn't reply, quieted by her hand moving up and down my back gently. I wanted her to keep stroking my back.

"Will you always be here?" I asked in a little while.

"I'll try," she said, keeping her voice light as a feather. When her voice was like that, I wondered if what she said could be true.

"Tell me again how I was born." I liked to hear stories of the time before I could remember. I liked to hear stories about the months I had alone with Mom and Daddy, before Betsy came. Usually she'd tell me about my dark eyes, my perfect ten fingers and ten toes, and my button nose, tracing the features of my face with her finger as she named them. "Your bow-ribbon mouth," and her finger moved around it, bringing it into being again.

Today, she traced my eyebrows and eyes and dotted in my dimples. Then she had a frog in her throat and cleared her voice. "I waited three whole days for you, you slow-poke," she teased. "It's not easy, that waiting. I was in so much pain."

Thinking of my mother in pain made me cry. My cheek went wet against her shoulder.

"Why look at this," she said, surprised by my tears, then pleased. She held me closer to her. "You forget the pain," she promised, but I was angry with her body and with mine for the pain.

"Penny for your thoughts," she asked.

"It's okay, precious," she said, cooing a little. We were alone together in her big bed. No one could take her from me.

The following Saturday, when I returned to her bedroom in the morning, again early enough for Dad still to be pulling his T-shirt over his head, she said, "Hello, honey," as I got under the covers. "Do you want to snuggle in and cry some more?" Mom said, reaching for me. Surprising myself, I pulled away. Something wasn't right. I could feel it in the room, and so I looked at her carefully. Tenderly, with emphasis, she repeated the question, glancing over at Dad, who was watching us.

"C'mon, Doyle," he muttered.

Tentatively, I slid over next to her, but I kept my eyes on Dad.

"How's my angel?" he said, looking at me, his voice lighter. I felt his words tug me toward him.

Pinned to my mother's mirror, just beyond where he stood, was a yellowing newspaper photograph of me and two classmates, Marianne Graves and Helen Rose, the three of us dressed as angels. The two teachers and the photographer kept telling us how to stand, where to put our hands, smile now, hold it, don't move. Mom was so pleased with the photograph, she let it stay on the mirror, yellowing. She said I looked just like an angel. She said I had been chosen.

In the pageant, all the first graders were to be multitudes of the heavenly host. We wore the organdy shifts our mothers cut out from patterns and sewed—or had someone sew for them, for pay. The teachers had made the wings, and they glittered, pinned to our backs. The night of the pageant, all the first graders and their parents had to sit along the row of windows on either side of the nave. When the third grader who was Gabriel raised her golden trumpet, we were to be in place on the window ledges of the tall, cold stained-glass windows. Without our coats and shoes, we stood in the windows while the mothers trained their flashlights on their transformed daughters. Across the nave, I saw the other angels in their ovals of wavering light, the wings taking fire.

That's what I look like, too, I thought. First there's darkness and cold, and then, "Suddenly there was with the Angel, a multitude of the heavenly host. . . ." Out of nowhere, here I was, held in the magnet of my mother's light, glad to be here, smiling as brightly as I could, and very uncomfortable.

When the newspaper photograph had been taken, I'd felt posed. Prompted and posed, and I felt that way in the church window during the pageant, too. And that's how it feels right now, I thought, as my mother stroked my hair and my shoulders and pulled me closer, all the while keeping her gaze on my father. What was she up to? I felt like a spoon—special and silver, but something you used.

But then Daddy shrugged and went out on the front porch to find the newspaper. With a clatter of running feet and a shout, Betsy climbed into the bed with Mom and me, pushing over her leg, then over the rest of her, coming to rest in between my mother's body and mine. "My turn," she said, but Mom slipped out of the covers and began dressing for the day.

At the *Amen*, when the flashlights snapped off throughout the church, I had heard my classmates scrambling down from the windows to find their families in the darkened pews. I lingered a moment in the dark window, trying to sense the edge of the sill, the edge of the firmament, afraid I'd fall. But then my father's arms reached up and lifted me down to my mother's body, and I fit into the space between them in the dark. As long as I was an angel, I remember thinking, I could have them both.

# 3

## *Thou Shalt Not Kill*

When Amma came to Richmond from the country for dinner, she liked to be kissed right away, with the door still open behind her. I wanted to stand and look at her first, because we didn't see her often. We never went to her house in the country, somewhere near Amelia, and she came to Richmond only to visit her grown children, four of the seven she'd given birth to right at the farm, not in a hospital.

"Without a doctor?" I'd asked Mom.

"No doctor, only the good colored women, but they took care of her. They took care of all of us in the olden days," Mom said.

In her dark serge suit and black lace-up shoes, ruffled blouse, and black hat with the veil over her eyes, Amma didn't seem to match the soft greens and pinks of the living room. She wore pearls and carried her large black pocketbook with the loud, shiny clasp before her stomach, her gloves folded neatly and tucked over the rim of the black bag. For all the elegance of her tight-lipped pocketbook, she was poor, like us. She stood so upright, it was like kissing a statue. Because she had slept in my bedroom once before, I knew that what made her stout body so firm was the corset she wore under the black serge. Mom said she was "a Lady," but I liked it best when she took off her dark clothes in the bathroom and padded into the bedroom in her bare feet and long cotton nightgown, her long white hair falling like a winter waterfall down her back. A waterfall in sunlight, her hair shone from the one hundred strokes with the hairbrush every night. She let me pat her hair before she braided it into the pigtail that hung all the way to her knees.

After braiding her hair, Amma would kneel down beside Betsy's bed to say her prayers, and I knelt down beside mine. Betsy was sleeping in the living room.

"What did you say?" I asked her afterward. Betsy and I always prayed the "Now I Lay Me . . . Soul to Keep" aloud, and we listed the names of those we wanted blessed. Because she was listening, I said Amma's name and then all her children's names in order: Uncle Billy, Uncle Theo, Adelaide, Uncle Ashton, Mom, Dennis, and Louise, whom we called "Too-Too."

"Prayers are a private matter, Margaret Leigh," she answered crisply. "Only God hears mine."

When I asked Mom what she thought Amma prayed for, before Mom could answer, Dad, who never said anything mean about people, said, "Herself, of course."

When Amma visited, our house seemed to shrink, and when she left, it took a big gulp of air and breathed easier. I didn't know why. Surely it wasn't just because she sucked her teeth after dinner. The little "pfitz" sounds, repeated in a series of three and four "pfitzs" every few minutes, were annoying only to Dad, who hid behind the newspaper like Dagwood in the funnies. When Betsy and I got the giggles, listening to "pfitz-pfitz-pfitz," we'd run to our bedroom, where we put our heads facedown in our pillows so no one could hear us as we let the giggles loose. During Amma's visits, Mom cooked more than anyone, even Daddy, could eat, and she washed dishes afterward until she "dropped."

After she arrived on the Good Friday of Easter weekend, Amma gave Betsy and me the gifts she'd made especially for us. "You won't find these in any department store," she said crisply. Mom looked very pleased. We never received gifts from Amma, not even at Christmas. Amma's children had had children, and these children had had children—too may begats to make it practical for her to give gifts.

The gifts were "Mammy dolls," Amma said. She had made them from dead Mr. Waters's black socks and from bits of Amma's worn-out aprons and blouses. Mr. Waters, Mom explained later, was not my grandfather. He was Amma's second husband, a postman from right there in the country. Mom's father had died when she was eleven, but she wouldn't talk about it, except to say that Amma had made a white linen dress for her to wear to the funeral, a hot day in July. Two days before, my granddaddy had overworked in the field, getting the barley in, and he'd had a stroke. So the Mammy dolls made me think about my grandfathers when I tried to play with them. My Mammy doll looked dead, but it smelled like ironing, when the cloth is hot.

During Amma's visit, Mom made me keep the Mammy doll on my bed, propped up by a pillow. The minute Amma leaves, I thought, looking at the dead-man doll black as night, I'll take it to the basement and hide it in the crawl space and say I'd lost it. Betsy decided to name hers Sookie-Sue, a maid who would cook and clean and put away clothes for her. Because Sookie-Sue worked for her, Betsy stole pennies from Mom's coin purse to pay her wages. After only two days, Betsy's doll had lost an eye.

Amma had attached mother-of-pearl buttons for eyes and sewn the mouths in a big smile of red thread. When she gave them to us, the dolls each wore a different colored bandanna, and in the pocket of the apron there was a single peppermint candy. While Betsy and I sucked the candy, Mom and Amma talked about the "darkies" in the country, back in the olden days. "In the olden days," Mom said, "a lady had help." They remembered Carrie and Bess and Lou and Aunt Sugar, who made the summer berry pies set to cool in a little box with screen sides and a screen lid. Then Mom remembered her pony, and the smokehouse, and the icehouse, and the heated bricks she carried to put at the foot of her bed in winter because there was no central heating. Then she remembered Brunswick stew, and the stew made her remember watching Uncle Billy and Uncle Theo and Uncle Ashton cut the field, mowing around the wheat in circles, until there was a little island in the center of the field. "Then they took their rifles and walked into the standing wheat to shoot the rabbits that had fled there."

"They shot the rabbits!" Betsy shouted. We were horrified.

"I know, I know," said Mom, glancing at Amma. "But they tasted so good in the Brunswick stews. Do you remember how we loved them, Mother?"

Amma's face turned to Mom's and she smiled, almost sadly. "You know, Mattie Leigh, I don't remember." Mom's face fell. When Amma said my mother's given name, the "e" sounds came out strong, and she ran the two names together. *Mattaleeee.*

The musical theme that opened *Boston Blackie* filled the living room. We heard hollow footsteps. Whistling. The silhouette of a man in a raincoat stepped into a dark city street, into a slick puddle of light from an overhead street lamp. He paused, turned his body toward us. A match flared. I saw his mustache and thick eyebrows. He lit his cigarette, the smoke curling over the brim of his hat. The man was a Yankee. I thought he must also be a murderer. I sat up straighter, chilled. But then came my mother, and with a flick of her wrist she snuffed out Boston Blackie and all his matches, too evil for us to see. The television screen went gradually dark, with a diminishing blotch of light in the center. Then it was fully dark. I always believed I could smell smoke as I rocked back on my heels on the carpet, breathing more easily, released from the ritual of rapt expectation and disappointment that was my fear.

I knew my mother was afraid of strange men. I had seen her put the hook on the screen door when a man she didn't know, a salesman with a suitcase of brushes and perfumes, rang the bell and stood on our porch. My sister and I should not open the door to any man or speak to strangers on the street. Our allowed universe extended only to Stonewall Court, no farther, unless we were invited onto Clark Road by a playmate, and to go there we first had to ask permission. Men stole children and sold them into gangs of white slaves. A woman's breasts had been sliced off by a man who had abducted her. When in hushed tones I told a girl at school about what happened to the woman's breasts, she put both hands over her mouth and ran off laughing so hard I knew she was terrified.

In Amelia County, away from the city of Richmond, my mother was more relaxed. Aunt T didn't have a television, there were no strange men. Everyone colored or white knew everyone else colored or white. Aunt T's old farmhouse, well off the road, wasn't stuffed with antiques like Mimi's Alandale, and we didn't have to be as careful inside the house, which fit like an old shoe, Mom said. Aunt T had a round face and a tidy body like a keg. Mom said her eyes had once been the blue of cornflowers and country sky, her hair the yellow of yellow corn. Before Harvie Hall, the big house, had burned down to the ground, Aunt T had lived there among finer family things. After the fire, she had moved into her brother Unc's humbler farmhouse whose paint was old, and she didn't care that the rooms were sometimes messy. An unlit, ash-smelling woodstove sat like a potbelly in the middle of her office, its long pipe running clear over to a little circle in the wall. Her desk was littered with torn envelopes, a riding crop, newspapers, advertising fliers, garden gloves, her winter hat—a perky brown felt with a peak in it like my father's hats—and her summer hat, a wide-brimmed straw hat with a darkly stained sweatband on the inside. In the middle of the mess on the desk, she kept a big ledger for her accounts. She wore starched print dresses and brown lace-ups and wound the braid of her now pale hair around her round head. Her glasses were also round, her eyes little blue orbs that peered sternly at the world—until she let out that hearty guffaw. Then her eyes snapped and twinkled. More often, she remained taciturn and shrewd, a woman who kept her own counsel, let the world outside her sphere run on as it had to, and didn't give a fig if she was an old maid. Within her own sphere, she was a crisp voice, morning, noon, or night, and everyone, even Mom, deferred to her. Mom said that she loved Aunt T, that she was "like a mother to me." She and Mom, years ago, had slept in the same bed, and even now didn't Aunt T move out of her big bed when we came to visit and let me sleep there? If sometimes I thought I should be afraid of Aunt T, I really wasn't. Her heart was as soft as the pillows on her bed.

But there were still snakes, black widows, the kicking end of the horses, and broom straw to look out for. Broom straw? Broom straw, my mother replied emphatically. A man who had been a neighbor, running across a field of it, had tripped, and a stiff shaft of straw shot up his flared nostril, piercing the soft brain. He had been found dead on his face in the field. Aside from not being allowed in the barn or the springhouse without a grown-up, once we were turned loose from Aunt T's house in Amelia, we were free to see whatever there was to see.

When Edwin killed a chicken, taking off its head with a hatchet, there was remarkably little blood. Killing hens, for my farm-bred mother, was an ordinary occurrence, and neither she nor anyone else thought to warn us. Later I would know the signs of Saturday and its ritual slaughter. Marie wore her most faded print dress into the kitchen. After getting breakfast, she put a huge black kettle of water for plucking the chickens on to boil, the temperature in the kitchen already near ninety, at not even ten o'clock.

Sometimes she wanted extra pay for Sunday dinner, a quarter, ahead of time. Aunt T grumbled, but out came the quarter from her change purse and into Marie's grip. To keep it out of sight, out of mind, Marie put it on top of the can of pork and beans on the second shelf. "Miss T, she got Sunday dinner. I got Saturday night to think about."

We slipped away from the breakfast table and ran through the kitchen. Marie was boiling water, paying us no mind. We banged out the back screen door, making as much noise as our bare feet could, slapping them down on the wood stairs. We were free until lunch. I wanted to go to the tin-top house where Aunt T kept the new broods of baby chicks. I was shy around the hens. When I was given corn to broadcast onto the dirt yard for them, I didn't cast it broadly enough. Or I forgot to be careful of my bare feet and wandered around in the feed area, fascinated by the lidless yellow eyes of the hens, the fierce and accurate bobbing of their necks after glints of corn, the flounce of burnished tail feathers, and the manner in which each yellow foot lifted itself, flexed its nubbled toes, spread them out, and set them carefully down in slow motion while the fury of the bobbing necks kept up their rapt staccato. The hens were as intent as I was neglectful. Why then was I surprised, each time surprised, when a hard beak found its way to my bare toes, or fell between them in a near miss that teased me with delicious terror? I might have seen it coming.

On this one Saturday morning, I saw Edwin in front of the open shed, in baggy overalls, no shirt on. He was Marie's husband. A hen fluttered and squawked in one of his hands. He had her by the ankle part of her legs, and her yellow feet stuck out the back of a hand as big as a baseball mitt. Sun flashed off the head of the hatchet that hung in the rung of his overalls. I stopped still and watched him intently. What was he doing? He was whistling.

Betsy was lingering at the old porcelain bathtub set out in the yard. Although we weren't supposed to, she was running water into it from the old hose, raising the level of the water in preparation for the cows and horses we always hoped would one day materialize from the pages of our books or from the pastures of more affluent farms in Amelia. She liked to sprinkle water on her toes and onto her exposed tummy, soft and pale between the little ruffled halter and the elastic band of her shorts.

I turned back to Edwin. He didn't let on that he saw us, but then he never did. Why should he have to deal with Miss Doyle's city girls? I didn't know anything about his life, except that he was married to Marie, came to Aunt T's to chop wood, and kept to himself.

They had a boy named Junior who had been hurt in the war. He had one arm and pinned the empty sleeve to the side of his shirt so it wouldn't flap. That's what Marie said he did when I asked her what about the empty shirtsleeve. I had seen Junior only once. You could ask Marie questions, and she would answer in her sharp, high, amused voice. She gave me little jobs in the kitchen, swatting flies when they got too bad, and she let me pat the rolls into place on the tin sheets before she put them in the oven. Marie, my mother said, had a lot of white blood in her. That's why her skin was so nearly white. Edwin had darker skin, and he was quiet. How burly his hand was around the handle of the hatchet, and how the sun lit the steel! The hen, only moments before a flap and a squawk of feathers, was now quiet, stilled perhaps by Edwin's gait, a lumbering that rolled as if he knew the earth were roundly curved beneath his feet, a stolid rocking along the ground that had taken him now to the stump of cut wood. Barely breathing, I let myself be drawn to the wood, coming near it with my body, going away from it with my mind. I must have known what Edwin was about to do.

In a motion so swift it was seamless, like light, down came naked arm, steel edge, and the weight of Edwin's determination to give Aunt T what she'd asked for—Sunday dinner. And these powerful forces met in the neck of the hen, which I knew from sucking one cooked in Brunswick stew was an intricately interlocked lace of bones, delicate. The hen's head went over soundlessly into the wood dust and pine chips at the base of the chopping block. The eye was yellow with a jet-black center, the beak hard and bright.

Next to me, Betsy was an explosion of giggles, pointing—for there in the dust, released from Edwin's grasp, the chicken, headless, ran its body in swooping arcs about the ground in front of the wood-shed, looking for its head. Wasn't it looking? It was blindly, accurately looking. It did not bump into the stump or into Edwin's legs. He watched the swooping hen without expression. "It dancing," he said flatly. Just then, it slumped to its side, near its lopped-off head. I inched nearer the stump. On the rim of the blade, on the cutting edge, there was a faint blur I could call blood. Then I saw two bright drops on the wood stump.

"Do another one!" my sister demanded. She was delighted with the dancing dead hen. Appalled, I never would have asked, although I was glad she had. I wanted to know if the frantic searching Edwin called *dancing* was what any chicken, headless, dead without knowing it, alive from the neck down, did.

"Miss T want two more hens for company Sunday," Edwin said. He wouldn't let us think he was to kill another just because two white girls from the city, who didn't know what they were looking at, the difference between life and death, had asked him to.

Marie plucked the hens in a large bucket into which she had poured water as hot as her hands could stand. I wondered if her palms were pinker than the tops of her hands and fingers because they were faded by the scald of hot water. I shook off the idea. Were that so, her hands would be entirely pink. Edwin's hands were light and dark in the same way, and so were the soles of his feet and hers. There were things no one could explain, and one of them was color. A girl in school had a rosy stain that spilled across one side of her face, a birthmark. In the Bible, God put a mark on Cain, a dark splotch as I imagined it. When your skin was light and you were marked, that meant sin and the Lord's punishment. But what about my grand-mother? Nanny, the palest lady I knew, Dad's mother and certainly no sinner like Cain, had a big mole on her neck, splotches of brown on her hands and on her bosom, and on her cheek a darker splotch that had drifted to the surface mysteriously one year and stayed. When I asked why it was there, the big mole, he shrugged and said, "Age, maybe." I was young, but I had a small mole just to the side of my nose. I checked it in the mirror when I brushed my teeth at night, to see if it would grow. So far it was only a tiny brown speck.

Marie sat on a stool, knees spread, the bucket between her legs, hunched over. The burnished red feathers turned dark brown in the hot water. The yellow chicken's feet turned yellower. Marie loved to suck the feet once they were cooked. She said they were "sweet." I worried about the toenails and never asked for the suck of one. Nor did she offer. "The feets is mine," Marie said, and she could have them, sticking up like broken witches' umbrellas, evil angles with small curved spurs. I hated the smell of blood and hot water and wet feathers. Sweat kerneled on Marie's forehead and slid down her neck into her dress, where it darkened the seams around the collar and shoulders. The feathers came out more easily in the hot water. Marie grunted softly as she yanked at them. I thought she had forgotten that I was there. Then she looked at me sharply. "Law, child—you gonna faint?"

Aunt T had smelling salts in her purse. I had gone into her purse on the sly to sniff them. She wouldn't allow the salts uncapped unless someone was light in the head. "They're powerful," she had said, "but each sniff takes the power off." The salts had turned out to be horrid things that made my nose prickle and tears sting my eyes, a kind of punishment for being devious. Although now I was in fact light in the head, I decided to duck out of the smell of water and feathers and blood. Just then Marie said, "Run along now so's I can get these hens done before it gets any hotter." That was lucky. It appeared that I was minding her, but I was doing what I wanted to do. And I wanted the day to be a scorcher. Aunt T would let Betsy and me fill the bathtub in the yard, and we'd go swimming. That is, we'd sit at either end of the tub facing each other and hit the surface of the water to slosh each other in the face. Or we'd put the hose down inside the bottoms of our two-piece bathing suits so that the water tickled and bubbled along the pale skin that never saw daylight, now that we were declared far too old to run naked. In Richmond, even in the summers, I kept on my shirt or wore a ruffled halter. In Amelia, we ran bare-chested in and out of doors no one bothered to lock.

Whenever my mother spoke of meals in the country, either in "the olden days" or at Aunt T's, she used the word *platters*. There were platters of fried chicken, platters of corn on the cob fresh from the garden. Garden peas or butter beans, sliced beets, shelled black-eyed peas, mounds of mashed potatoes, or new potatoes cooked in their skins, quartered and bathed in butter. These came to the table steaming in bowls. But when my mother said *platters*, bowls and gravy boats were included in the largesse of the word. When she said *platters*, I could sense her mouth watering, could smell the crispy, oily chicken. Marie served the food, bringing it to the table on platters once everyone was sitting down and the blessing mumbled. The food was blessed because it helped us to serve others. But Marie served the table, Aunt T served the plates, and everyone else ate too much, even in the heat. "Loosen your belt," my mother sang out, an instruction that included unbuttoning the top button of my shorts if need be. I *should* eat; that was the commandment. My father had a belly, Betsy was born chubby, my mother squeezed herself into her girdle and struggled with the hooks of her broad bras. Daddy helped her to hook up. The day before we were due to leave the country, I'd hear my mother's voice, high as a blue jay's shrill imitation of a field hawk, call "T?" She meant her voice to carry from the kitchen, past the phone that rang two shorts and a long, and into the office where T did accounts. "T, let me have one of these chickens to take home to feed my girls." And T would have Marie pluck her a hen. Again the voice, nearer the time of our departure, would ring out, "T," and a request would follow, this time for the snaps simmering with the ham bone in the stew pot, "for my two girls." I hated snap beans cooked until their seams split and the beans turned a washed-out, flaccid olive drab. But Aunt T promised a ham hock—Mom could cook up her own green beans.

In Richmond, at home, dinner was not served on platters. Mom fixed our plates in the kitchen, and we brought them to the table. Meals in Richmond included fare I never saw at Aunt T's farm, and that was why Betsy and I thought Aunt T was rich. At home, Mom made ends meet with navy bean soup and soft Nolde's bread, spaghetti with crumbled hamburger, and the dreaded salmon cakes with their tiny circlets of bone and little slimes of skin lurking somewhere in the patty, no matter how long it was browned in the skillet or baked firm in a mask of white sauce. I knew that we didn't have much money because Daddy didn't make much. That was why he stayed in the army reserves and went away for a week each summer. If we were stretched, how, I wondered, did Marie, who was poorer than anybody I knew except colored Annie who had twenty children and did Aunt T's washing and ironing, make ends meet? In Marie, who was stout, ends had visibly met. She liked her stoutness and patted herself on the belly like a drum, to let me hear what the hollow inside sounded like. I couldn't figure out how Marie got stout. My father praised her pies, especially the lemon chess. But if he wasn't careful, he could keep trimming away at the pie on the dinner table until I squirmed, knowing that Marie wouldn't have much of an extra piece, if any, to take home in a carefully folded napkin in her purse, along with the extra rolls.

Marie's house was down a deeply rutted red clay road. The car jounced in the ruts, and red dust filmed the windows, no matter how slowly Daddy drove the car. Marie's house looked as if it had slunk into place and hunkered down, a slouch of gray and black tar paper and planking with a screened porch in front that had bits of cotton or newspaper stuck in the tears in the screening so mosquitoes couldn't get in. Smoke came out the chimney even in summers—Marie had a woodstove, too. She had a well out back, a kind of miracle down into which we peered fearlessly to see what appeared to be the glint of a coin at the bottom.

"Can I go to the well first? Please?" I asked Mom.

"May I," she replied. Then she said no. We had to stay in the car.

I didn't know why we were going to see Marie anyway, I thought as I slouched back grimly into the upholstered cushion of the Chevrolet. The car was packed for the trip home; my sister and I had struggled over who sat where in the backseat. There was a best side of the car, the side that passed the most animals in the fields. We counted animals on each side of the car. Whoever had the most won. I could count higher than Betsy could, and I had the advantage unless I sat on the side where the graveyards were. Whenever the car passed a graveyard on your side of the car, all the animals you had were killed. We knew where the fields with the most cows were. We knew where the graveyards were. Just by picking the right or left side of the car, we knew at the beginning of the journey who would finish triumphantly and who would not. Today, I had the best side. Ready to win, impatient to start home, I whined silently to myself. We'd already said good-bye to Marie after the Sunday dinner, which had taken too long because Aunt T sent the roast back because it was pink when she carved. We'd packed, but no one had been able to find the two cigar-box banjos my father had made for us to play, twanging rubber bands as we sang the refrain to "Oh Susanna" loud enough for everyone in the house to hear. We wouldn't see Aunt T for a whole year.

Mom and Dad went into Marie's house by the front screen door, after warning us not to go near the well. Since we didn't know why they were stopping to see Marie, we couldn't guess how long they'd be inside or judge the time we'd have to sneak to the well, lean over the rim, and get back to the car before they came out frowning. I was halfway through counting empty cans on Marie's back stoop, many of them Crisco cans, when my father came out with his hat tipped back on his head, grinning. He had a large, rectangular wood-and-wire box in his hand. On the box a door flapped open. "Come on," he called heading back of Marie's house, past the well, into the feathery green pine and scrub hardwoods.

Marie had rabbits! Marie had millions of rabbits—nearly thirty. White, brown, and gray rabbits, black ones and some with mottled brown and white fur. We could each choose a rabbit, whichever one we wanted, and they were coming home with us to live in hutches Daddy would build, he said, out back in the stand of three dog-woods at the edge of the backyard. No, we could not hold them in our laps on the way home. Yes, we could put them into the pen at our feet and pet them. We both chose white rabbits.

The rabbits would not fly away over Miss Conrad's crepe myrtle and apple trees as had the bantam chickens we'd brought home after last summer's visit. We had been told they flew away. I wasn't so sure. I had heard dogs in the yard before dawn and their growling haunted me. Would the rabbits tempt neighborhood dogs? I remembered that our dog Rusty had been hit by a car and had hidden to die under our mother's bed. Now we would have two white pet rabbits instead of Rusty.

In building the first rabbit hutch and placing it on wooden legs high off the ground, my father was like Noah making an ark for animals two by two. The hutch was not lifted up and set high because we expected floodwater from the James, but because rabbits that lived on bare ground might sicken and die. The bottom of the hutch was wire with square holes the size of the checks in a gingham blouse I wore. The holes were small enough that the rabbits had secure footing, large enough that their tidy, admirable pebbles of dung dropped through to the ground. From there my father would shovel the droppings onto the flower beds. Dad was happy with his hammer and saw. And I was happy thinking how much better off our two rabbits would be than those who lived on the earth, barren or grassy. I was glad that we had been able to make for them a refuge, an ark.

I named my rabbit Peter. Betsy named hers Snowball. We named them without knowledge of their genders, nor were we encouraged to peer beneath their puffs of tail. Such areas were private. We called ours "privates," and we weren't to show them to anyone, Mother said. *Private* meant none of your business. Two houses up the street lived Susan Dortch, who called hers a "cotton tail" even though hers, like mine, was bare skin, no frizz. Once, when she wanted to see mine, she said, "If you show me your powder puff, I'll show you mine." It took me a second or two before I knew what she meant.

Soon there were six rabbits. Then eleven. Twenty. Too many to name. But how serene the original Snowball rabbit was. She could sit unmoved for as long as I could remain quietly watching her, only her fine, quirky nose twitching like the winter shivers. I suspected that the nose was connected directly to the heart of the rabbit, which I had felt thump with a terrifying rapidity when I held her up once by her chest to measure how tall she'd be if she stood up like the bunnies in the Easter books. I was as frightened as she was, breaking the rule that we were not to take the rabbits out of their cages. Didn't we remember what had happened to the bantam hens?

Peter and Snowball produced rabbits that were brown and gray and white and black or a mix of those colors, and they huddled together in the hay we stuffed into their hutches in the winter. The more there were, the warmer, especially the little ones that tumbled over each other and slept pell-mell with their paws and tails on top of other rabbits' heads as they burrowed into each other's fur.

After church on Sundays, our family came home and we got quickly out of our good clothes. Betsy and I shrugged ours off, silk socks to the floor of the closet, patent-leather shoes back in their boxes, our dresses and coats hung on hangers. My mother audibly sighed out of her clothes, the flesh pent up inside her girdle gratefully released as she unzipped it at the side. Then she leaned over to unpin the hosiery from their little tabs and wire hooks, so that the soft brown nylon fell to her ankles. She'd flip off her high heels and then carefully, so not to run the expensive nylons, uncover her feet. Next the girdle. She'd scoot it off her hips to thigh level, a final tug, and down it would come. Flesh the girdle hadn't been able to tuck behind its elastic grip, and which had ridden up into rolls between the girdle and brassiere, would come melting down. These rolls—she called them jelly rolls—were what Marie's turnovers turned into.

Before church, Mom put a pot roast into the oven or she baked a hen in a dented roasting pan that had a snug lid. She loved soft bread, meat that was fork tender and fell off the bone, potatoes that steamed open and crumbled with the gentlest pressure of a fork. I was given white meat, my sister dark, her preferred piece a drumstick. Mother took breast and thigh, leaving my father with a leg, the back, the wings, and the pope's nose, the last part of the chicken over the fence. It was a triangular plump piece that resembled the nose of a boy I knew after he'd fallen smack on his face. I nibbled the pope's nose, shyly, once—just once. It was fatty, and I spat it out. But the fat, my father said, was what made it "sweet."

We hadn't had pot roast for what seemed a long time. Never mind sirloin. Steak was a sale at the Safeway or a special occasion, like my birthday. For an eternity of Sundays we'd had chicken stew, chicken hash, chicken in lumps in a cream sauce on rice. One Sunday night, when we were playing cards, only a half an hour from bedtime, Mother drew a card from the pile after Betsy sniggered, "Go fish!" She fanned out the cards in her hand and said, "You know, Marie and Edwin wouldn't do as well as they do without their rabbits." I thought about Marie's house, smaller than ours. What did "doing well" mean for Marie and Edwin? They were colored, and the country seemed far away from us in Richmond, where the only coloreds I saw regularly were women waiting for buses in the afternoon on Grove Avenue, or the maids in white aprons and gray uniforms pushing strollers around the block. "They'd be a lot hungrier if it weren't for Aunt T's goodness to them, and their rabbits." Suddenly I understood. Rabbits were how Marie got stout and made ends meet. From the depths of this insight, I heard her say that rabbit meat tasted a lot like chicken. I shivered, suddenly afraid that there was something I shouldn't ask. My father, I noticed, was frowning. We finished the card game and said the prayers that gave our souls into safety for the night, and then we slept.

On the next Saturday we drove with our parents to the egg farm on Three Chopt Road. This farm was the nearest thing in Richmond to Aunt T's farm, a white frame house that needed painting, a dirt road that raised clouds of dust behind the car, and a half dozen tumbled-down outbuildings here and there behind the big house. Mom bought her eggs here because they were brown and fresh from the oven of a hen's body. Brown eggs tasted country. This Saturday she bought extra eggs for the meringue she would make for a special pie on Sunday. I begged for chocolate. "Chocolate it is," she promised, overriding my father's plea for lemon.

That Sunday we were allowed to eat dinner in our shorts. Early April was warm, and Betsy had already been up to something in the backyard. She had plans for a new hideout underneath Miss Weeks's tree that wasn't a willow but drooped over like one and made a dark tent inside. In the shade of this tree she was planning to spend Sunday afternoon, letting me in only if I knew the password. Since Saturday night, she'd been taunting me about what the password might be. I didn't know what it was—she wouldn't tell me—and I pretended not to care. I was above passwords; she could hide out all she pleased.

Dinner came to the table on plates prepared in the kitchen. The chocolate pie with perky peaks of meringue was sitting on the stove like a kept promise. I carried in the glasses of milk and sat down. On my plate was a mound of potatoes hollowed out, with a well of gravy in the center. Also corn niblets from the can with the green man on the label. And chicken. My piece of breast meat looked queer. Instead of the crispy tapered end where I usually found the soft fold of cartilage that held the tenderest meat, this breast was blunt at both ends. I turned it over to see if there were the ribs I liked to suck, but Daddy said not to play with the food. He was about to say the blessing.

After his voice had stopped rumbling over the words we knew too well to listen to, I looked around to see if it was okay to poke my fork into the chicken. Perhaps it was a thigh. I would have to eat dark meat and watch out for the thready vein that reminded me of blood. Chickens didn't fly, that's why white meat was tender. White meat was lazy, dark meat was used muscle—in fact the last muscle the hens used, dancing about without their heads.

Suddenly Betsy's face turned red and splotchy. Tears spurted from her eyes and splashed on her chin, missing her cheeks altogether. "Snowball," she cried, pushing her plate into the middle of the table. In the middle of the table was a large white Wedgwood bowl I liked because two rams' heads faced off in opposite directions. Inside the bowl my mother put a clever disk with sharp needles. She called it a frog, but it didn't look like a frog. She had daffodils stuck into the tines, and these nodded out of the ram's head bowl, nodding in assent, agreeing with my sister's allegation and outraged grief. Her lower lip trembled. She looked at Daddy with a lowered brow that would butt like a goat's at anything in her way. Tears streaked her face now. My father's eyes met my mother's smack over the daffodils.

"I can't eat Snowball," I murmured and put down my fork. I felt pale and cold. I had been about to eat, and I knew it. I remembered the rule: eat what you're served. But Betsy had known what I'd only been on the brink of knowing. Not quite knowing, believing whatever my mother said, I would have obediently eaten the mother of all the little bunnies in our ark.

Mom pushed back a wild frizzle of gray hair and began to explain that we had to eat, money was tight just now . . . but my father interrupted. He said her name. Would he look at her the way he looked at me right before he took me down to the basement for a strapping? I knew without looking that his eyes never left hers as he said to my sister, "Don't cry, honey, just eat the potatoes and corn and forget the rest."

After lunch I ran out the back door into the yard to check the hutches. Peter was there. Several smaller bunnies were nibbling on greens. That meant Betsy had sneaked carrots and lettuce from the icebox to the rabbits before our lunch. We had been warned that the rabbits were "eating us out of house and home," and Daddy was put in sole charge of feeding them before he left for work. A man's work was mostly outside the house, even what he did at home. I thought about Edwin in his overalls, sun on his brown arms, the hatchet bright in his hand. I thought about the sharp and heavy tools Dad hung in the basement, awls and screwdrivers, hammers and saws. There was a gun locked in the desk, right in the living room, near the front door, just in case. Betsy had touched it once, before he put it away in the drawer and turned the key.

There were young rabbits—many females, Mom had said recently —and lots of baby bunnies. Peter was there, but Snowball was nowhere to be seen. She must have been missing when Betsy fed the rabbits earlier. Betsy hadn't asked about the missing old mother rabbit, perhaps because she was afraid of being whipped for taking food to the rabbits without permission. How Snowball got dead, whether she slumped or danced in her blood and her white fur, I forgot on purpose to think about. I forgot so intensely, and so thoroughly, that later I couldn't remember if I, if anyone, spoke words of comfort to my sister, who went to her room and wouldn't come out, not even for chocolate pie.

4

## Christmas Dinner

A great fire, high and red, flamed in the fireplace. Careful of the great heat and the crackling noises which now and again exploded into a spew of sparks, Daddy poked at the logs, tapping them, pushing them back, as if he held roaring tigers at bay. Mom had moved our empty stockings away from their hooks over the hearth and was standing at the ready with the fire screen.

"When I was a girl, the Yule log burned all day and all night—a single log!"

"Yule?" The word sounded like *yowl*, a word for wild beasts crying in the wilderness. And *Yowell*, a man at church with a double chin. *Yule, yowl, Yowell.*

"It's English for 'Christmas.'" You know the words in the carol, "Yule-tide bright." I didn't know the carol or the word, but I was pleased to learn it. A new word was a gift. "In the country, we cut our own trees for the logs, and my brother Ashton brought in holly and running cedar, and he shot mistletoe from the tops of oak trees and hung it over the entrance to get a kiss!"

A burst of sparks sent a large flaming cinder onto the hearth, and Daddy stamped on it. The other sparks winked out against the dark bricks in the fireplace or floated up the chimney.

"Too much kindling," Daddy said to himself and shook his head, as if the sparks were sinful.

"If Dr. Belk were here, he'd quote Scripture: 'as the sparks fly upward,'" Mom said.

"What does that mean?"

"A man's life is like a spark, bright, and then it flies upward."

*To fly upward*, then, meant *to die. To burn out.* There were many ways to say *die*, without saying it.

44

Any minute now Dr. Belk, our minister, was coming, with Mrs. Belk, too. The house smelled of turkey and gravy. There was also a sweet spice smell from the oranges Mom had stuck with cloves and put in a dish on the mantel. The potatoes Mom called "I-dee-ho" were mashed and whipped and warming on a low eye.

The doorbell rang, and Betsy, who had been looking at presents under the tree, sprang for the door. "They're here!"

I glanced at the manger scene. All the holy figures were in their right places on the cotton snow. On the dinner table were little plates of special pickles, a dish of celery, a dish with sliced rounds of the canned cranberry sauce Betsy adored. It wasn't time yet for the candles to be lit on the dining room table. That would come just before the blessing. Beneath the chandelier, the thin goblets, Mom's best glasses, sparkled. If you wet your finger with the water and rubbed around the rim, the glasses sang like a soloist in the choir. Soprano. Mom let Betsy and me rub the rims in the kitchen, so we wouldn't do it at the table. What was wrong with making the glasses sing at the table?

"Maybe Dr. Belk never heard glasses sing."

"He has," Mom laughed. "And he's done some singing in his time, too. But you be quiet and watch at the dinner table. And listen. You might learn something!"

"Will he preach?" Betsy asked.

Mom had been emptying cans of tiny green peas into a saucepan. Everything was going to be perfect, and no sermon would be needed, she said.

Perfect meant "going the extra mile," the Sunday school teacher said, but now Dr. Belk and Mrs. Belk had come that extra mile to our house and were being helped out of their coats. Betsy and I were to take the coats and scarves to the bedroom and put them on Mom's bed. It was hard to hold a wool coat and curtsy.

Dr. Belk, our minister, was a only hair's breadth taller than my father. His hair was thinly combed over his broad head, and he wore gold-rimmed glasses. When he moved, he seemed ready to bound or leap forward with the contained grace of a powerful animal. I couldn't decide if he was old or young. He seemed youthful and old at once, like Abraham or Moses, those ageless patriarchs of the Bible stories. Dr. Belk had a paunch like Daddy's, the stoutness that thickened the waist and made a man a man, Mom said. The way to a man's heart is through his stomach, she would laugh, and Dad would pat the bulge around his belt. This was their little joke. Dr. Belk was the minister who had married Mom and Dad at the Mattoax Church in Amelia—he was also, therefore, responsible for my life. Life began with God and ended in God. In the middle, Mom said, we followed the direction of God's servant and messenger. To be a minister sounded to me like being a kind of guardian angel and then some.

Mom had told me how Dr. Belk had visited in Amelia County, coming up from seminary in Richmond with his spotted dogs to hunt doves. I had seen a photograph of him as a young man, and I could see him striding across the yard, the chickens fluttering out of his path. His whole name was J. Blanton Belk, and grown-ups at St. Giles called him "Blanton." Betsy and I always said "Dr. Belk," and when we passed through the greeting line at the close of the service with Mom and Dad, we were to curtsy and then stand quietly while Mom talked and Dad smiled at his two girls and his wife. "Give Daddy something to be proud of," we were told.

Dr. Belk's wife was tall and thin, elegant and dark-haired, gracious and pale, and she smiled as she sat in her pew at St. Giles. She was a Real Lady. I couldn't imagine her laughing or talking about Dr. Belk's girth. Until tonight, I had never seen her without her hat and her dark blue suit with the white flower the church gave her to wear every Sunday. The ladies' eyes would glance at her hat or her pearls. Mrs. Belk kept her gloves on and always had her hymnal open to the hymn when she stood up to sing, barely opening her lips as she sang, and she never stood up too soon or too late. We weren't supposed to look at the people seated behind us in church, but I liked to snatch a glimpse of Mrs. Belk as she was walked down the aisle and was seated by an usher. No lady could come in on her own. When Mom wasn't singing in the choir and sat next to me, I'd turn toward her, pretending to watch the beady-eyed little minks chase themselves around her neck, playing tag, the one behind with the tail of the one in front clamped in its jaws. Gradually, I'd turn ever so slightly past the minks until I could see Mrs. Belk. She inhabited her place like a magnolia tree, deeply rooted, darkly elegant, untroubled by wind.

Most of the time I was happy to face forward and watch Dr. Belk in his robes. He and the choir entered the chancel from the two side doors, one by the lectern, one by the pulpit. The organ, which had been playing softly, would swell louder, and the choir, two purple and gold ribbons of song, would furl into the chancel and the choir rows. Dr. Belk would enter last, taller than anyone in his black robe with the red and gold scarves that hung long down the front. His glasses flashed in the lights overhead, and he walked in holy light. He was the smartest man in the world. When he stood in front of the big Bible to read, he hardly needed to look at the words. He knew the words by heart. When he concluded the reading by saying, "The Word of God," his was the voice of God Almighty. When he raised his hand to bless the money taken at offering, all the silver turned to gold. When he strode across to take his place in the pulpit just before he gave the sermon, the hem of his robe swayed like palm trees in the Holy Land. When he stood over the congregation and preached, I didn't dare move. I didn't want to move. Although I couldn't understand what he said much of the time—I was too young, Mom said— the words he spoke rolled richly over me, an ocean current that buoyed and crested, now smooth, now harsh and tumbled, vast as thunder. I liked it when he retold stories in the Bible with the broad, dramatic gestures the Bible called for: "Get Thee behind me, Satan!" He made his voice tender when he told the Christmas story and imagined being born to a young girl far away from home, no place to lay her head but on hay for the cows. I thought *virgin* meant *poor*.

"Will he wear his robes when he comes for dinner?" I had asked Mom, who was making wine jelly and custard and mincemeat and lemon chess pies for dessert. Two more hours to go, she had been in a "swivet." Mom had the recipe for wine jelly from Mimi—the only alcohol she would serve. Mincemeat was Dr. Belk's favorite pie, lemon chess Daddy's. "Will they eat both the drumsticks and then there's none left for Santa?" Betsy had asked repeatedly. She didn't believe it when Mom said they wouldn't leave Santa with nothing. Each year we left a plate of sugar cookies and a turkey drumstick for Santa to snack on after he brought his presents for us down the chimney. Christmas morning, the cookies were eaten and a bare turkey bone angled neatly across the top corner of the plate. That's how we knew Santa was real: he brought gifts, he ate food.

Even without the Belks coming for dinner, preparations for Christmas brought fresh energies into the house, which swelled with pride, much as my father did when he leaned back in his chair, his shoulders back, both hands patting his belly. "Now that was a piece of pie," he'd exclaim. Being happy suggested taking up more space. At Christmas the house breathed in cold air that smelled of spruce and pine. At Christmas, our small house became in spirit a big house. Already I knew, though I couldn't have put it into words, that a man's home place was an extension of himself. Mom made our door wreath from pine boughs and magnolia leaves from Mimi's Alandale. Nanny, Daddy's mother, sent to the house her famous fruitcake. Laced with bourbon and shut in a tin, the cake was put reverently on the cold attic stairs to "keep" until the bourbon "ripened" it. Bourbon, which smelled simultaneously bad and sweet, was the medicine Dad took in a glass with water. Bourbon was "medicine" in a glass, but it became an exotic flavoring, like frankincense and myrrh, when it was in a fruitcake, changing an ordinary cake to "food for the gods."

And here was Dr. Belk, God's minister, come to enjoy it.

In the living room, the fire had settled down. Dr. Belk and Daddy sat in the wing chairs, Mrs. Belk on the sofa admiring the tree, the fire, the manger scene, the room. Dr. Belk had something for us, he said, and he withdrew two small mesh Christmas stockings filled with hard candy from his pockets. They were sewn at the top. Mr. Hardesty, whose company made the candy, was a member of St. Giles.

"You can put the stockings under the tree," Mrs. Belk said. "I'm sure your mother doesn't want you spoiling your supper." She was very pretty, even without her white flower. Tonight she wore a fake little peppermint candy cane on the lapel of her suit jacket.

"We're nearly ready," Mom called out, returning to the living room and backing up to the fire, lifting her skirt a little, the way she did. Dr. Belk teased her. "The country in you is showing," and that got Mom to talking about the Yule log.

Out of nowhere, Dad said that he wasn't allowed to tell war stories at dinner tonight.

Dr. Belk laughed as if he understood. "War for the women back home," he said, "was a different story." He winked at Dad. "We can keep ours to ourselves tonight." Dad nodded. They were choosing sides, men against the women.

On her way back to the kitchen Mom suggested that Betsy and I show Dr. Belk the dolls Santa brought us last Christmas. We had put them in little rockers by the hearth, so that Santa would see them and know how well we had taken care of them. And he would leave us two more each, Betsy said.

"*Two* this year?" Mrs. Belk repeated, smiling.

"Maybe just one each," I said quickly, and now Mom was leading us all to the table.

"Now, Blanton, you there. And Jenny . . ." she gestured to a seat next to me. She nodded to us to sit down as soon as the Belks were settled.

"My, look at that bird!" Dr. Belk exclaimed. "Done to a turn."

The turkey was before Dad's place at the table. He had sharpened the knives in the afternoon, making a scraping with a lilt in it at the end of the stroke, a skirling. It made a little song, too. Dad lifted the sharpened carving knife and the fork with a flourish. Then he put them down. He looked at Dr. Belk, who didn't need to hear words to know what to do.

"Bless this food to our use and us to Thy service, O God. Enter our hearts this Christmas and bring us new life. We thank Thee for this gracious hospitality and the ceremony of the Christmas table. We thank Thee for the gift of Thy son Jesus Christ Our Lord, and for this bounty."

Usually Daddy said only the first sentence and ended quickly, saying, "In Christ's name we pray." Dr. Belk made up his own blessings, the way he made his prayers in church. His blessing was an act of gratitude to God, but it was also southern courtesy.

"Didn't want to go on too long, Doyle," he joked. "The feast awaits, and it shouldn't get cold."

He was enjoying his meal already, and he hadn't had a bite. That was manners.

Daddy carved and Mom added mounds of whipped potatoes and deep wells of gravy, and the Belks helped themselves to peas and cranberry sauce. Mrs. Belk admired the ring of tomato aspic salad, which had slipped without a hitch out of its mold and now sat on green lettuce, dollops of mayonnaise and sprigs of parsley at intervals around the ring.

Betsy spoke up for the gizzard.

Mom said the sauce in the creamed onions was a bit too thick.

No, it wasn't, Dr. Belk countered. Everything was *perfect*.

At the word she wanted to hear, Mom's body relaxed and breathed, taking the word in as if it were manna.

"Take a biscuit," she advised. "The best ones are on top."

"Pass the gravy," Betsy asked Daddy, who reached over with the gravy boat and spooned more on to her turkey, speckling the white cloth with a splash of the gravy. Mom didn't see. Did Jenny need gravy, too? she was asking.

"No, thank you," Mrs. Belk murmured. "I've plenty here. More than plenty."

Was there too much? I looked at my plate and began to eat. Everyone was eating hungrily. Then Dr. Belk said he would have to go back to Amelia to find biscuits as light as these. Light as angels, light as air, he said.

"Use your napkin, John," Mom said quietly, and Mrs. Belk asked Dr. Belk about his Christmas sermon.

"New life!" he said heartily, helping himself to another pat of butter, waving off the cranberry sauce.

"All my sermons contain in one way or another four questions. *Who am I?* That's one."

Mom said immediately *a child of God,* but Dr. Belk was on to question two in his list and didn't hear her.

"*What do I love?* That's two. Both are questions we ask ourselves over and over, sometimes giving the wrong answers. Think of the Prodigal Son."

"What did he love?" I asked. Dr. Belk looked at me, surprised to hear a child's voice. I put down my fork. I had forgotten just to listen, but Dr. Belk didn't mind. He liked, he said, a curious mind, as long as it wasn't, he laughed, too curious. The Prodigal Son was too curious.

"He ran away from home because he loved food and drink and all manner of pleasures. He squandered his birthright and ended up having to sleep and eat with the pigs, he was so poor, so destitute."

I had seen the pigs in the pen in the country, a huge sow on her side in the mud and little pigs sucking.

"We saw worse poverty than that during the . . ." Dad was going to say *war,* but I saw the *W* become a *D,* and Dad said, "*Depression.*"

"Seasons of wealth, seasons of poverty," Dr. Belk said, dismissing good times and bad times equally. "We remember those bad times, don't we, John?"

Mom nodded.

Dad carved more turkey and scooped out stuffing from the turkey's belly. I could think *belly*, but I couldn't say it aloud. Mom had told me that *belly* was a rude word. Colored people said *hog belly*.

Dr. Belk said that questions three and four were *Given that I will die, how shall I live?* and *What can I give to the family of the earth?* Because Christmas was the season of giving and receiving, he would spend more time on the question about gifts in his Christmas sermon.

I let the phrase *family of the earth* stay in my mind, on my tongue. My family was right here at the beautiful table: Mom and Daddy, Betsy and me. Mom had decided not to invite Dad's family—Mimi and Uncle Bud, Uncle Allan and Ruth—who, with no children at home, usually went to the Country Club. But when I asked why they weren't coming, Mom said Allan didn't go to church, and so dinner with the Belks wasn't a good fit. St. Giles is our family, she said, as if Uncle Allan, Mimi, and all of Alandale were not.

If St. Giles was family, was Dr. Belk also my father? I kept the question to myself.

"I have an announcement," Dr. Belk said importantly, as Mom served the tomato aspic salad, cutting the ring as if it were a cake. Each slice jiggled and threatened to tear, and there were several jokes about the jolly old elf.

"An announcement," Dr. Belk repeated, and all eyes turned to him. Daddy, who seemed to know what he would say, motioned to Betsy to put down the little piece of gizzard.

Dr. Belk drew himself up until I thought his head would touch the tulip lights of the chandelier as he said that he'd supported the nomination of my father to the position of Sunday school superintendent. "And I'm sure he will be elected easily," he nodded.

Elected! Like General Eisenhower, who had won hands down.

Dad's face brightened, and he smiled across the holly at Mom. I knew that Mom, across whose face had fallen a shadow, wanted Dad to be a deacon, not Sunday school superintendent. Deacons were the men who marched down the center aisle with empty plates while the choir sang, took up the offering, and then marched to the altar with the full plates while we sang the doxology. Dr. Belk blessed the money, and then the deacons took everything out, and the superintendent of the Sunday school counted it. Dad would count the money in the vestibule.

"I won't say anything important during the opening of the sermon," Dr. Belk joked, "so you won't miss anything before you slip back into your pew."

"Your father is an honest, good man," he said to Betsy and me, and his concluding remark made Mom smile. But she didn't say "Thank you, Blanton."

Mom and Mrs. Belk cleared the plates. While Mom was in the kitchen preparing to bring in the pies and the wine jellies, Dr. Belk talked to Daddy about his plans for the church. The church had to grow, to add new members—new life! And what better way than for St. Giles to be active in Moral Rearmament?

Dad nodded. He knew the phrase, but I must have looked puzzled. I liked it when grown-ups explained things before I had to ask a question, breaking the rule of silence. Catching my eye, Dr. Belk said to me, "Moral rearmament means this. There are forces in the world *for* God and forces *against*."

"Commonists," Dad said, nodding. Dr. Belk nodded back, and his deep voice continued, speaking of revival, renewal, spreading the Word of God. Betsy said, "Onward Christian soldiers!" and waved her fork.

I focused on the word *Commonists. Common* was the word Mom used for women who didn't know better. *In common* was what you said when you were like someone else. About Betsy and me, sometimes I heard grown-ups say we didn't have much *in common.* But why were *Commonists* bad people?

I listened to see if I could tell. Then I heard the words *Joseph Stalin,* and Dad said a new blurred word that began with a B, had several syllables, and rhymed with *fist.* During my puzzlement, Daddy switched gears, now talking about his commanding officer in Berlin after the war. He stopped abruptly, interrupting himself, and said, "Well, anyway, to understand that, I have to go back to . . ." and then Mom came in with the pies.

"None of that," she warned gaily. "Not around the children. Not at Christmas. You boys promised."

Mom had just called Dr. Belk, a man of God and our minister, a boy! I watched his face carefully. "She has us, John," he said. "We'll have to fight the Communists another time." He pronounced the word *Communists,* not *Commonists,* making the word sound a little like *communion,* the meal Dr. Belk served in church to remember

Jesus. Communists must be people who were against communion. I had heard Dad say that the Commonists were godless. They must have lost a child's faith, I thought, watching Mom help Dr. Belk to a generous slice of lemon pie.

"Mmm," he said, taking a forkful even before everyone else was served.

When we all had our desserts in front of us, Dr. Belk said, "Let's toast the chef!"

The grown-ups lifted their crystal glasses and held them over their plates. Mom was red in the face with pleasure.

"To the chef," boomed Dr. Belk.

They drank a sip of water, and Mom said the coffee was nearly finished perking.

"Another toast," Dad said. "To the soldiers of the Faith," and Dr. Belk's glass went up.

Mrs. Belk lifted her glass and wet her lips.

"And let's honor our family," said Dr. Belk. Did he mean the church family? He nodded one way down the table to Mom, the other way to Daddy. "To Doyle's family," he nodded, "and to John's." Then he looked at Betsy and me. "To our children and our hope," he continued. And then he said, "And let's drink to all those who are not here."

Did he mean Mimi and Uncle Bud, Uncle Allan and Ruth? Yes, and all the others in our family not with us at the table. Amma, who loved mince pie. Nanny, with her fruitcake. Uncle Ashton, who had once gathered the Yule log. Mom's Aunt T. Dad's sister Billie in South Carolina. *All who were not here.* Even the dead ones? When grown-ups said "not here," they sometimes meant "dead." So then, Mom's beloved sister Adelaide and both my dead grandfathers were included in the toast.

Perhaps *all who were not here* meant *the family of the earth.* I remembered seeing fields of tall grasses and other fields with clipped grass and white markers for all the dead soldiers. Then Dr. Belk said, as if he were reading my mind, "All flesh is grass." *All flesh is grass,* only I also heard *glass,* seeing suddenly all of us there in the lamplight as transparent figures who could never hide anything. We were all crystal and shining, and as the rest sang a hymn of union for the living and the dead, I wet my finger and ran it around my lips until they rang as clean as the tone of crystal, *Amen.*

# 5

## *C atechism*

Where Mom and Dad purchased the only piano we could afford I don't know for sure, but by the time of my second lesson, the piano—a dark, somber wood with still-white keys—was delivered. Mom didn't play the piano, but when I saw her spread her hands over the keys, I knew she was giving me what she would like to have had herself. An upright—the word Amma used for well-behaved—it just fit the wall in the dining room, making a narrow walkway between it and the chair at my place at the table. If I pushed my chair back too hard when I got up after dinner, I'd hit the piano bench. I was to practice every afternoon for an hour. Mom called it "the music hour," and while I found middle "C" or ran a scale or perfected the position of my right hand and my fingering, Betsy wore her tap shoes or took her baton out to the yard to make throws and catches and twirls. Wasn't I sorry I had to stay inside and practice?

I wasn't sorry. For my first piano lesson, Mom had walked with me out the back gate, through a neighbor's backyard, down a driveway, and onto the sidewalk on Clark Road. Count six houses, and we arrived at Mrs. Bishop's house. Mrs. Bishop's voice was soft, and she sat close to me and said, "Pretend you have an apple just under the palm of your right hand." She wanted me to hold my wrist at a certain angle, make a curved spaced under my hand, and be able to wiggle my fingers freely. "Relax them, wiggle them, *Now!*" When she said *"Now!"* I was to strike a note clearly. She was very gentle and let me try again and again, pleased even when the note blurred. She gave me a three-note tune to play, and she said I had mastered it. When she took the bench alone to play the piano, a Steinway, I was unprepared for the music she brought out of the keys, the speed and precision and power of her hands. The music was stirring, and

I felt tears in my eyes to think that I might, as she said I would, learn to play the piano, to make music like that.

When I left Mrs. Bishop's house, I was so excited that I ran all the way home without a thought of my not knowing the way. My body knew the way home, the way Mom said a horse did if you dropped the reins and let it go on its own. Not even a glimpse of Molly Taylor's freaky white sister Elsa, white as an albino rabbit and with pink eyelids, could stop me, out of breath when I reached the backyard gate, where Mom met me.

"Did you like it?" she asked, delighted. She could see for herself. Nor did I have to answer when she asked, "Did you lose the way?" *Here I was,* back home from my piano lesson, a child of music to come. I gave a little jump of happiness when she asked if I liked it enough to take more lessons.

"You're such a big girl," she said, saying *big* in a way that meant *good.* It was the music in her voice that made the word change.

One afternoon when the backyard seemed to float on its own scent, lilac and peony and plum, I paused at the backyard gate, unwilling to leave the yard even though I wanted to play for Mrs. Bishop the complicated little piece I had practiced all week. Pausing at the gate was a ritual. Making that pause, I cleared my mind, so that all the way to my piano lesson I thought of nothing at all. Then the music I'd learned filled me completely, like water poured to the lip of a drinking glass, about to overflow. After three years of lessons there was so much more to flow over that rim. Today a sonata, but once, I remembered, I simply wanted to show Mrs. Bishop that my left hand could strike its few notes and move down the keyboard into deeper tones and at the same time my right hand could go confidently up keys into higher and higher notes. When the different notes fit together, though some were high and some were low, Mrs. Bishop said, there was harmony. In the little song, my left hand was to stay near middle C, and my right to travel further into the treble, going away and returning, going away and returning until finally both hands came back to middle C, which was home.

The backyard gate was still my middle C. Standing there waiting to hear the click of the latch that sent me on my way, I could see myself unfolding like a row of paper cut-out figures, making a linked path from the piano at home to the piano at Mrs. Bishop's. It was as if going to Mrs. Bishop's I never left home, as if, going off for lessons on my own, I held hands with myself each step of the way. The Margaret who paused at the backyard gate, waiting in the drifts of fragrance, was linked with the Margaret scuffing her sneakers on our neighbor's gravel driveway to see the little stones leap, and she to the Margaret tagging up on the honeysuckle bush in a solitary game of tag, and she with the Margaret who withdrew the little thread from the honey-suckle bloom to release the drop of sweetness on her tongue, and she with the Margaret who paused at the sour-smelling boxwood at Mrs. Bishop's, then to become the leap and three strides over the mossy bricks, up the steps, the doorbell ringing its three-noted "Come right in." All these Margarets sat down together on the piano bench to release the music of a week's practice, to try her skill.

Mrs. Bishop was as strict about music as she was kind, and she became particularly strict during the weeks that led up to her piano recitals. Standing at the backyard gate, unwilling to set off, I was, without knowing it, hesitant about another recital, a form of dress-up during which I played the piano for an audience, careful not to make mistakes, only vaguely pleased to receive the compliments that made me study the tips of my shoes. None of this was truly *playing the piano*.

When Mrs. Bishop played the piano, the skin on my arms shiv-ered, and I became excited and quiet at the same time. When she played the piano a great listening opened and took me into it. There was no gate to this listening, to this music, only entrance and inti-macy and space. Listening to Mrs. Bishop play was a listening so complete I felt neither big nor little, good nor bad, skilled nor unskilled. I was not Margaret, not even my mother's Margaret. The cut-out row of paper Margarets dropped their hands and fluttered off in the wind like the scraps of paper they were. Not that I disap-peared. There I was, sitting on the hard chair in Mrs. Bishop's living room, all of it part of the great listening.

To listen like that was like being propped in the rough-barked Y branch of the backyard plum tree, the entire tree thick with the tiny clusters of purple flowers that nestled along the branches. With the branches above me mysteriously distinct against the vivid blue of the sky, wind stirring the petals, I was swept into plum shade and sunlight, buried in blossoms, in so wide a solitude between earth and sky I had no way of telling how long I was there. My back fit the branch of the plum tree, flower fit branch, sky fit earth. The wind soared. Everything fit.

The light was slanted along the grass when I climbed down. I heard my mother calling and calling me in for supper, calling my name, the word rising on the last syllable as if it were a question, a chord that needed to be resolved by my return. I turned and looked at the plum tree. The backyard gate had been left open. Returned home from piano lessons, I was supposed to close it. But no, just now I wouldn't. I was very still inside, and I liked that stillness. Let everything stay as it is, I thought, just as it is. I turned and walked quietly over the cool grass, along the brick walk, and around the hackberry tree toward the kitchen door.

In Sunday school Betsy and I were learning to answer questions from the *Shorter Catechism*. Sunday after Sunday, Mrs. Treadway would ask a pair of questions, and when we didn't know, she would say the answer very slowly, as if she were teaching us how to spell. She repeated the questions in review each week before asking the new ones. That way she checked "our progress in the Lord."

*Who made you?* God. *What else did God make?* God made all things. We learned, Mrs. Treadway said, by asking and answering aloud. Answers were to be said aloud because then the teacher would know what you were thinking. "Everyone says precisely the same words," Mrs. Treadway explained. "If you recite the words daily, you'll learn to think just what you say." Thereafter, your life, she said, was "living the answers." When we lived the answers, we would be disciples. To help us learn the names of the disciples of Jesus, she had showed us how to fold paper and cut with scissors so that, when we finished trimming, we each held a row of paper dolls holding hands. The heads were round as lollipops, blank and identical, until we wrote the names of the disciples where the eyes should be. When I collapsed the row of disciples into one white figure, I could open and string them out into a line again, in and out, like an accordion. There were a dozen disciples—who looked like eggheads, Betsy said. I put my disciples in the top drawer of the dresser in our bedroom.

I liked to imagine prayers leaving my fingertips like candle smoke, the smoke floating up beyond the ceiling and roof of the house into the sky, carried by the wind to God. Because God was a Spirit, He was everywhere.

*Can you see God?* No, I cannot, but he always sees me. *Does God know all things?* Yes. Nothing can be hid from God. I liked saying the questions and answers to myself before I went to sleep, and it didn't matter if I fell asleep in the middle of a question or an answer. Nothing was incomplete. God knew the answer to every question, the question before every answer. Every question had an answer that fit. God was invisible, and so was the soul. They belonged together. The catechism didn't say so, but it made sense to suppose that my soul and God had been separated at birth. My body was what kept my soul separate from God.

If my soul belonged to God, my body belonged to my mother. She made my dresses and cooked my food. She washed my hair, and we took baths together to save water. I liked to see her body. She would lie back in the curve of the tub, and I'd sit near the spout to run more hot water into the bathtub when the water cooled. Then I'd swish the hotter water Mom's way, sharing it, watching the waves against her thighs and belly and the thatch of hair I didn't have yet. Her breasts shone with soap and water. Her belly button was a little well.

"Did I come out of your body *there*," I asked, pointing.

"Who told you that?" Mom wanted to know.

"Nobody."

"You just knew?"

I nodded.

Mom covered herself with a washcloth, saying she'd tell me more when I was old enough.

Already the bumps on my chest were larger than those of other girls, whose little brown penny nipples were flat on a flat surface. I hadn't yet told Mom that one warm day in the neighborhood a bunch of us had gathered to take off our shirts, look at our chests, and compare.

I had waited until we were in the tub together to tell Mom about being teased for not taking off my shirt in front of the neighborhood boys and girls.

"Why didn't you?" she asked me gently.

I looked at Mom's large breasts, which she sometimes called seals or sea lions—one of our private jokes, bathtub talk. Mom said I would look just like her when I grew up.

"Was it because you felt modest?" she asked, and I nodded.

"It's private," I whispered, meaning all of my body.

Mornings, if I had the luck of waking before anyone else in the house, I lay in bed listening as I waited for the room to grow light. Slowly, vague outlines sketched themselves into air, becoming the solid things I remembered. I named each one as the world of my room reassembled. Because Betsy and I sometimes played "blind," closing our eyes to find everything by memory and touch, I knew where the sharp edges of the dressers were, bedposts, closet door knob, sash at the window, light switch. As darkness became light, the morning was first a tarnished silver. Then, like water, the early light would gather in the window, pool in the mirror—a rising tide—and I floated on it, listening.

I was listening for God. Since God was a Spirit who was every-where, but invisible and very quiet, I had to listen carefully. *Everywhere* condensed into a bird in the dogwood tree by the window, another far-ther off, in Miss Conrad's yard, or in the Medkiffs', or the Eastons'. There were layers of birdsong. Betsy breathing. A faint, high humming in my ears, called ringing, but more like the last note on a violin held and held and held, fainter and fainter until you thought it was gone, but no: there it was, inside you. God's voice—and He must have one because He answered prayers—would be like that faint, high hum at first. There might be words next, or no words. Each morning, as I was waiting to hear God, I'd hear a human mumble, or the weight of a footstep on the floor, or a shift of blankets, and then I'd feel Betsy's fin-ger poking me. It was time to get up. I promised myself I'd listen for God throughout the rest of the day, but I forgot by the time I took fresh underwear from my drawer and matched my socks.

Some mornings, I'd wake up empty and frightened. I didn't want to hear God's voice, afraid of what He might say. *What is sin?* Sin is any want of conformity unto, or transgression of, the word of God. *What does every sin deserve?* The wrath and curse of God. Some mornings I was sure I was a sinner. On those mornings, God rattled his skin and bones in the bedroom closet. Dr. Belk said Christians were God-fearing, and I was afraid of what God would do. God was hidden from me, but I couldn't hide myself from God. He must have known I liked to fall asleep on my stomach with my hands underneath me: *there.* Hands that only moments before were pointed to heaven in prayer were also hands that knew how to bring the rub of pleasure, an unbidden, startling pleasure I knew I shouldn't tell anyone about. On the mornings I didn't want to see or hear God, deliberately I confused my parents with God, thereby making Him nearer and more kind. Even my father, buttering toast, was God. My mother, humming a hymn from choir practice as she washed the breakfast plates, was certainly God. On those mornings, her alto was the only voice of God I wanted to hear.

Touching myself was sin, my mother said when she found my hands there once during one of my afternoon naps. She held my hands away from my body, and she gripped my legs by the ankles, lifting me as you'd lift an infant to put a diaper under. Holding my legs in the air, she talked to me about sin. I was too young, she said. I was hurting myself, she said. Little girls who did what I had done, some of them, when they married, couldn't have children. Some of them died. You can't fool God, she said. I went numb and blank while she talked so that I wouldn't be angry at her and angry at my feeling of shame.

At night, my hands found their way *there.* In the morning I listened. Between the birds' songs, there arose only silence, and deeper silence. My mother said forgiveness meant *say you're sorry,* and sorry meant *stop the sin.* But my prayer hands beneath me in the dark did not understand. At night I tried to distract myself by retelling myself Bible stories or by repeating catechism questions and answers. For greater discipline, I lay on my back looking up at the stars pasted to the ceiling. God was off among the stars that hung in cold fire above the backyard plum tree. Far away and yet near. If He saw what my hands did under the blankets, He never said a word.

"Are they sitting in pews?" On the screen in black and white were rows of older men who looked like deacons and elders.

"No, indeed," Mom answered. "That's the United States Senate, and that is Joseph McCarthy at the table. It's a hearing."

"What's a hearing?" I asked. Betsy was in the bedroom by now, changing into her dungarees. Back from school, we were going to practice hitting croquet balls through wickets in the backyard. We had just enough time before homework and supper.

"After all these years Senator McCarthy's committee is still asking questions to find out who the Communists are. They're hidden away in Hollywood, and in all walks of life." *All walks of life* was a strange phrase. "Everyone's under suspicion until we find out who they are."

"Show me the Communists," I asked. "Is that one?"

Mom laughed. I had put my finger in the face of a man who helped Senator McCarthy ask the questions.

"They're saying at church that there may be Communists on the Supreme Court," Mom said. I had heard grown-ups at St. Giles talking about the courts and the schools and the Negroes.

"Why are Communists bad?" The face I had pointed to was moving its mouth angrily, pulling the corner of his lower lip into a shape like a square. Now he was shaking his pencil at another man. He wasn't a Communist, but he looked dangerous.

"They don't believe in God, that's why," Mom replied. "But this is a grown-up matter. You're still a child in the Garden of Eden," she laughed, snapping off the television. "You don't have to carry the weight of the world, not yet."

"But if Adam and Eve hadn't sinned," I said to Mom, who was going to the kitchen, "they wouldn't have left the garden or had children, and we wouldn't be here."

Mom was looking out the dining room window into the backyard. Betsy was swinging her mallet and yelling for me to hurry up. "But they did, and we are," she replied. "That's part of God's plan for the coming of Jesus Christ." She turned back to look at me. "It's too bad you can't come to the evening services during Revival Week. But there will be two special services next weekend, to bring everything to a climax. You can come to those. I've got to sing in the choir every night this week!"

She looked amazed and resentful and pleased. She also looked tired. Mom had gray hair because she was older than most of the mothers of children in my class at Collegiate, and that was why she took a nap every afternoon, I thought.

"Does every church have a Revival Week?" I was annoyed that Mom and Dad would be leaving the house again at night, leaving us with a babysitter, even if it was sweet, owl-eyed Miss Weeks from next door, who came for free, doing Mom a good turn. No, Mom said, not every church had Revival Week. That was Dr. Belk's genius and Moral Rearmament's plan, to have a week of services that would draw in new members—like Hazel and Lance Phillips, who lived in a big house in Ashland. Since finding the Lord on Tuesday night, they had been driving all that way to services each night. They had signed the pledge of membership already, and the week wasn't even over! Mom was excited. A Christian spread the word. A Christian brought more lost lambs into the fold.

During Revival Week, Dr. Belk was preaching on the parables of Jesus, and the choir was singing anthems and hymns. At breakfast Mom would be still humming the hymns from the night before, and sometimes she sang the words softly while she stirred the oatmeal or turned the bacon. "O Master, let me walk with Thee, in lowly paths of service free: Tell me Thy secret, help me bear the strain of toil, the fret of care." Betsy and I could almost remember all the words to "Onward Christian Soldiers," but Mom, it seemed, knew the words to every hymn. "Lead on, O King Eternal, the day of march has come," she sang, swerving from the soprano melody when the notes got too high and dropping down into the harmony. "God of Grace and God of Glory, On Thy people pour thy power, Crown Thine ancient church's story, Bring her bud to glorious flower." I liked how music stretched out some of the words. *To* became "To-ooh." *Moment* became "Mo-oh-ment" so that all the notes would fit. "Once to-ooh-ooh every man anh-anh-and na-a-shun, comes the-uh-uh mo-oh-ment to-ooh decide." This, Mom said, was a hymn about choosing between good and evil, light and dark. Dr. Belk asked that hymns of decision be sung at the end of every service, she said, so that everyone would be called to be on God's side.

To prepare for the Saturday night service, Mom said that Betsy and I should try not to fight with each other all day, so that we would be in the right frame of mind when it came time to go to the service, and I decided the best way not to fight would be to hide. If I played by myself all day, I wouldn't be tempted by Betsy into a fight. After breakfast, when Betsy was ready to go across the street to find the Dortches and the Mansons, she couldn't find me. I could hear her calling and calling, but I stayed quiet in the thickest part of the bushes between our yard and Miss Conrad's. After I heard her close the gate, saying "You'll be sorry!" I smiled to myself.

But what was I going to do all by myself? And was I a sinner already for hiding myself in the bushes, putting my light under a bushel? I decided to look for four-leaf clovers in the backyard and to offer one to Betsy. We were always looking for them, rarely finding any. Honeybees, little amber buzzings, hovered over the clover blossoms, and I was careful not to put my bare feet on them or to brush them away and make them angry enough to sting. Squatting down in the clovers, I moved sideways like a crab at Virginia Beach, parting the blossoms, looking for a leaf that wasn't in threes. If you found a four-leaf clover, you had luck. Mom said you could also make a wish, and I knew what I'd wish for: *a change of heart*. A change of heart was a gift of the Holy Spirit. No one could make it happen.

The sun was hot, and there were so many bees, so many clovers. After a while I crawled over into the shade of the lilac bush. The lilac no longer bore its perfumed purple cones. The lilac wouldn't have bees. I would be hidden from the sun and from my sister, in case she came back to find me or wanted to play croquet. From under the lilac bush, hidden away in the shade, I could hear Dad getting out the push lawn mower to cut the grass. I could see him, long legs in brown pants, and parts of a shirt, although the browns were patched with the winking sunlight of open places and green leaves, the screen through which I now saw the world. A catbird landed on a branch above me and made its hoarse, odd, repeating notes, a song with squeaks in it. It ended with a whining cat's meow. A catbird was all gray, but now that I was down low to the ground, *under* the bird, I could see that beneath its tail there were brown feathers. What else would I learn if I stayed by myself under the lilac bush? No one knew where I was. Running away from home wasn't just going across the street into the stand of dogwood and tall evergreens with Daddy's knapsack from the army stuffed with my books and a peanut butter sandwich. Running away was as simple as hiding yourself, even right at home. I could run away and not leave the backyard. I could run away just by being quiet. It felt good to be out of sight, thinking what I wanted. *How do you know that you have a soul?* Because I can think about God and the world to come.

Simply to do something, I picked a lilac leaf. I held the leaf into an opening of sunlight that came through the thick branches, and I twirled it between my fingers. The leaf was a dancer, twirling to the notes of the new song I was learning to play for Mrs. Bishop. I thought about Betsy and looked through a break in the lilac leaves. Why did I not like my sister? That I didn't like her bothered me, but I didn't know how to like her. Why was I thinking this thought? I twirled the leaf and pretended it was Betsy, then stopped. I didn't want to think about my badness. It bothered me, what I'd done in the auditorium at Collegiate School as Betsy sang the Lord's Prayer, standing by herself, solo, on stage during the talent show. What I did had hurt her, and I should pray for forgiveness, shouldn't I? She *was* my sister.

Without wanting to, I remembered my heartless laughter and embarrassed self-consciousness at seeing my sister stand on the stage at Collegiate School, trying to sing "The Lord's Prayer" solo. Mom had told the teachers she could do it, and she could, singing with the record player at home, or in the bathroom by herself. Our neighbor Miss Conrad had told Betsy she "sang like an angel." Miss Conrad must have stood on her kitchen stoop, out of sight, just across from the bathroom window, and listened to Betsy's voice float through the screen, through the leaves of the rose of Sharon, over to her kitchen door. Betsy sang like an angel when she thought no one was watching.

But on the stage at Collegiate, meant to perform, Betsy couldn't find the right key. She started off too high. She stood with her legs together like someone who had to pee, and she stumbled through the prayer, breaking off to catch her breath after "Give us this day." Did she stumble because she'd noticed that the girls I was sitting with were laughing? Hand over my mouth, I had slipped down in my seat, also giggling, in league with my friends and their unkindness, faithless and a coward, heartless and hating the laughter, unable to stop it, and hating it. My friends were watching me, too. I wanted to stop laughing.

But how did one have a change of heart while everyone watched? It seemed impossible.

Only once had I felt changed. The feeling had lasted only as long as it took me to walk home from spending the afternoon in the dogwoods on the edge of Miss Anne and Miss Eileen's yard, that leafy shelter from which I could watch cars whiz around the corner, or see Mrs. Meizell walk to the store to buy candy for "Thumper," whose real name was Phil. Booty Easton sped by on his bicycle, scattering gravel in a wheelie, a wild grin on his face. Miss Weeks swept her side porch. In the vacant lot on the far side of her house, the ruffians from Clark Road, as Mom called them, tore through the bushes on a race to who knows where. No one saw me in the enclosure of the dogwood and pine, honeysuckle and holly. Was this what God felt like, invisible to everyone on earth but seeing their lives unfold and move swiftly by? I didn't know. No one could know God's thoughts, Dr. Belk said. Only the Bible, his revealed Word, told us. All the rest was idle thinking.

And yet, after an idle afternoon in the green shade and scatter of sunlight through the leaves, as sheltered as a lightning bug asleep on the underside of a leaf as it waited to be a floating spark in the thick summer night, I was surprised to feel alive in my skin in a way I had no words for. For hours I'd been watching what wind would do in the branches overhead, a rhythmic swaying sometimes matched by the passing procession of clouds, sometimes not. After saying no words aloud for hours, my whisper, "Time to go home," startled me. I was new in my skin, a girl of green shade and scattered light, a girl of wind and hushed, shuttered honeysuckle scent. I belonged to myself, and I didn't really want to go home. There I'd be recognized immediately, fixed and fit into a pattern of requests and schedules. There I was obligated, also obliged. Once I crossed the hot tar and prickles of gravel, light and leaf shade would slip from me the way a clover blossom necklace slipped its knot and fell away. I'd be who they expected. I'd do as they expected.

Under the lilac bush, I kept my eyes on the still leaf. It was shaped like hands in prayer, thick at the bottom, swelling out midway, and rising to a narrow tip. I held the leaf into the sunlight again, putting my eyes closer to it, looking through the leaf, which was shining now with the sun through it. Inside the leaf there was a bare tree. I looked again. Inside the green leaf was a tree shape, like trees in winter with no leaves at all. Mom had been talking all week about the parables Jesus told. Was the leaf a tiny parable?

It struck me suddenly that Daddy was busy pushing the mower around the yard, starting at the edges, making a square of mowed green, then cutting in and in to the center. If I didn't come out of the bush right away, soon there would be no clovers. I wanted to shout "Stop!" But I knew Daddy wouldn't stop mowing. The best I could hope for was that he'd leave a small patch for my search. If I couldn't find a four-leaf clover, I could still tuck the lilac leaf inside a book and make it into a little green fan. I could give the little fan to Betsy, or I could keep it for myself. After all, I had promised only to give her a four-leaf clover, if I found one. I was lucky to have found the tree in the leaf. I waited until Daddy came closer with the mower, and then I jumped out of the bush to surprise him.

"Where have you been?" he laughed. Then he frowned. "You'd better go tell your mother where you are. Betsy's telling her you've run away from home and now Mom's fit to be tied."

As far as I could tell, the Revival Service was just like regular church. In church, part of the drama was watching my parents perform their parts in the pageant. Daddy wore a glazed smile as he led the way down the aisle, at the pew extending the program so abruptly to a man he was seating that his gesture seemed a poke in the ribs. Other times, he forgot to offer the program. Mom's face lit up in a reverent smile when Dr. Belk stood up to do anything—read the Bible, accept the collection, cross to the pulpit, preach—and especially when he offered prayers. Mom's face shouldn't be seen in public like that, I thought. I'd duck my head and study the little pencils and cards on the back of the pew in front of me, cards for visitors to sign. We weren't allowed to doodle on them, and I never wanted to except when I saw Mom smile like that. If I had a change of heart, would I look at Dr. Belk the way Mom did?

I liked to become a note in the hymn the congregation sang, a speck of color Dr. Belk saw when he looked out into the congregation. Even as I became nothing in particular, I could still make out my mother's voice. I could see her lifting her voice, as she'd lift her eyes to the hills, *from whence comes my help. My help comes from the Lord.* That was her favorite psalm, and she said it when she was tired out. "Do you have to sing so loud?" I wanted to ask her, unable to say how her flexible and expansive voice, rising and falling, was too moving to be heard over the humdrum voices of the congregation, in whose ragged hymn singing I could pick out the shrill, the off-key, the bumbled, the mumbled. Mom's voice lifted into rapturous grieving or praising, whatever she felt the hymn required. "When I Survey the Wondrous Cross" had her near tears. "A Mighty Fortress Is Our God" had her in confident proclamation. "The bod-dee they may kill, God's truth abideth still, on Earth is not his ee-ee-ee-qual." "All Hail the Power of Jesus' Name" had her in a crescendo of triumph. "And crown him, crown-own Him Lor-or-ord of all."

Throughout the service, I waited and waited to feel a change of heart. But the moment was like playing the piano when you hit all the wrong notes or hold the pedal down too long, slurring the notes. I couldn't make it happen. *Who can change a sinner's heart?* The Holy Spirit alone.

If that was true, I wondered, what about all of Mom and Dad's efforts? Were they in vain, too? Daddy wrote prayers word for word in his notebook, transcribing from the church program into a little black binder. He never talked about God, except to say that he served the Lord. Daddy said, "I can't s'press myself," and then he would make a long face. Mom talked for him, and she found her words in the Bible, in sermons, and in *The Robe,* which she read and reread, a tender, possessive smile on her face, as if the words she read were hers.

To keep us apart on the long ride home from Amelia, heading back from the country late one Saturday night from a week at Aunt T's, Mom let me lie down in the crescent of space between the rear window and the backseat, up high and with only glass between me and the night. Betsy would have the whole backseat to herself. She could lie down, or not, as she pleased, and she had the cushions. I could only curl my body into the curved narrow space, but Mom gave me a baby pillow for my head, and I lay with my back to the inside of the car. Behind me, my parents' heads were dark against the windshield; my sister was out of sight, out of range. I watched telephone poles outside along the country sky at blue dusk, the heads of trees blown back against the stars. I felt the road through the car tires, the sway of the car around curves. I couldn't see ahead,

I didn't care where the car was going. I saw the night country rushing away from me, and I was at home in that rushing away. Nothing now but trees, a barn roof, a house roof, backlit clouds, cool glass, star by star more stars, a swaying, a shudder, a branch of floating lights, blue-black night light, a whirring, no lights, no light, then nothing.

My father lifted me and carried me to the front porch, where he put me down, the cement cold beneath my bare feet. I stepped on an acorn and moved farther from the door and the sound of the keys. Dad was looking for the key that fit the front door. Betsy was still asleep in the backseat, Mom waiting in the car with her, but I didn't think about them. Drawn toward the sky, I looked beyond the stars. Beyond everything visible, *there* was God.

What if—the thought came swiftly—what if there were no God?

I stood very still.

What if there were absolutely *nothing*? Anywhere, *nothing*. Everywhere, *nothing*. Nowhere, *nothing*.

Could there be nothing?

A jangle of keys, cool cement, oak leaves in the wind. Porch and house melted into the *nothing*. There was *nothing*, and a great emptiness stretched out into the sky, beyond sky into no-sky, no-stars. *Nothing*, until *nothing*, as swiftly as it had appeared, rushed back into my body. I became *nothing*, which was, I discovered, the feeling of being everything. Of being everything looking. Simply looking. Then a sensation of relief, followed by a tingle of thought. *There could never be nothing, not as long as I was here to think: nothing.*

Here I was, thinking it. *Nothing*.

In the click of the door latch, my father's voice said my name. Then I felt his arms, and a lifting up as he carried me into the dark house.

The house was dark, and I was light. Everything had an edge of light to it now. *Everything* and *nothing* embraced, the wind soared, bearing us along, the earth rushing from dark to light to dark. Everything fit.

## 6

*Stonewall Court*

"Fetch me an iced tea, slave," murmured the queen.

"Susan, wait. . . ."

"Immediately, slave!"

"But you're supposed to give me a name. What's my slave name?"

"And bring plenty of mint, Hettie Lou." Queen Susan stretched back in the privileged and languid shade of the green privet hedge.

She yawned. Then she ordered slave Betsy Jemima Manson to fan her.

"Faster, slave, faster." Betsy Jemima, who was pale even in the middle of July, fanned harder and faster.

The iced tea and the glass, the mint, the sugar, and the lemon were all make-believe, but I pantomimed making and serving the iced tea on a silver tray, bending at the waist as I entered the shade. I curt-sied, but my humility wasn't deep enough.

"Kneel, slave." Queen Susan had to be severe with me, because I was next oldest in our gang, and her rival. Given our bargain, I would be queen tomorrow afternoon, but I knew that tomorrow we might choose to play jump rope or Mother-may-I or jack rocks or kick the can, and I'd miss my chance to be a tomboy queen.

"Stonewall Court," between Grove Avenue and Cary Street Road, was our kingdom, a neighborhood of young families and grand-parents and old maids. Mom said that Lexington and Albermarle roads, which formed a loop, were like the primary grades at school— they were where you started in the West End. When you had enough money, you moved up to a bigger house on Oak Lane or Ampthill or Cary Street Road or in Windsor Farms. Or you stayed put—unmar-ried or too poor to move—and you just got older.

Between the backyards of the houses were green alleys, a tangled territory of morning glory and privet, prickle bush, honeysuckle, and stick-burr weeds that hitched to our socks. In this no-man's-territory, we had our forts and hideouts and our secret trails to Bumper Hill, where we coasted our bicycles down into the street, and you were chicken if you used the brakes. As long as we were in a fort, our mothers couldn't find us or see us. When they wanted us home for lunch or for dinner, each household had a whistle and a whistle code. Mom's whistle was three longs. If we dawdled, the three longs stretched into a blur of six, a long line of shrilled insistence that reeled us in.

"Did you see the coronation on TV?" I asked Queen Susan. I had slipped out of character momentarily, and she glared at me.

We had assembled in the living room as a family to watch the coronation of Elizabeth the Second take place, because, as Mom said, we might not see another coronation in our lifetime. Mom said that had her mother's family stayed in England, the women would have been called "Lady" this or "Lady" that, and they could have been ladies-in-waiting at the court. It was so far back that no one remembered exact names and faces, but the family was her mother's: Castleton. I made no reply to her quiet boast because she'd recently told me that my middle name was the same as Robert E. Lee's last name. Susan Dortch received more allowance than I did, and, refusing my request for a raise, Mom wanted to lift my spirits—money didn't matter when you had a name like mine. And my spirits did lift for as long as it took me to see in my mind my middle name—*Leigh*—set next to *Lee*. It wasn't a match.

Taking my silence at the coronation for the doubt it was, Mom went into the desk in the living room and produced a letter as proof. It began, "My dearest niece, Your family in England is an ancient and honorable one." Because I wanted to believe the letter my mother had received from one of her aunts, I put it into the family scrapbook I had begun to keep.

During the coronation, I could see that the throne had a large flat stone tucked under the seat, the Stone of Scone. Ferguson was a Scots name.

"We should dig to find a stone to put under your throne," I suggested to Queen Susan, who liked the idea. Then she'd rule Scotland, too. Jeff was sent off home to find a shovel. We'd dig!

"Like the slaves in Egypt," my sister Betsy said. She'd been ordered to make a honeysuckle crown for Queen Susan, and we'd already sucked the flower throats for honey. "Let's change countries."

"We will not change. It is not our wont," sneered the queen. "I'm queen for today, and I choose England. When you're queen for the day, it can be Egypt."

On the television, at the end of *Queen for a Day*, the TV host in the dark suit gave the queen a new washing machine or a Buick. The queen would clasp her hands or cover her mouth in shock and laughter. I liked it best when the queen was surprised by someone she hadn't seen for a long time, a friend or a relative brought there by the TV show. Many years into the future, I might be queen, and the TV show would reunite me with Susan Dortch, my best friend. We wouldn't have seen each other for years. I would be a famous pianist, and she'd be a movie star. We'd have three children each.

Betsy kept insisting on Egypt. "Keep on," announced the queen. "Just keep it up, and it'll be the Tower we build, and I'll have you put in chains."

"No, we won't have a jail," I said quickly. If there were jail, Betsy would end up in it. I'd have to protect her. That was a rule now, after what happened two weeks before in the vacant lot next to Miss Weeks's house.

We didn't even know their names, although we were to learn that Mom knew how to find out when it came time to confront their parents. The Clark Road Gang wasn't allowed on Lexington, just as we weren't allowed off our home street, but they had fooled their parents into accepting the vacant lot on the far side of Miss Weeks's house as Clark Road territory. Betsy and I believed that the lot was on Lexington, and from its dense brush we could spy on whoever was going to the Stonewall Court market and drugstore. On Lexington or not, the vacant lot was dangerous ground, or so Mom ruled. Too near the corner. She didn't want us there.

Whenever we could, we'd sneak along our back fence and Miss Weeks's back garden border into the wilderness of weeds and tall trees with grapevines tangled in them. The grapevines made fine

Tarzan jungle swings, although we didn't let our feet more than one or two feet off the ground when we hitched a ride on them. Betsy double-dog-dared me to climb the maple and swing down the vine from high up, and I took the dare as far as the third limb up before I thought better of it. The maple, I told her, jumping down, would make a great tree house, and we should head home and beg Daddy to build us one. Daddy enjoyed making things "with his own hands," as Mom put it, proud of the dresser in their bedroom and the new book-case in the living room, which now held volumes waiting for me to be old enough to read them, books by Dickens and Twain, Thackery and Hawthorne. She was saving pin money for an encyclopedia.

"You ask him," I suggested to Betsy. "He likes you best."

"*You* ask. We're not supposed to be in the vacant lot, remember? If I ask, I'll get taken to the basement." Playing for sympathy, she made a face that mimicked the wet-cheeked outrage that made her scream as much for effect as from pain. At her last belt-whipping, I'd run up the street each time she'd screamed, just to see how far her voice carried out the basement windows. How many neighbors could hear her? I got past the Dortches' house and stopped. If any-one asked me what I was doing, I'd be caught.

> *Eeenie meenie my-nee moe*
> *Catch an Indian by the toe*
> *If he hollers, let him go*
> *Eeenie meenie my-nee moe.*

We'd said nothing to our parents about the tree house, but each day we checked the vacant lot and the maple, deciding the number of planks we'd need and how many steps had to be nailed up the tree trunk. If there was an opportunity, I promised Betsy, I'd ask them—first Mom, then Dad. I could always get Mom on my side, and I hadn't been taken to the basement for two years. While we were stalling, however, the Clark Road Gang began digging fox-holes and trenches in the vacant lot. They even put up a single strand of wire and hung a sign on it that said DMZ, NO TRESPASSING. They were serious about their war games. Betsy found rope and some staves she called lances. Sharp, they were certainly a kind of weaponry. We pulled down the wire and threw it into one of the fox-holes. We covered the staves with leaves. Then we ran home.

When we returned, next afternoon, entering by way of Lexington Road, Betsy shot ahead of me, although I'd warned that we should stay together. I had a funny feeling, and that feeling was confirmed as I jumped over a foxhole and saw in it, crouched for ambush, a girl about my age. Ahead of me, Betsy was quickly surrounded, and the taunts began. The girl in the foxhole jumped me, and she and her brother wanted to tie my hands behind my back. I grew cold, but I smiled.

"Not a good idea," I said to her. "And anyway, I'll walk along with you. You don't need the rope." Then I asked her if she went to Mary Munford School, the public school where I might have to go for fourth grade. She started to answer me, but her brother glared.

"No talking, prisoner!"

"Yeah, you got no rights," said the girl, recovering her meanness quickly.

Betsy, I could tell, had been chiding her captors, teasing them, calling them names, threatening to tell on them. I tried to catch her eye. She shouldn't make them angrier. She should keep still.

"What's this all about anyway?" I asked, my voice light with friendly innocence, my fear camouflaged so well I didn't feel it.

Betsy, red-faced and crying now, had been backed up to a telephone pole, and the boys were tying her with rope: ankles, knees, belly, her arms at her sides.

"Quit hollering, or we'll hang you," yelled a boy, his face so close to hers I could imagine his breath and the sting of spit. He put the rope to her neck.

The girl who was my captor looked uneasy. The others were picking up the staves and making the noises of natives in the jungle. "You tell your friends," I whispered to the girl, "to leave Betsy alone, and I'll promise you we won't come into your fort again."

"Cross your heart."

I crossed it.

"Cross it again."

When I did, she ran over to one of the older boys and whispered to him. He made a face and turned away.

Betsy looked at me. *"Do something,"* she yelled. Her captors thumped their staves, and one of them picked up a handful of dirt.

"Make her dark as a nigger," he said. But the girl to whom I'd made my promise was talking to another girl, and they nodded.

"Leave them," they commanded. "Time to return to command post number one!" And for no reason I could understand, the entire gang flung themselves back through the weeds and hedges and disappeared into Clark Road.

"Remember!" yelled the almost friendly girl over her shoulder. "Remember your promise or next time you eat dirt mixed with your own blood!"

The knots on the rope were so tight I couldn't loosen them. Betsy was still crying and her nose ran.

"Don't leave me here," she pleaded.

"I have to. I have to get a knife. I can't untie you." Now that the Clark Road Gang was gone, I was feeling my own fear, and my voice was terse. I didn't want to pee in my shorts.

"Don't leave me," Betsy cried out again.

"If I don't, you'll stay tied up. I can't get the knots."

"Yes, you can."

I tried. When I couldn't, I just ran home, ignoring her cries, which followed me.

Mom found me rifling through the knife drawer, sweating and pale as a ghost, as she later told the parents on Clark Road. The whole story came out.

"You stay here," she ordered, taking a knife from the top of the stove to go cut Betsy free. I wondered what Betsy would tell Mom. Whatever she said, it wouldn't matter that I'd negotiated her freedom, even if I couldn't get the actual rope unknotted. Mud was what you might could call my name.

Mud for sure and maybe a trip to the basement when Dad got home.

It wasn't fair.

"It's all her fault," Betsy would say. "They were going to make me eat dirt, and she just stood there."

There was little I could say or do. I'd be tongue-tied, as much in bondage as Betsy had been tied to the telephone pole. We'd have to spend a few days, or longer, with all other territory but the backyard off-limits. Everyone else, all my playmates, would be off-limits, too. We'd have only each other. I was stuck with Betsy, I concluded angrily, and I decided to blame her for what the others had done to her.

It was her fault, and I knew it.

One day a few weeks later, Mom announced that, in July, we were adding on to the house a bedroom, a bathroom, and a screened back porch. Betsy and I were both excited. "Where did the money come from?" Betsy wanted to know—a question no one would answer, of course. Mom and Dad didn't talk about money in front of us. I thought Mom had read my mind: I wanted my own room.

I was excited about the new rooms. Their outlines were traced in the backyard, marked by string and little stakes. Our house wouldn't be a "big house," but it would be bigger than it now was. Already Betsy and I were picking out wallpaper, turning the pages of samples in heavy books with shades of every color, stripes and flowers, masses and swirls. A man we called "Red Cap" because he wore one would be doing the construction in a few weeks. He called Betsy and me "Missy" and touched his red cap, even though he was a white man. That was because, Mom said, he worked with his hands for a living.

I was also glad for the addition to the back of the house because the house would no longer be a bungalow. *Bungalow* was the word I heard Mrs. Harrison use, surprised that Mom and Dad were raising us in a bungalow. Having moved from Atlanta to Richmond, she and Mr. Harrison, old friends of Mom and Dad's from army days, had driven their car around Stonewall Court before they bought the two-story brick house on Albermarle, its backyard just through the green alley behind the Dortches'. "My stars," Mrs. Harrison had explained. "When I looked you up in the phone book and discovered you just around the corner, you could have knocked me over with a feather." She'd forgotten the number of the house, #37, and so on her scouting mission she'd picked out our house by eye, a house that "looked like us," as she put it. She had picked the Mansons' house, a large brick colonial with new swings in the backyard. Descended directly from President Harrison, Mr. Harrison had come to Richmond to be president of C. S. Sauer, which made vanilla and was located in a building right next to the FFV cookie company, which sold lemon thins in blue tins. FFV meant First Families of Virginia. Their only daughter was named Courtney Carrington Harrison. Mom showed me a picture of Courtney and me, both in snowsuits, sitting on a wall in the winter sun. "She was your first friend," Mom said. "Funny, isn't it, how the world works."

The Harrisons had moved into their new house in February, while I was finishing third grade at Collegiate. Asked to spend the night at their house, I packed my new green suitcase, *Little Women*, and my new pajamas—all three were birthday presents from Mom and Dad. *Little Women* was too hard for me to read, but I packed it anyway. It was the first time I'd spent a night away from my parents. Mrs. Harrison couldn't get over that.

"Is your mother hiding you in the closet?" she laughed.

Mrs. Harrison's question made me realize how little Mom let me out of her sight. Just like that, Mrs. Harrison's question made me feel older and able to meet the world. But it also made me tongue-tied, and I couldn't answer.

Mrs. Harrison was a woman who set a great store on appearances. Courtney's clothes were expensive, even though she was starting off in public school. It would take some time to get her through the waiting list for St. Catherine's, Mrs. Harrison said. My clothes were secret hand-me-downs which Mom obtained from Mrs. Black, a lady whose daughter Nancy, one year older, attended St. Catherine's. I was not to speak of the fact that my favorite red jacket and most of my dresses had been passed to Mom over the front fence by Mrs. Black's maid, who was cleaning out closets every season, looking for whatever had been outgrown or was no longer admired. Mom knew Mrs. Black from the country, and they were both Presbyterians. Mom wore one of Mrs. Black's sweaters, the one with the seed pearls, and that was a secret, too. When Mrs. Harrison praised the sweater and asked where on earth Mom found such a treasure, Mom just smiled.

When I spent the night at Courtney's house, Mrs. Harrison had the table set with her best china and silver, and she lit candles. She and Mr. Harrison sat at the grown-up ends of the table, and Courtney and I sat across from each other with the flower arrangement blocking our view of each other's faces. Mrs. Harrison reached slowly over her empty plate and rang a silver bell, at which the kitchen door opened and a short, elderly colored woman brought in the thick broiled steak on a platter. "Thank you, Minerva," Mrs. Harrison murmured to the door as it shut behind Minerva.

Minerva, I was told, had been with them since Courtney was born. As I would learn later that summer, Courtney bossed Minerva around, and she had even slapped her once when a dress had been improperly hung in the closet. I couldn't imagine slapping Marie. I couldn't imagine wanting to. Neither could I imagine asking Courtney why her mother let her slap any person who was older, no matter what her color. By July, Courtney had earned the title "Queen Courtney." Queen Courtney was so completely a queen that she found it beneath her to play queen and court with us in our hideout. Her home is her castle, Mrs. Dortch sneered, and I wondered what Courtney had said to Susan that made Mrs. Dortch so touchy. That's the way it seemed to work. If the children had a tiff, the parents had one, too.

I watched Mrs. Harrison lift a doll-size coffee cup to her lips and sip what a doll would sip. I watched Mr. Harrison carve the sirloin faultlessly, giving me too much because I was an honored guest. They're treating me like a grown-up, I thought, and I felt pleased. Then I felt awkward. I didn't really know how to play the part they'd assigned me. Wasn't I really just a child? I was more comfortable being ignored, or nearly so, and I almost envied Minerva. For the Harrisons, Minerva didn't seem to exist as she passed the vegetables to our left, waiting silently as we took what we wanted. It was as if the silver dishes floated around the table on a current of air. In Amelia, Marie put the serving dishes on the table directly, and Aunt T talked to her, and Marie laughed and answered back and teased and rubbed her belly. She told us to save her some now, don't eat it all up. Minerva was, by comparison, a silhouette.

"Do you eat dinner like that every night?" I asked Courtney upstairs in her bedroom as we unpacked my new green suitcase.

"Every night. It's awful."

"At least you can take how much you want. Mom serves my plate."

Courtney said. "It's our station in life. That's what Mom says. She bought new dessert dishes just because you'd be coming to dinner, and she wanted the cherry sauce to be set off by the blue border. She's just that way."

When Courtney came to our house to spend the night, Mom cooked spaghetti and we ate it at the kitchen table because that was our way on Saturday nights. But she did make a special chocolate cake. We ate early and by ourselves, so that there would be light left in the backyard for croquet. I wondered if Courtney would be miffed that Mom fed us in the kitchen. Only Minerva ate in the kitchen at the Harrisons'. But Courtney seemed to be relieved, especially after asking Mom to pour her more milk, and Mom said, as polite as you please, "It's right there in the refrigerator. I'm stirring the sauce. Would you just help yourself?"

In the beginning, Mom and Mrs. Harrison talked on the phone two or three times a week, but I wondered if they really were friends. They never got dressed up and went anywhere together, except the one time Mom asked for a ride to the Safeway on a Wednesday, Mrs. Harrison's shopping day. Once Mrs. Harrison was at ease with her move to Richmond, she rarely called. Richmond was a hard city to move into, she said. It was like Charleston society. You were either in, or out.

She asked me to let her nap in peace. Her head was splitting open.

Worried about Mom, I stood quietly next to the bed she'd returned to shortly after breakfast. It was only early morning, not yet hot. Nevertheless, she had said to Daddy as he left for work, "It's too hot to think about it." When he leaned over to kiss her, she'd pretended to see something on the rug and bent down, so his lips had only grazed the air. Then she'd burst into tears.

What could be wrong? "Your mother has the blues," Daddy had explained the night before, saying what I already knew. Sunday, we hadn't come home for midday dinner as usual after church. Instead, we'd driven to Byrd Park with Lance and Hazel Phillips. Dad and Mr. Phillips walked with Betsy and me around the lake as we fed bits of crumbled bread to the ducks, but Mom walked away from us with Mrs. Phillips, who put her arm around her. Mom was crying.

"What's wrong with Mom?" I whispered to Betsy, who widened her eyes and shrugged. But we were both absorbed by the mystery. Mom had moods that filled the house, usually at nap time, and those moods made the clocks run slower, the house fill with shadows. I had never seen her let someone outside the family walls see her cry. Now this morning, after she'd gone back to bed, I'd entered her room to ask what the matter was. Mom mumbled something about a bad dream, about living in a bad dream, but she wouldn't say any more, so I left the room. She acted as if I were Betsy, coming to her at an inconvenient time. She never turned me away; this morning, she had.

I thought about Mom and Betsy and me. It wasn't out of the ordinary for the summer heat to make us quiet and solitary. In it everyone retreated, slowed, got quiet. Any motion was just too much. Betsy drew pictures or played jack rocks by herself. Mom read *The Robe*; Mom made lemonade. I could sit for hours with a book, seeing the story unfold the way dreams did, in colorful pictures. *The Black Stallion. Satan. Son of Satan.* That summer, I was reading horse books, as many as the library would let me take out at a time. During the sultriest hours of the afternoon, I read. On the front porch. On the back porch. In the crook of the dogwood tree in Miss Anne's secluded clump of trees. Before a storm broke, when the wind rose and the trees flipped up the undersides of their leaves—a sure sign—I'd run home to help shut the windows. On the new back porch, Mom would be moving the new chairs away from the south screen as it filled its little squares with rain spatter. Unless the lightning was severe, I'd stand on the front porch up close to the rail to see how close or how far away I'd have to inch before the rain and wind spray dampened me. I'd wait for the storm to end, then for the ten minutes more Mom required after a storm passed. We waited to make sure no last lightning threatened, then Betsy and I would run into the rivers of rainwater that coursed down the sides of the street, wading in water so deep it covered our ankles and splashed up our shins. After the rain, this release from suspended motion was thrilling. As a storm gathered, there was a concentration I relished and a stillness that was hypnotic. I didn't know which I liked better, the time just before the storm or just after.

Soon after the morning Mom wouldn't talk to me and moped in bed, Daddy asked Betsy and me to come with him to Betsy's bedroom after dinner. We sat down on the twin bed and Daddy leaned against the windowsill, clearing his throat. He said we must have noticed how upset Mom had been in the last few weeks.

"She's had a disappointment," he said. He paused. "Your mother didn't have a happy childhood," he said quietly. His eyes, brown like mine, were dark and sad. "And she wants to make sure yours is happy."

He said Mom was better now. But you will, he added, be going to Mary Munford for school this year. That was no longer a possibility, it was a fact. And perhaps we'd have to go to public school every year after that. "It wasn't what we wanted for you."

We nodded. I didn't really understand why this had made Mom sad for weeks.

"Public school isn't safe anymore," Dad said. "It's not like it was when I was a boy." I still didn't understand. Then he said *Plessy ver-*

sus Ferguson, our name. And three words more, separate but equal. He shook his head. "It's looking like that won't hold."

"What's versus mean?" I asked.

"It's Latin for against. It's the language the courts use."

After Daddy left the room, Betsy and I looked at each other to see who understood more. "Big deal," Betsy said. "Now I bet we can walk to school with Susan and Jeff. No more Miss Moon. I hate Collegiate."

Then, her voice lower, "Daddy didn't tell us everything."

"What's there more to tell?"

"I know something you don't." Singsong words.

"Then tell me." I knew she wanted the suspense, but I didn't want to wait through it. This was about Mom.

"Mom thought she was going to have a baby. I heard her tell Mrs. Phillips before we left church that Sunday."

"Is she?"

"No. That's why she's feeling better. She found out she made a mistake."

"How do you know?"

"When Mom tells us she's napping, she makes phone calls. I heard her talking to Too-Too. You had your nose in a book."

"So, so what did she tell Too-Too?" Too-Too was Mom's younger sister Louise, and in those years our families were close.

"So she wanted to get a job teaching at St. Catherine's and have us go to school there. She couldn't apply for the job because she thought she was pregnant."

Betsy amazed me.

"Grown-ups don't tell you anything," she explained.

I looked at her with a new respect, only momentary because I was still thinking about Mom. I was glad she was feeling better, and I didn't care about having to go to Mary Munford. But what had Dad meant saying that Mom didn't have a happy childhood? These words made me see her in a new way, as if she were a character in a book, as if I could stand away from her and see hers as a life that had been, and still was, apart from mine.

"Do you like your new bedroom?" I asked Betsy. My mind was still on Mom, but I wanted to show Betsy I was glad for what she told me.

"Yes, I do," she nodded fiercely. "It's a lot bigger than yours." She said *yours* in the way she always had—*yo-ees*. And indeed it was bigger. When the new addition was finished, I had been surprised to see how much bigger her new room was, compared to our old room, now mine. I was envious of Betsy's room, and Betsy knew it.

A door from Betsy's room opened onto the screened porch, and the heat wave deepened, smoldered, and refused to break—even after dark. Even Mom and Dad had gone to bed early. Dad was exhausted from digging up the blue hydrangeas we'd brought from Amelia and transplanted into our yard. They had bloomed in cloud puffs the color of blue sky. One of our neighbors had commented dryly that they were "colored people's flowers," and I had seen hydrangeas in a colored neighborhood off Cary Street downtown. I had never seen any blue ball bushes in the West End, but I liked them. But Mom and Dad insisted: the bushes offended a neighbor, and Dad would dig them up.

That night, the hottest on record, one by one we each made our way out to the screened porch late at night to sleep. The trick was to get there first and claim the glider. Betsy was stretched out on the glider, and I was in a folding chaise that would leave little stripes on my skin by morning. But there was a breeze, and we'd soon be sleeping. Then Mom came out with sofa cushions, and Dad set up his old army cot. They settled in and whispered good night to each other. Betsy and I said "Good night!" to them in one voice, and all four of us laughed.

"Good thing we spent all that money so we could have separate rooms," Mom laughed. Her laugh, when it was deep and throaty, meant her eyes were watering, too. I was relieved. The summer heat had us all together in one place, the new porch itself hardly separate from the backyard's lightning bugs and stars. We barely fit, but we were together, laughing, and the hot night was sweeter than the smell of the newly planted crepe myrtle.

From the top of the hamper in Betsy's new bathroom, I took several copies of *Reader's Digest* to flip through, looking for anything to read to while away the time I might be spending on the toilet. I was there on Mom's orders. Bread to push it through, a regular time, and patience—that was her advice on the subject of "doing your duty." Were I not dutiful, I'd face the enema bag, having to lie on my back on the fluffy rug in Mom's bathroom while she filled the rubber bag with water. I'd be dreading the tube she'd put into me, the gradual swelling, the embarrassing urgency and lack of privacy.

I was done with counting all the hot pink squiggles in the bathroom tiles, erratic zigzags, like electric pimientos, that hadn't been included in the single sample tile my parents had been shown and had approved. They had been dismayed when, with the work half done, they saw the irregular markings. Red Cap, the carpenter, had said he thought it was artistic. Mom did not agree. She pouted and blew air from her nose, a show of frustration. The tiles were half up, they couldn't afford to pay for the extra labor and new tiles. What could she do? She called the marks lipstick trails a disobedient child would make on walls.

I had already taken out the toilet roll and put it back. I'd examined the scar on my knee and a fresher scrape from a spill off my bike. Finally I turned to the *Reader's Digest*. I read a few jokes and then began a story in which two colored people were taking a train. I hadn't been on a train since I was nine months old during the war. According to Mom, I'd flirted with the men in uniform as they passed up and down the aisles. At ten, I couldn't imagine flirting with a uniformed man, with any man. Reading slowly along, I came to the moment in the story when the colored man leaned over and kissed his colored woman wife—a tender moment, affectionate, like those teasing moments in the kitchen when my father would put his hand on the back of my mother's thigh as she got the butter from the icebox. The colored man was more careful than my father, perhaps because he was on a train, visible to the public. I stopped reading just as his lips found hers, struck by the warmth of the moment, into which these words formed in my mind: COLORED PEOPLE KISS.

I was shocked.

If they kissed, they were like us.

I stared at the erratic wisps of pimiento in a tile. I leaned over and cracked the venetian blind, just enough to see out the slats, through the dogwood branches, and into Miss Conrad's yard. But I couldn't shake the strange idea.

I reread the sentences in which the colored man kissed his wife on a train going north. He had to lean over the picnic basket between them on the seat. I could smell the fried chicken in the hamper, still warm, its oil soaking into the napkins. I could smell Marie's kitchen in Aunt T's house in Amelia, and I could feel Marie's breath hot along my cheek when she said, "Whew!" bending over to flap a hand towel past my ear, flicking a fly off the pan of turnover rolls she'd just pulled out of the woodstove. I could smell the yeast, the trail of Marie's sweat along her dark arms, the colored skin smell of the colored man on the train, and his wife's perfume, maybe Evening in Paris from a fancy cobalt-blue bottle from the Amelia Courthouse drugstore.

I pulled up my cotton underpants and play shorts, torn but good enough for the backyard. I thought, excited, that I should tell my mother. She should know what I had just found out—did anyone in Richmond know this? *They were like us.*

I stopped short of clicking open the bathroom door, *Reader's Digest* in hand, my index finger in it to mark the page on which a colored man and woman were kissing. But what if she already knew? What if Mom knew and, never mind knowing, still explained that the colored people should sit in the back of the bus because they might have a disease? What if she knew and, never mind knowing, reminded me that there weren't colored ladies, only colored women? What if she said Unc was right to call Marie's husband *boy*, when anyone could see he was older than my cousins Johnny and Leigh?

What if she knew that colored people were like us, and the knowledge made no difference?

And how did I know I was right?

I slipped my finger from between the pages and put the *Reader's Digest* back on the hamper. I knew what I knew, but I couldn't think how to tell anyone. *Colored people kiss.* Of course they did, even if I'd never seen it, even if no one spoke of love between them, only of the number of dirty children they had on dirt floors, children who could barely fit into the little houses with the blue-ball bushes in front. What if colored people kissing proved nothing to anyone but me?

There was a Rule about keeping colored people separate, so how could my knowing that they were just like us make a difference? I'd only get in trouble. Mom kept secrets. For the time being, tucked out of sight in the new bathroom no colored person would be allowed to use, I'd have to keep what I knew secret: *colored people kiss.*

Mary Munford School occupied a cleared area between Grove Avenue and Cary Street Road only four blocks from Stonewall Court. It appeared that houses had, in a variation of *Monopoly,* been lifted off and a school lowered into the space the houses had occupied. I wondered if I was going to school on what had once been hideouts and houses and yards with badminton set up for contests after supper. The school had a flat roof, a broad horizontal sweep of windows, and a wide entrance with two aqua doors. The playground offered a few swings and jungle gyms and painted lines for hopscotch, a couple of basketball hoops. Susan and Jeff, Betsy and Ellen Manson, Courtney, and my sister and I walked to school every morning it didn't rain or snow, keeping on the sidewalks along Grove Avenue, skipping over the cracks that would break our mothers' backs. Simply walking to school without our parents made me feel that a change was coming into my life, or had already come, although I couldn't say exactly what it was.

At Collegiate School we had never said the Pledge of Allegiance, and I had to lip-read it from Mrs. Sims the first two days in my new classroom at Mary Munford. Promptly at 8:30 in the morning, we stood beside our desks, faced the flag, put our right hands over our hearts, and said the words it took me two days to learn. Mrs. Sims was as full-breasted as my mother, and when she pledged she put the palm of her hand slightly under her heavy breast. A few of the boys in the class smirked at each other, but with boys you never knew what the joke might be about. I had never been to school with boys. My mother said I was attending a "mixed" class, although everyone I saw was white.

Other girls pretended to have boyfriends or to have crushes on boys who ignored them. Susan's boyfriend was Todd Dabney, a blue-eyed blond boy who couldn't sit still during multiplication flash cards practice. Susan liked him because he was handsome. I told Susan that my boyfriend was Billy Perkins, a tall shy boy who reminded me of Robert Wagner, who was Prince Valiant in the movies. Billy would move to Chicago in December. We never quite got up the nerve to speak to each other, and I was relieved when he moved.

Courtney was placed in the other fourth grade classroom, and Betsy's third grade classroom was on a different floor in the building. We rarely saw each other during school hours, not until all of us from Stonewall Court reassembled by the flagpole to walk home together. We had to walk home together—that was the rule.

Every report card, I received straight As. We were asked to take the cards home and have our parents sign them, then bring them back to Mrs. Sims. Teachers had usually been pleased with my work, or Mom said they had been, but I had never had proof: a paper in hand to look at, typed, official, with the signature of the principal and my teacher. I was proud and also a little ashamed of that pride. Except for having to learn to write script and to give up the printing Collegiate taught, I found fourth grade at Mary Munford easier than any previous school year. Perhaps, Mom suggested, I had more confidence in myself. I finished tests in half the allotted time, and Mrs. Sims let me practice script or read to fill in the extra time. Soon she was satisfied that I knew how to write the officially prescribed script, which she said was more grown-up and looked like everyone else's.

Betsy's report card was a different story. She wouldn't let me see it, even though she showed it to others and laughed at the low marks. When Mom asked me to help her with her homework, using flash cards for addition and subtraction and early multiplication tables, Betsy pretended it was a game like Go Fish or Old Maid, and she would cheat. How could I help her if she acted like that? I was dismayed, then scornful. Because I felt bad that I couldn't help her, the scorn changed to a contempt I hid from myself because I knew I could cheat, too—although not at school—and cheating was shameful. At school, cheaters were sent to the principal or sent home. *Sent home.* I couldn't think of anything more shameful than walking home all alone, knowing you had to give the principal's letter to your parents. He would call home, too, just to make sure the letter arrived. At Mary Munford School I began to see how easy it was to be judged, to let a quick mistake become the way others knew you. At school, seen from the outside, known best by my schoolwork, I was no longer the girl with the Ferguson height, the Doyle nose and dimples. I was no longer a sum of family members. I was a sum of whatever others saw or thought they saw when they looked at me.

"Are you Jewish?" an older boy from the sixth grade asked me, leaning on the bike he had skidded to a halt beside me, his smile masking the accusation, or what felt like an accusation.

I denied it.

"But you have such thick eyebrows," he said and pedaled off, laughing.

I did have thick eyebrows.

Did Jews have thick eyebrows?

In my whole life, I'd seen only one Jewish boy. He was in Courtney's classroom, a boy with blue eyes and brown hair. Peter Soloman, and his eyebrows were thin wisps along the brow bone. The boy on the bike didn't know what he was talking about.

"He's just flirting," Susan said. "It's courtship, dummy."

"Fine way to flirt," I replied, and made a face I knew Susan would laugh at. I was cheered by her interpretation, but not so cheered that I couldn't see something I didn't like: *I was prejudiced against Jews,* even though I didn't know any Jews. How had that happened, I marveled? I didn't think I disliked Jews, although I'd learned the word *prejudice* at church, where some kids said that the Jews killed Jesus, didn't they?

But what else could my not wanting to look like a Jew mean? I was stunned that I could be what I hadn't given myself permission to be. It was like being fat without eating. It was like being blindfolded, without a physical blindfold and without agreeing to it. I was simply unable to see the darkened way of the world right in front of me.

It was odd. If I wasn't the mirror's sum of family traits and features, if I wasn't what others saw and graded, appraised and labeled, then what was I?

All by myself, alone in the dark, what was I?

I imagined looking into a dark, open sky. I saw no one, nothing I could call my own. I was No One.

"What are you shaking your head about?" Susan asked.

"Margaret talks to herself a lot," Betsy teased.

I frowned at her, and she ran ahead of us, jumping on the cracks in the sidewalk. She didn't care.

I wondered if Susan would recognize the blindfolded feeling, if I described it. Had she ever seen herself as No One?

But I didn't dare ask.

One afternoon, Mrs. Harrison's car, a new Buick like Uncle Allan's, pulled slowly to the curb in front of school. Susan and Courtney and I were waiting under the flagpole for the younger ones who walked home with us. It was late fall and breezy. Soon we would need our winter "woolies," as Mom called them, and in fact Mrs. Harrison was dressed in a camel-hair suit, a pale gold color. Courtney said it was a new suit and cost $200 at Montaldo's, maybe more. Mrs. Harrison also wore a hat to match, with a little veil over her eyes. She was a handsome lady, I thought, but there was to be no standing about and admiring her today. She raised her arm, a gesture of full authority and grace, bent her hand at the wrist, and motioned us over to the car.

"Come on, girls, I can't wait all day. Courtney and I are expected at the Boyds. Hurry along, now!"

I looked behind me—were the others coming? In the surge of third graders leaving the building, I saw Betsy, then Betsy Manson, then Jeff.

"Hurry up, Jeff," urged Susan. "We're getting a ride in a new car!"

Mrs. Harrison supervised our getting into the car. Courtney up front, no shoes on the cushions, four in the back, come along now, that's it. And then she stopped. Jeff, Susan, Betsy Manson, and I were seated in the back, jostling each other. My sister stood outside the car, waiting for us to move over enough to let her in.

"Oh dear me," Mrs. Harrison murmured. "There's no more room."

I looked at her. Then at Betsy.

"Now you stop that, Jeff Dortch," said Mrs. Harrison, peering into the backseat with a severity I had come to recognize as the iron she was made of, beneath all the chiffon and fine wool, silk and lace.

"There's room," Betsy said.

"No, I'm afraid not," Mrs. Harrison corrected her. "The law is one child up front, only four in the back. I can't fit you in."

"I can fit," Betsy insisted.

Mrs. Harrison looked at her directly. "No, indeed," she said. Then her voice got lighter. "You can walk home dear. It's not far, and you know the way, don't you?"

Slipping into the driver's seat, Mrs. Harrison shut the door and turned the ignition. I watched Betsy's face as the car pulled slowly off. She was already in tears, but the word *wait* stuck in my throat. Worse still, far worse than my reluctance to interrupt Mrs. Harrison, I felt a triumphant flash leave my eyes as the car began to move. It said, "You don't fit. There's no room for you, only room for me." I hadn't meant to gloat, but there it was. It flashed out, and Betsy saw it.

I was made to spend a day in my room, I lost my allowance, and movie privileges were removed for two weeks, even though *The Robe* was coming to the Westhampton Theater and Mom had planned to take us on a Sunday, because it was a Christian movie.

Mom called Mrs. Harrison before dinner. "*Any* mother should know better," I heard her say before she closed her door. After the phone call, Mom went into the bathroom, and I heard the click of the medicine cabinet, the shaking of the aspirin bottle. That's what the sound had to be. Then she slapped the bottle down on the sink.

"I *never*," I heard her exclaim to the tap water that needed to run a bit before it was cold enough to wash down the tablets.

Next day in school, Courtney found me at recess. "Mother says we can't play together any more. I'm not even allowed to speak to you!"

"For how long?"

"Forever," she said dramatically. "And Mom's going to drive me to school now, every day, and sometimes we can give the Dortches a ride, but never you or Betsy. It's not fair. She says Susan has to be my best friend now."

At home, Mom said, "That sounds about right. Queen Courtney and the dowager Empress! You don't need that friend, and neither do I."

I was sorry, but I knew there was not a thing I could do about Mrs. Harrison. I could pretend to ignore Betsy until she got over it. Months of silence would pass between Mom and Mrs. Harrison, and then one of them would relent and make a phone call. That was how it had gone when Too-Too and Mom lasted an entire year without speaking to each other. It had taken Uncle John to melt the frost.

"Enough is enough," he said, and drove the entire family over to our house on Mom's birthday. They brought a cake and walked right in the front door. I was glad to see my cousin Johnny, still serious and polite, and also Leigh the cutup. Susan had grown a lot and now wore fancy French braids. Mom and Too-Too cried, and then they went into the kitchen to pour iced tea. Johnny and I picked the mint in the backyard, shy with each other as the grown-ups settled their scores by not saying anything about them.

There was plenty of iced tea, Mom said, or there should be, and plenty of ice and mint and sugar. She filled the glasses with ice, making sure there was enough tea to go around. "This is no time to run short," she exclaimed. "It's a celebration!" But in fact two glasses came out with less tea in them, I noticed when Mom carried the tray out to the table on the screened porch.

"Oh, this is soooo nice," Too-Too was cooing in her high-pitched voice. Mom had said that Too-Too's voice could make a rug jump with excitement.

Mom confessed that a few glasses came up short on tea. "I didn't know you were coming," she explained, but Uncle John waved her off.

"Everything's fine," he said. "There's a plenty for everyone."

Leigh took two glasses of iced tea, one filled to the rim, the other filled three-quarters of the way. Cleverly, he held the glasses next to each other, not rim to rim for a true measure, but tea-line to tea-line. "See," he said, "they're equal!" Everyone laughed.

Then he took the full glass and put back the one with less. "Everyone's equal, but some are more equal than others," he said, and we laughed again. It was good to laugh.

But when Mrs. Harrison came to tea in the late spring, she and Mom were cordially stiff with each other. Mrs. Harrison ate only half of her slice of cake. Like good servants, Betsy and I helped remove the tea things, leaving the room tactfully when the two adults settled in for "our first good chat in a while." Courtney had made new friends in fourth grade, and so had I. For a while, we had waved at each other every day across the playground, but that hadn't lasted, nor had we disobeyed our mothers.

Mom's white-and-gold china teapot had a chip on the spout. Mrs. Harrison's teapot, I remembered, was silver.

## 8

In the fall of 1954 Mom landed a job teaching second grade at St. Catherine's School—the most respected school in the city of Richmond, she told me proudly. All the best people enrolled their children in the school, which had a long waiting list. It was owned by the Episcopal Church Diocese. St. Stephen's Church was just across the street, and the Country Club, where Uncle Allan played tennis with the editor of the *Richmond Times-Dispatch,* was only a few blocks away. All the houses in the neighborhood, she said, were big houses. Many girls attended from kindergarten through the twelfth grade, and then they left for college. Their path marched them, Mom believed, directly into a future that was secure.

St. Catherine's had begun in the 1890s when a maiden lady named Miss Jennie Ellett opened a school for young ladies in her living room in downtown Richmond, the first woman in Richmond to take seriously the education of women. In those days, young women hardly ever went to college, Mom said. Why, she wouldn't have gone herself had it not been for Uncle Percy, a doctor in Norfolk, from whom she had borrowed money, leaving home at the age of sixteen. Mom had graduated with a Certificate of Education in 1928 and gone to Amelia County, where she would teach for ten years, living with Aunt T at Harvie Hall, until she married Dad. With Mom now returning to teaching, I felt a strong wind from her past sweeping through the house, pushing Betsy and me into the future.

But it was only Betsy, stepping back a year and repeating the third grade, who would go with Mom into the future. I was not to go to St. Catherine's—not yet. There wasn't an opening in the fifth grade, Mom explained, and so I would return to Mary Munford. I didn't want to show her how left out I felt. Mom and Betsy would go off in one direction to school, and I in another. But what could I say? There was no room.

Betsy was frightened by the coming change and also pleased to have something I couldn't have.

"Now you'll know what it feels like," she taunted.

I shrugged. "You won't know anyone, and you'll have to make new friends," I returned.

A week after starting school, Mom made Betsy change her name to Elizabeth. It turned out there was a girl named Betsy Fergusson in the fifth grade, and though her last name, with an extra s, was different from ours, Mom didn't want her daughter confused with this other Betsy, said to be a poor student and a troublemaker. "It's a new name for a new start," Mom told Betsy, whom now I had to call Elizabeth, even at home. The name was a mouthful, and it didn't suit her. But Mom was adamant.

The waiting time for me to go to St. Catherine's fifth grade melted swiftly away. In two weeks, a girl in the fifth grade class suddenly had to move to Texas, her parents divorcing. While divorce was shameful, and I shouldn't be thankful for another person's sorrow, still I could be grateful for the opportunity. "See how God works in mysterious ways?" Mom preached. But I hardly had time to think about God's mystery. Now Mom was saying that my clothes had to be made ready for my first day—the very next morning. I wouldn't even have time to tell my classmates at Mary Munford good-bye.

"When it rains, it pours," Betsy-Elizabeth snickered.

Every other girl in Mrs. Keene's fifth grade class was seated at her desk when I entered the classroom, dressed at Mom's insistence in my Sunday best. The other girls looked at me like the stranger I was, but they seemed friendly enough. A girl who would later ask me if I always wore silk socks to school—her name was Corbin White—smiled at me in a way that seemed friendly. Mrs. Keene had big brown eyes made rounder by the magnification of her glasses, and her dyed reddish brown hair made crinkly waves that nestled into a tiny knot at the back of her head. A kindly fairy godmother, she seated me near the front but on the second row, not far from her desk. "Now girls," she said, "it's time for the test, put your books away." I looked under the lid of my desk and saw stacks of new books, a pad of paper, and sharpened pencils. How did they get there? Mrs. Keene smiled, and I knew she had put them there for me, along with a little note, "For your mother." That had to be the bill for the school supplies.

The test was an end-of-the-week examination in arithmetic. I looked over the test uneasily, finding two rows of problems I'd never seen before. When Mrs. Keene gave the signal to begin the test, I raised my hand.

"I haven't been taught how to do these yet," I whispered, pointing at what she would tell me were problems in long division.

"I'll show you," she said, also whispering, and did the first problem for me, drawing a little flat roof over the number to be divided and showing me how to divide, multiply, subtract, and bring down the next number, until all the numbers were used up and there was the answer, sitting on the roof like a line of birds in the morning.

"Now you try on your own."

When I hesitated, she said, "Here, I'll start you off."

Later when I switched my paper with the girl at the next desk over and Mrs. Keene read out the answers, everyone wrote an X or a C for correct next to the answers. Sarah Everson missed two. I missed none, although one didn't count, I told her. Mrs. Keene had done it for me.

"Are you good at hopscotch, too?" she wanted to know. "Corbin and I play hopscotch at recess." Then she said, "Aren't you a little dressed up for school?"

I nodded. "It's my first day here, and my mother was excited."

Sarah understood. Mothers were like that.

"Who's your father?" Carolyn Rawlings asked, her hands braced on her hips as she leaned her face forward intently, a little frown leveling her eyebrows into a line that underscored her query. No one had ever before asked me who my father was. In Stonewall Court, my friends knew Dad's crooked grin and the pipe that stuck out of his mouth at a cockeyed angle. They would know his patience, teaching us how to hold badminton rackets and hit the birdie or how best to line up a shot through the wicket in croquet. He also raked a heaping big pile of oak leaves in the fall and didn't mind if a half dozen children jumped in, even if it meant more raking afterward.

At St. Giles, Dad was the tallest usher with the most hair. Mrs. E. R. Patterson, whose husband, Pat, was bald as an egg, called Dad "a brown-eyed handsome man" right in front of my mother.

Right under Carolyn Rawling's nose, Dad had driven away from the Lower School parking lot, having let out Mom and Elizabeth and me for our day at St. Catherine's. Carolyn and several of her friends since kindergarten days watched me emerge awkwardly from the backseat of Dad's black Chevrolet, a company car now five years old. Carolyn judged the car too old and, with only two doors, inconvenient for those in the back. Why didn't we have a newer car? Why didn't our mother drive us to school? No one else's father brought them. Who *was* my father? The question was harder than doing long division. I didn't know what to say. Who was my father? My father was . . . my father.

When I thought of Dad, he inhabited first a family world, then a church world, then the mythic world of World War II, the war that had taken him across an ocean. Before going to St. Catherine's I hadn't felt the need to think of my father as someone important or rich or polished, except perhaps around Uncle Allan. Although Dad had been to college and had his degree from VPI, Uncle Allan's membership in the Country Club seemed to count more. He wore a suit or pleated slacks with a silk tie tightly knotted above a soft cashmere sweater, and he kept his cigarettes in a little gold case. His manners were, Mom said, impeccable, although I had seen him condescend to Dad in front of other adults.

I could never make heads nor tails of Dad's stories about his time in Europe. He told stories the way Nanny did, all twisted and turned, and just when you thought you understood the story, he'd say, "Well, anyways, to understand that, I'll have to back up and tell you . . ." or he'd say, "Funny thing was . . ." and I could never get to the punch line, the place where the laughter could be released. The story was never funny. The story usually had to do with a swamp of misunderstanding and guilt, resentment and a confusion of detail. I understood only the broadest details of his time overseas. Too old for the fighting itself, Dad had worked in "supply" and later, when the war in Europe was over, he had been in "intelligence."

But all that information about Dad was too much to say to the parents of my classmates—who also asked the question—and not what they wanted to hear. *Who is your father?* was a compass reading, a means of getting one's bearings. Asking *Who is your father?* was also a way of saying, *Who are you?* I couldn't be anyone unless my father was someone. It was a question with many others huddled behind it, among them *Should I know your family?*

To the troublesome question, most often I would reply by giving just Dad's name. "John Ferguson."

"No, I don't believe I know him," would come the puzzled, faint response. Or, "I know an Allan Ferguson." That Allan Ferguson, as often as not, turned out to be a man with the same name as my uncle, but no relation.

When Cookie Lewis's mother asked, "Who is your father?" she broke into a smile when I said, "John Ferguson, Allan Ferguson's brother." She knew the family, she said. Her brother had dated my Aunt Billie. She knew the Bon Air crowd. She smiled at me warmly. Cookie and I were already forming a friendship. We were tall, awkward, shy, and we had early breasts that embarrassed us. Soon after Mrs. Lewis knew who my father was, I was asked over to spend the night.

When my father's name didn't ring a bell, sometimes a grown-up would ask, "Where does he work?" and I'd reply, "Southeastern Underwriters." If the face continued to look blank, I'd tell them where the office was, on Main Street, two blocks from the State Capitol. I knew that Dad's office was bare wood and humble, and I also knew that Mom didn't like people to see him in the clothes he wore to make inspections. But she didn't have to worry. Where Dad worked was a mystery to the parents of my friends at St. Catherine's. The job, he said, was the first good one he'd gotten in Richmond, and, having been through the Depression, he was glad to have the job—afraid not to have it, as he put it. He never looked for another one. By his lights, he had no call to look for a better job, not even one that would give him more respect. I was beginning to understand that he needed more respect, even from Mom, who looked at him now with the eyes of social St. Catherine's, a gaze that made my tall and handsome father look insignificant.

No one asked me who my father's father might have been, but I already knew that it would have done no good to say he was a white-collar worker for the Chesapeake and Ohio. White-collar was the only collar at St. Catherine's. I thought it curious. Before attending St. Catherine's I didn't know I didn't know who my father was—or that

I couldn't say it in a way these West End Richmonders would recognize. It hadn't occurred to me I didn't know who my family was or what class we were. Anyone, however, who had the right answer to "Who is your father?" stood on firm ground. Those who asked and those who knew how to answer had confidence, old money, important jobs, new cars, and new clothes. As I watched my father drive away from St. Catherine's in the morning, the black Chevrolet seemed like the storm cloud a cartoonist might draw over a character's head when there was trouble brewing. Without knowing fully why, I began to feel sorry for my father and to wonder if the reason he was shy—often tongue-tied—was because he didn't have the right answers either.

Even though Dad's father had held a white-collar job and the Fergusons entertained with a butler at their occasional dinner parties, even though Bon Air was an up-river country resort community where the wealthy families of Richmond came in the summer to escape the mortal humidity of the city, the Fergusons were not a family of means. My sister would tell me how sorry she felt for Dad. While the other boys were given bicycles to speed around on, Dad had a pony and a cart. I thought about going fishing on the Rappahannock once with Dad. Dad loved to fish, but he wouldn't buy any equipment. Either he borrowed a pole or he lowered a drumstick tied on a string to attract blue crabs. At dinner Mom gave Dad all the bony parts of the chicken to eat—backs and necks and wings—but he never complained. He'd sing out praises for Mom's cooking and laugh the laugh that embarrassed Mom in public—a high whinny noise. His deeper laugh, the one I deeply trusted, came rarely. To hear that laugh was like listening to a fire in the fireplace: soft crackles of kindling, a quiet roar of wind and fire, then a spreading warmth throughout the room.

*Fourscore and seven years ago our fathers brought forth on this continent a new nation, conceived in Liberty, and dedicated to the proposition that all men are created equal.* Sitting on a straight chair with my ankles crossed, ill at ease in the living room of the town house belonging to the Carter family, I rehearsed what I could remember of the Gettysburg Address. Mrs. Keene had assigned it to the class to memorize, word for word. *The world will little note, nor long remember what we say here.* Slowly I remembered, then tripped over a later sentence which I knew had in it the words *brave dead* and *our poor power.* In the hall, Elizabeth was playing dolls with Gigi Carter, who talked baby talk to her doll. She acted younger than a girl in third grade should, Elizabeth later told me, adding "Gigi is a pill." Mom and Dad were sipping sherry with Mr. and Mrs. Carter in the parlor before going in to the table for Sunday dinner. Mom had Gigi's younger sister in her class, and she and Mrs. Carter had concocted this family Sunday dinner. We were still in our church clothes, having made a rushed exit from church and a beeline down Grove to the Carters' house. Except for Elizabeth and Gigi, everyone else was being careful and proper, the way you are with people you don't know and you don't want to ruin it by making a mistake. Mom saw my lips moving silently and smiled, then hurried on to explain to Mrs. Carter what I was doing.

"She has the whole speech pretty near by heart now," Mom announced proudly.

I shook my head. Not yet. There were blank spaces I couldn't bridge.

A little bell tinkled, and a heavyset colored woman in a black dress and starched apron opened the door between the sitting parlor and the dining room. The town house on Grove Avenue, in an older area called "The Fan," had been built before the War between the States. It was "antebellum." Gigi and Elizabeth came ripping around a corner, playing tag, and Mr. Carter spoke sternly to them as we were getting seated, Mrs. Carter pointing out who should sit where. She put Dad opposite her at the head of the table. When we were finally seated, though some of us children were still squirming, and as I was eyeing the forks to determine which one I should pick up first, Mrs. Carter asked Dad to say the blessing. We bowed our heads and looked into our laps. "Heavenly Father," Dad began, but his voice sounded strained. Mom said that how you behaved at the table at home revealed what you'd do out in company, and she had been teaching us about knives and different forks and different spoons, how to use them correctly. The blessing we said every night, and it was a short one. *Bless this food to our use and us to Thy service. Make us ever mindful of the needs of others, Amen.* Dad, however was beginning with "Heavenly Father," fancier words for the hosts and guests seated around the roasted chicken and the rice with gravy. "Heavenly Father," he began again, "bless this food to . . ." and he stopped cold again. I tried not to stir in my chair, but I peeked over at Dad. Was he slurring his words? "Bless this food to . . ." He looked over at Mom, his jaw slack with disbelief. He was at a loss.

". . . to our use and us to Thy service. Make us ever mindful of the needs of others, Amen," Mom chimed in with a clever lie, saying, "At home we do it as a duet," her voice like a descant over the others who were still saying "Amen" in unison because they were Episcopalians, and Episcopalians sounded out their Amens, while Presbyterians let the minister do it. Dad's face was sweaty, and he was blushing. Mr. Carter busied himself with his task of carving, and Mrs. Carter with hers, which was rice and conversation. I don't remember what anyone said, and like my father I couldn't speak, caught up by the surprising new sensation of being inside the dark silence of what my father must be feeling.

At least, I thought, no one had gasped. No one had stifled a laugh, as now at St. Giles some of the older children were doing on those Sunday sermon times when Reverend Rainwater, Dr. Belk's new assistant pastor, melted forward into a fish-belly-white, dead-as-a-doornail collapse onto the pulpit. He had fainted now three times, on the three separate occasions when he was to give a sermon himself instead of sitting there like the rest of us listening to Dr. Belk.

"Poor man," Mrs. Parke Lecky had murmured to Mom. "He's just plain scared to death."

Reverend Rainwater never got beyond his opening paragraph before, as someone unkindly put it, he drizzled out. On the third fainting, Mr. Floyd Abbot, one of the elders, volunteered to speak extemporaneously, and the congregation hung on his every word, rising to applaud him before the final hymn was announced. What a man!

Having muffed the blessing, Dad was now having a hard time keeping up with the small talk. He was dwelling on his mistake. When the vegetable dishes were passed, he reached to take more rice, reaching across his body to the left with his right hand and slightly back to where heavyset Gracie was extending the dish, when the serving spoon he was using flipped like a live thing with its own mind and fell to the white rug, taking down with it bits of rice and gravy. Dad made it worse by scrambling to pick up the spoon, ignoring Mrs. Carter's plea to let Gracie take care of the spill. I knew she didn't want Dad rubbing the goo into the white rug with his linen napkin, but Mom was talking gaily to Mr. Carter about, of all things, *Poppy the Fairy.* The diversion seemed to work because everyone wanted it to. I saw Dad's hand shake as he resumed eating. After lunch, as soon as it was polite, Mom made doing homework our reason for going home. "Don't want to eat and run," she said to Mrs. Carter, "but the girls do their homework in the afternoon before Sunday night waffles and Roy Rogers. It's a school night after all!"

I couldn't be sure, but I thought the Carters were relieved to see us go. Home, I went to my room and shut the door. That way, I could concentrate on the Gettysburg Address. *Now we are engaged in a great civil war, testing whether that nation or any nation so conceived and so dedicated can long endure. . . .*

The Westhampton #15 had its last stop at the University of Richmond, in a wooded and hilly area where my friend Cookie Lewis lived. Her mother and, finally, mine agreed to permit us to ride the bus together downtown, where we would get off at Miller and Rhoads Department Store to look into the festive windows whose autumn scenes showed mannequins in new bright wool scarves and wool pleated skirts. We could go to the Miller and Rhoads tearoom—not to the lunch counter, the tearoom—and buy a Coca-Cola, then board the bus just outside Loew's Theater and come back home, all this by ourselves.

On the bus you saw every sort of person, white and colored, babies in their mothers' arms, and old men—some wearing suits and vests, their handkerchiefs puffed, their hats cocked at an angle on their heads, others with stubble on their chins and rips in their trousers. Old ladies wore white gloves to go downtown, and we gave up our seats for anyone elderly and white. Recently on the bus, two colored women had boarded and sat down in the first row of forward-facing seats, so close to Cookie and me I could smell the starch in their summer skirts and the cool autumn air on their wool jackets. They wouldn't move to the back of the bus when an elderly white man got out of his seat and asked them to reseat themselves—*if you please,* he said, but his tone didn't mean *please*. The women were very nice about it, and they smiled, but they looked straight ahead and wouldn't budge. I had to elbow Cookie to keep her from edging into a fit of laughter, even though it was more interesting than funny. The man finally gave up repeating his request and sat back down in his own seat, scowling. Cookie didn't bust into it, but I knew she could any minute, because I'd seen the wings of her nostrils flaring in and out, the way they did when she was about to have a fit of giggles. The old man must have made her anxious, and we agreed later, and too grandly, that it was fine with us to sit near colored people—why not sit where you wanted? We sat in the back now, too, and didn't have to stand when all the seats up front were filled. Before, we wouldn't have moved to the back had we seen an open seat. Now we could.

These days, *before* and *now* were words that were making sentences seesaw back and forth. *Before,* there was respect; *now,* there's more than a body can endure, I overheard a lady say, getting on the bus in front of Loew's Theater, the wattle of her white skin trembling as she spoke. *Before, this; now, that*—that's how the sentences went, and the bus made its circle, mostly down Grove Avenue, then back west on Franklin until it crossed Stonewall Jackson on Monument and regained Grove. There were enticing views of the spacious houses of the wealthy on the streets off Grove Avenue in the West End and on Monument Avenue, but there were also whole blocks downtown, before you got to the downtown shopping and business centers, where I could see tiny bungalows next to small rundown shops or boarded-up buildings. Sometimes the bus would take a detour and cut through a colored neighborhood where, even now that it was cold, the colored men sat out on the sagging front porches in their summer T-shirts, holding brown bottles and smoking cigarettes while children—a man with a pug nose and a fight-me look called them "their get" and spat into his handkerchief as if it were the floor of the bus—shrieked and tumbled in the dirt yards my father called "black dirt" even though it was red clay. Long-legged teenage girls hung around the front of the little grocery at Meadow and Grove, looking into the window at their reflections and yanking their hair into almost straight sheets of shiny black.

"Everything's changing," Mom announced, standing behind me as I practiced Handel's *Largo* on the piano. I hated it when she stood behind me, watching intently. Was she waiting for me—I complained—to make a mistake? "With all that's going on these days, all I ask for is a little music, a little peace," she announced to the attic door as she retreated past it, and I felt instantly guilty for snapping at her. Handel was for her a source of pleasure and peace and solace. Solace I knew she particularly needed.

Shortly after we'd entered our classes at St. Catherine's, Mom met us at the front door one afternoon, watching me carefully to study my response to her telling us that Aunt T had died—gone back to God, she said. "I am sorry," I'd said, knowing that the three words weren't enough. Taking my words and holding them close, Mom said, as if excusing their poverty, that Aunt T hadn't been, even when we were younger children on summer visits, the T she knew from her girlhood days. Now we wouldn't be going back to Amelia in the summers, she added. The house would revert to Gordon and French and. . . . Her voice trailed off. She cleared her throat. And, it wouldn't be home anymore.

"Won't you go back for the funeral?" I asked, suddenly understanding more than I could feel or say.

She shook her head.

"It's tomorrow. I have to work, and so does your father."

Before, we went to Amelia; now, we no longer would. Now Amelia would be merely a historical marker on Route 60 West, a sleepy, poor county with big houses and colored shacks, the rolling land the Confederate Army had trudged through on its slow retreat from Richmond to Appomattox. With Aunt T dead, now Amelia was the buried past, the Grand Retreat, and the Depression rolled into one. When something died, you buried it. Everything ended— except for the War between the States, about which everyone was distant and polite and intractable.

In a moment, in a twinkling of an eye, we would all be changed, according to Saint Paul and Handel's *Messiah*. "You bound for Glory, girl?" Georgia asked acidly when I showed her the Revised Standard Version of the Bible with my name on it in gold, which I had been given when I was received as a member of St. Giles Church. Georgia came to clean once every two weeks, and she refused to wear a uniform. She left a little early, to show Mom what she thought of our money, and she didn't do windows. When Carolyn Rawlings phoned and Georgia answered in her low dark voice, "Ferguson residence," Carolyn commented to me, even before saying hello, "Well, you're coming up in the world."

A good student, I knew how important it was to get good grades. The report cards at St. Catherine's were amazing and thorough. They evaluated not only academic subjects and effort but also, in great detail, one's attitude and character. A tally of the report card would show eighteen As and seven Bs, for example. These report cards we were to take unopened home, but the following day, all of us in Miss Keene's class compared grades—at least the smart ones did. I was surprised by this competition, more so when a sallow girl I'd never met, Melissa Banning from the other fifth grade, stopped me in the hall and asked to see my report card. I showed it; she nodded and pressed on into the lunchroom without showing me hers. Before long, I had a reputation for being a good student. I don't know if I was "shining" about it, but my mother certainly was.

"You can be proud just to be you," she said, a not so subtle criticism of my having recently become Janet Leigh as a craze for movie stars swept Miss Keene's class. We spent our allowances on going to the movies, on buying movie magazines. Bonnie Buford was Mitzi Gaynor; Sarah Everson was Audrey Hepburn. Carolyn Rawlings wanted to be Janet Leigh, but clearly, as a brunette, she wasn't. I also had the breasts, I thought grimly. Cookie and I were the only girls in the class who wore bras and "needed" them. I'd started off with a size B and was very careful to avoid being teased. As Janet Leigh, I could bear the changes that were coming to my body, changes promised in detail by a movie on menstruation that showed cartoon drawings of the uterus and the fallopian tubes and the monthly passage of the egg through that corridor. No one in my class had as yet "started." But the scripts for the pageant were available, good sensible advice about hygiene. The rest was left to our mothers, who called it "the Curse." Janet Leigh must certainly have the Curse, but she was beautiful. I considered her "family." Weren't we linked by the same name? Cookie, who wanted to be less shy, was told by her mother to be Katharine Hepburn. In the garage apartment back of their house, the four of us—Cookie-Katharine, Margaret-Janet—pricked their thumbs, pressed them together in a blur of blood, and became blood sisters.

My sister's responses to me were more like Georgia's. She knew who I really was, and if I could rise in the estimation of others, well and good, but I couldn't pull the wool over her eyes. At recess one day as I was standing alone, she came up to me with a friend from her third grade class and said abruptly, "Here, I want you to meet my awful sister." She looked embarrassed immediately, as if the words had just slipped out. How would Mom handle this? I wondered, and an image of her face, flustered and offended, floated to mind. I chose to be Mrs. Lewis instead, and I lowered my voice, ignored the insult, and replied to Elizabeth's friend, "How do you do?" They skipped away and were gone in the mass of churning bodies at play.

At home by myself, I opened the closet door in my room to hang up my clothes and just stood there. How could she have done that? My bewilderment changed swiftly to a fury so black and deep it frightened me. *This is what you feel when you want to kill someone,* I thought. Who was I, who could feel like this? There was no one I could tell about this fury. I watched it boil. Then I stepped away from myself and watched from a distance. Then I stopped watching.

Elizabeth was, I knew, having a hard time in third grade. A reluctant student with inventive and wily excuses, by spring she had earaches so bad she couldn't hear in class, not a word the teacher said, even when she was moved up to the front row. I thought she was faking the deafness. Was that right? On the playground, I saw Elizabeth taunt her classmates, then blame them when they called her "Fatterson." Was that right? From time to time, Mom came home with a sweater that had lingered for too long in the Lost and Found and was ripe for a change in ownership. Was that right? And—truth be told—when a parent of a classmate gave me a ride home for the first time, I would have them slow the car and let me out in front of Miss Anne and Miss Eileen's house, saying it was ours, because it was bigger. Lying worked well with strangers and people you'd just met. They didn't know you, so you could use words to change yourself in a twinkling of an eye to something better. Was that right?

I stood outside my family and appraised them. Mom said family loyalty was the highest virtue next to family honor, but too often I felt ashamed. I didn't feel as if I belonged to the same world as my classmates. Even at the Lewis's house, where I spent many weekends and was treated affectionately, I found myself observing them as if they were exotic plants in the Florida room where Mrs. Lewis was pleased to relax in the afternoon with iced tea and the newspaper, lying on a chaise longue. From whoever I was, I felt distant.

Even when I gave piano recitals, no matter how correctly I played the music, a part of me flew outside and hovered behind the piano bench. I began to skip my afternoon practices, even though these were the only few moments I had of a fine and focused solitude. I practiced less so as not to risk bringing dark judgment into the rapture I relished. I could still bring music into being at the touch of my fingers on the keys. To save music from what I might do to it by standing outside it, I eased myself away from its presence, or possible presence, saying nothing to anyone, not even to myself until it was too late, and I had, it seemed, decided to give it up. Now I would have to figure out a way to say *why*, a way to open and close a door so quickly that I could slip through and no one would know, nor would I, that I was stealing away from the deepest part of myself.

"Mom," I said one afternoon, helping her to snap the green beans. "Next year, I'll be in Miss Stites's sixth grade, and she gives tons of homework."

So much work that parents in former years had complained.

So much work I'd need all my time after school for homework and reading.

Mom listened, and we decided together. Lessons were expensive and one should, given the expense, practice. It was, Mom said, my choice. To study or to play piano. Since she was helping me make the decision she thought I wanted to make, perversely now I wanted her to tell me I must continue with music, I must not ignore my great gift. But she was only saying, "You really like to study, don't you?" And I had to admit that I did.

"Shall we keep the piano?" she wondered. Was this her way of checking my resolve?

I snapped off the end of a green bean and tossed the plump bean into the colander Mom had in her lap, announcing with outward confidence, "Let's sell it."

"We could use the money," Mom replied softly, and I wondered if I was feeling her sadness or my own.

This is my first real choice, I thought. My choice. Even more than joining the church—the choice that was prechosen and predestined—this nearly wordless decision to stop my piano lessons and practices and recitals came from within me, from that mysterious inner space from which grown-ups made their choices and gave their directions and seemed so sure of themselves. I was surprised at the mixture of grief and other confusing feelings that accompanied the pleasure and the relief I also felt.

Then Mom said. "You'll always have the music inside you. That never goes away."

That night I emptied the piano bench of the sheet music and gave it to Mom to give to my piano teacher. At night before sleep when I found myself practicing a complicated fingering maneuver, I made myself stop. Gently, I touched instead the callus on the middle finger of my right hand where, as I did my homework, the pencil pressed.

As early as fifth grade, the petite and perky girls in my class—Anne Cabell, Nancy McBryde, Kinzie Haskell, Betsy Fergusson—began attending pre-cotillion parties with boys from St. Christopher's, readying themselves for the cotillion that all of us as surely as day follows night would attend in sixth grade. In sixth grade, the parties before the party continued until a week before cotillion. Taller than most boys my age, I only wondered about these fabled parties held in the paneled dens and formal living rooms of houses off Three Chopt Road and River Road, thrilling more to the names of pharaohs of Egypt and the exploits and discoveries of the Chaldeans, the Babylonians, the Assyrians. I was moved profoundly by the extraordinary clarity of sentence structure as revealed in the art of diagramming sentences: everything fit. You could see it. Elizabeth, who was interested in the parties and in the cotillion that was two years in the future for her, charged that I was much too serious about gerunds and infinitives, Egyptians, Persians, Greeks, and Trojans.

"Want to see something funny?" she teased, hauling me into the bathroom. Fastening one of Dad's Trojans—where had she found it?—onto the bathtub faucet, she turned the cold water on with a fast twirl of the knob and the condom puffed out like a balloon, like a blowfish. Elizabeth rocked back on her heels, her nostrils flared wide, snorting with hilarity. "Do you think it's like that in bed?" she giggled, and I shook my head, laughing at my sister's brazen impishness, but trembling in a way I couldn't understand.

I knew that inside my body, even as I knelt at the tub's edge with my sister, within one of the sacs of eggs, a single egg was swelling, readying to burst the horizon of a membrane and tumble into what would become the palpable presence of a uterus that had prepared for the egg with a thick mush of blood. Because of that blood, I thought, because of that egg, the line in the basement is hung with white crinolines, pre-cotillion parties are in swing, and the short girls in the class are learning to waltz. Mom said menstruation was glorious: the bleeding meant I would one day have a baby. It meant I was no longer a child. It meant grave responsibilities as I "saved myself" for the man I would eventually marry. Edmund Purdom in epaulets and a cape as the Student Prince. Robert Taylor in riding breeches and a safari hat before the pyramids of Egypt. Thinking about it made me numb. Later I would be glad when the first signs of the auspicious and wondrous moment turned out to be little more than a hollow ache and a faint rusty smear in my underpants.

Before "the Curse" commenced, however, there was the first season of cotillion. With the orchestra on stage playing a stirring and spirited melody, the Grand March commenced in the ballroom of the Women's Club in Windsor Farms, the most elegant neighborhood in the West End. Mom and Dad were in the balcony to watch, along with other parents, as the daughters and sons of old Richmond marched toward each other, toward the initial good or bad luck of a dancing partner. Who would it be? The boys lined up on one side of the room, the girls on the other, and the lines inched forward. Miss Cleiland Donnan and her dashing partner stood in a glitter at the head of the room, where the girl and boy would meet, join hands, and parade down the center of the ballroom to stand awkwardly until everyone had passed through the line and all were paired. Girls and boys who knew each other and wanted to be partners counted back in the line across the room and shifted places in line until their intended partners were assured, as long as no one cut in or dropped out of line ahead of them. The boys wore suits and white shirts with ties and handkerchiefs. The "fast" girls whose mothers would let them wore lipstick and stockings. The old-fashioned others—most of us—wore silk socks, but we all had on new party dresses. I was wearing the fanciest dress I had ever worn, a skirt of plaid taffeta and a dark blue velvet top that made me anxious: a bra strap might slip into view.

The Grand March was an agony. I had counted back and knew that my partner would be one of the shortest boys in the room. His head would barely reach my collarbone, and where would his eyes naturally rest as we faced each other and attempted the box-step waltz, the fox-trot, the samba?

Miss Donnan had demonstrated these dances and promised us step-by-step instruction. She wore a peach-colored chiffon dress with rhinestone straps, and when her transparent high heels touched the ballroom floor, lights flashed in the high clear plastic heels. Tap-flash, tap-flash! The fire in her being shone in her feet, and she threw back her head and gazed into the face of her tall dancing partner as they moved flawlessly, effortlessly across the floor. They were as shining as a meander of water, as inevitable as planets in orbit, as romantic as Fred Astaire and Ginger Rogers. Miss Donnan was like no old maid I'd ever imagined, and she gave directions in a clear, deep voice that brooked no nonsense, offered no reprieve, and promised success all at once. The art of the dance was the art of life, and she called to us to follow her lead past the uncertain knowledge our bodies currently held, beyond innocence, into the experience of dance which, because of its firm patterns and sense of design, would release us to fly into the lilting rhapsody of music itself, into the heart of music, where we would be free.

Freedom, I decided, would have to wait until I discovered how not to step down hard on my partner's feet. His name was Lowndes Nelson, and I was supposed to follow his lead, but he had the lead wrong, and when I followed him I ended up on his toes. It was proving difficult, this rhapsody of the dance. Counting 1–2–3–4, back–2–3–4, making small talk, and taking care that my partner's nose didn't graze the smooth velvet over my young breasts was hard work. After cotillion, Mr. Rawlings was driving four of us girls to the Clover Room for ice cream cones, a tradition for many young initiates into the dance, a way to descend from orbits of tension and delight.

I knew that my mother would be sitting on the living room sofa waiting for me to come home, waiting to help me out of the finery that had, I knew, caused her to sacrifice something essential in the budget. Her eyes would be shining, and she would tell me what I had not been able to see earlier in the mirror as I dressed for cotillion—that I was beautiful. That watching me at the ball was better than her dreams, better than a movie. I was her girl, and this was my life.

Mattie Leigh Doyle, age eighteen.

109

Mrs. John S. Ferguson, 1940.

Mom and Dad, 1944.

Mom, Margaret Leigh, Betsy.

Cousin Jane, Betsy, Margaret Leigh,
37 Lexington Road.

Margaret and Betsy with Marie Hill in Amelia.

Margaret and Betsy with Snowball.

Margaret, age eighteen (1962).

Elizabeth, age nineteen (1964).

Dad and Mom at the Chesterfield, 2004.

## 9

# The Queen of Hearts

Shetland sweaters were a must, but they were expensive, especially at Steve and Anna's, the select little shop in Westhampton where St. Catherine's girls bought their clothes. My mother rummaged in an attic trunk and found a sweater, dusky rose in color, with the large-yarn look of a Shetland, and she gave it to me. She had worn it in college, she said proudly, and since I was tall, it just might fit me. Wearing it and my fashionable new shoes—clunky boats of brilliant white leather with saddles of brown and broad white laces—I made my way toward my assigned desk in the Middle School's study hall, avoiding the ring-binder notebooks that edged into the narrow aisle as a few intent girls finished their homework assignments. There was no talking in study hall, except during morning announcements and morning chapel, when only the teachers talked.

The seventh graders sat one behind another in long rows that abutted matching rows of eighth graders. My desk was next to eighth grader Armistead Merriweather, to whom I had never spoken because I saw her only in study hall. Armistead was as exotic to me as a movie star. Her skin looked velvety, tawny. Hers were the largest, most liquid brown eyes I had ever seen. She had fingernails—polished—and a little gold ring. Her clothes came from Steve and Anna's.

Our teachers counted on their authority to keep the silence in study hall, but it also helped that, to a seventh grader, most eighth graders appeared to be unapproachably mature and experienced. I wouldn't have dared begin a conversation with an eighth grader. When I looked at my seventh grade classmates, I saw the bodies of girls still coltish and unsure. The eighth graders wore their sweaters and skirts with grace and style. Lipstick wasn't allowed at school, but we knew that many older girls had a tube of lipstick hidden away in their pencil cases for a quick swipe once they were released onto Grove Avenue at three o'clock, when the eighth graders gathered at Doc White's pharmacy on the corner of Grove and Maple to talk with the boys from St. Christopher's. If a boy had a crush on you, he was "snowed." From the bus stop on the opposite corner, I watched the crowd at Doc White's, and like most of my friends, I was gawky, tongue-tied, and envious.

In field hockey, an eighth grader's body followed Miss Fleet's instructions with apparent flawless ease. I stumbled over my stick, failing to send the ball with a confident crack to its destination in the field. How did they do it—Kitty Anderson, Marty Davenport, Lucy Day, Isabel Rawlings? In their short yellow uniforms with bloomers, they couldn't have looked more comical, and yet, given their skill, they managed to give off a gritty allure. Studying them from a distance, I imagined my own body into existence, burgeoning toward a maturity that wouldn't have to think about itself.

With a swift, sidelong glance I studied Armistead Merriweather. She was perfect.

Perfect, but not a top student or a top athlete. Perfect, but with a most peculiar manner during morning prayers, the time I had my best look at her. During chapel at our desks, I couldn't take my eyes off Armistead, even though my head was bowed, and my mind supposedly focused on an omniscient Triune God with the same concentration I gave to ungovernable fractions. Together, both grades prayed what we had memorized from the Book of Common Prayer, reciting by heart the required General Confession: *Almighty and most Merciful Father, We have erred and strayed from Thy ways like lost sheep. We have followed too much the devices and desires of our own hearts.*

As she spoke the words softly, Armistead's head bent so low to her desk that her mouth met the wood. Her full, generous mouth opened slightly, an open-mouthed kiss that skimmed the surface, not quite kissing—but what else was it? I heard small gasps of breath. *We have left undone those things which we ought to have done. And we have done those things which we ought not to have done; And there is no health in us.* The desk was a dark mirror. I could almost see Armistead's warm breath upon it. Was she kissing herself? An imagined boy? God? Now her mouth opened wider and her lips rested on the wood, murmuring *Spare Thou those, O God, who confess their faults.*

I held my breath as Armistead's mouth married her faults to the study hall desk. She was the carnal embodiment of the words we had recited in the call to prayer: *O Lord, open Thou our lips.* To which we had responded, *And our mouth shall show forth Thy praise.* Whether it was praise or plea, Armistead Merriweather—and all of us—concluded the confession: *That we may hereafter live a godly, righteous, and sober life, To the glory of Thy holy name, Amen.* As we straightened in our chairs, Armistead looked at me and smiled, gathering her books. Did she know I adored her?

Miss Hood, our history teacher, was an elderly elf in tweeds, her body a tidy little barrel on bird stilt legs. She wore lace-up shoes that seemed too large for her little body. She wouldn't hurt a fly, if one judged from the sweetness of her face or, less charitably, from the wavering warble of her speaking voice. And yet there was a ferocity to occasional remarks and predictions. "If your parents think the Russians are bad," she warned, tapping a map of the Middle East, "let them look to the desert. *Here* is where the future wars will be fought." She lowered her voice an octave. "Oil," she said, and the heating pipes in the old bungalow, one of the three original buildings, knocked and hissed.

Melissa Banning dutifully wrote down the word *oil* in her notebook. Cookie Lewis was still my best friend, but it seemed as if the classroom seating assignments in Middle School had been designed to part friends and scatter cliques. I saw Cookie only from across the room, rows of classmates between us. By chance or design I was placed next to Melissa Banning in history, biology, and math. I was getting used to showing my grades to her at her request when our papers were returned, and she occasionally phoned me at home. Among the first in our class to wear saddle shoes and pleated wool skirts, she seemed to know everyone and even had a friend among the eighth graders, Meade Davidson, for whom the study hall had risked Miss Thruston's ire by breaking into applause when Meade emerged from the bathroom with a triumphant grin that every eighth grader and many in the seventh knew how to interpret. Slight and underdeveloped, Meade was the last in her class to menstruate.

Everyone knew she was waiting for Mother Nature to bestow on her the physical maturity which even most seventh graders had attained long before. Her waiting was a physical trial, each month another chapter in a series of suspenseful moments. Her triumphant grin could therefore mean one thing only: finally! Her friends applauded, then everyone else did; Miss Thruston sputtered, shook the wattles of her chin, and grew red-faced. "Girls!" she cried. In her maiden outrage and Victorian body, she resembled a hen turkey. "Girls!"

Melissa Banning, graceful only on the athletic field, was gangly and unformed. In the classroom she twirled a bit of hair with one hand and took notes with the other. She bit the side of her cheek during tests and moved the leg crossed over her knee up and down like a manic wood saw. Often chosen as class captain of the Gold team in our Gold-White rivalries, this year Melissa had been elected president of our class.

"Be careful," prim Kathy Pinckney cautioned, as we rode home on the #15 bus. She had noticed Melissa's attentions to me, but would say no more than those two words. "Ask Susan Abbot," she finally offered, closing the conversation firmly. But Susan was not in any of my classes, she lived on Patterson Avenue—too far to visit after school—and she was close to being another one of the outsiders in the class, those mysteriously unpopular, disregarded girls like Patty Wells, Shirley Fairgrieve, invisible Mary Hogue, or Annie Coleman. I tried to figure it out. Was it that Shirley's voice was too shrill, her body too scrawny? Was it that Annie always said the wrong thing and wrung her hands? Was it that Patty's clothes were too small for her and Mary's skin so freckled that she slunk into the shadows for camouflage? Their lack of popularity hung on them like a faint sour odor, untraceable but persistent.

I thought of the scatter of stars in the night sky, some clustered, some far-flung and solitary. I thought of jack rocks—the jacks thrown up and spilled randomly on the floor. Some jacks fell into clusters, some skidded off alone, too remote from the others to be gathered in. Considering that I was a relative newcomer to this class at St. Catherine's, I was grateful for my friendship with Cookie Lewis, and I protected it.

Was I going to the slumber party at Bear Island? Melissa wanted to know as we changed classes. *Good*, she replied, when I nodded. Bear Island was the country home of Cookie's grandparents, the

Parrishes. Cookie and her cousin Kathy Parrish were hosting a sleepover, and Cookie had invited, predictably, her neighbor Sally Everson and me. Kathy had invited Melissa, Page Fitzgerald, Mary Tyler, and Corbin White—popular girls chosen from the athletic, brainy clusters in the class. It was my first slumber party with a large group of girls, and I was excited and a little nervous, more accustomed to the intimate and nearly familial weekends at the Lewis's house, our rituals of movies during the afternoon and card games at night.

Kent, Cookie's older brother, had to cross through Cookie's bedroom to get to his own. Saturday nights, he would knock, wait, and knock again as Cookie and I leaped into bed, pulling the covers to our collarbones. As Kent crossed the room and entered the sanctum of his own room, my cheeks glowed hot, a heat that gradually reached what must have been my heart. Clearly, I was *snowed*. Snowed and terrified that Cookie would guess it. Had she known, our friendship might have altered, and I knew that rompish, shy, awkward Cookie needed me as much as I needed her, lest we both be loners to whom no one talked at lunch. The years would pass, I imagined, following the movie in my mind, and Kent would notice me. We'd marry, and Cookie would be my sister until death parted us.

I liked the expression *snowed*. It didn't snow in Richmond often, but after gray skies and the rush of snow came winter's clean bright air and a changed world. Snow was beautiful in the air, treacherous underfoot, and like any weather uncontrollable. You could neither summon it nor dismiss it if it came. When I said *snowed*, I could ignore the raw terror and reluctant pride I felt in having a maturing body which, one day, I'd promise to a man. One man only. "Snowed" deferred commitment. In the flurry and rising wind of the storm, "snowed" masked feelings, just as whenever other girls dared speak of sex, they used exaggerated tones of comic and tragic awe to mask what they might really be feeling.

This mixed awe lurked in Melissa Banning's voice as she let me know that Corbin White had promised to bring to Bear Island the book her mother was reading: *Lady Chatterley's Lover*, written by an Englishman. "Just wait until you read the passages that sizzle," she said Corbin had warned, relishing her power to bring us the forbidden. "He writes about *intercourse*," Melissa said in an impressive whisper.

"I wouldn't know," my mother replied when I asked her what was so awful about *Lady Chatterley's Lover*. Why, no one she knew would read such a book! Airy and too easily dismissive, she forgot to ask me why I was asking. Perhaps she trusted me, or perhaps she had something to hide. And so it was with a little guilt that, on a hunch, I searched her dresser drawers the next afternoon as she walked down to Stanley's Market, and I found the forbidden book. It was giving off heat in her slips and stockings. As I turned the pages, reading quickly, I listened for mother's returning footsteps on the front porch. Lady Chatterley's lover was the gamekeeper of her estate, and he lived in a cottage, which she would visit. When they were naked, he touched the two openings between her legs and said, "And I don't mind if ye shits or pisses. I like a woman who can shit and piss." His ruff of pubic hair was red. I read as much as I dared and replaced the book in its hiding place. Then I made a resolve. I would tell her I'd found it, but I wouldn't tell her I'd read any of it. We could both have our lurid little secrets.

"It's not as terrible a book as they say," she told me, after a pause.

"Now don't you tell your friends your mother's reading it!" she exclaimed shortly.

"That man, that man in the book, he really knows what a woman likes," she mused. The smile on her face stunned me. It was tender, as if she had made the man in the book her lover just by reading the book. Mistaking my expression, she added, "Your father's a little rough."

*She shouldn't be telling me that,* I thought, wishing I hadn't tried to trip her up, catch her in a lie, shock her with my knowing her secret. She possessed, I realized, secrets I couldn't hope to fathom, secrets that tipped into view in the quick lightning flash of words that gave me a glimpse of the woman my mother was, the man my father was. In that flickering light, I'd see but I wouldn't know what I'd seen, and then it would be dark again. Telling me once about her wedding day, she described her dress, the church, Aunt T's house made festive with greens and flowers, the box of baked sweets the cooks sent them off with, the smell of the ocean when she and Dad arrived at Virginia Beach. "We were so happy," she said. Then, "And next morning on the boardwalk I could hardly walk, I was so sore."

*She shouldn't be telling me that,* I remembered thinking. Mom didn't talk to my sister like this. Mom needed a friend, I realized—and I was it.

Becoming a woman appeared to be a process of repeated shocks and perplexities. I had existed until now in a lull. Until now I had floated in shallow waters. Now the tide was in, bringing with it a stiff undertow, and I was borne by currents I couldn't anticipate or govern. My body had a mind of its own. I could obey Commandments, school regulations, my parents' rules. I could keep to schedules and codes, I could follow Proverbs and not call my sister a fool, I could say "Yes, Sir" when my father's eyes darkened and he could no longer be teased by "Poor Daddy, all alone in a house with three women!" But I couldn't ask my breasts to stop growing. I could tweeze the random hairs that sprouted between my eyebrows, but I couldn't ask the monthly blood not to stain my bedsheets.

In the summer, I longed for the simplicity of earlier trips to Virginia Beach. In earlier years, I would run on the beach, shoot the waves with Dad, eat a full plate of Mom's rare sirloin and new potatoes, roughhouse with Elizabeth and her black cocker spaniel who chased fiddler crabs into their sand holes on the beach. Now I worried that my Kotex showed in the crotch of my bathing suit. *Take frequent showers,* counseled the pamphlets on female hygiene, but Mom rationed water, Kotex, shampoo. Now at the beach we dressed up in the afternoons and attended "dances" with the famous Lester Lannin band. Invited to dance, or not, all the wallflowers and short boys joined in a daisy ring of follow-the-leader—the band called it the "bunny hop." *Dah de dah de dah dah, dah de dah. Dah de dah de dah dah. DAH DAH DAH.* The rhythm pounded like surf as we kicked and hopped, holding on to each other's waists. I worried that I smelled like rotting fish. Elizabeth and I refused temptations of saltwater taffy and Coca-Colas, spending our money on perfume, powder, bobby pins, and deodorant. Mom and Dad had rented a cottage on the cheap, owned by the unmarried aunt of a St. Catherine's girl

Mom had taught in second grade. "Divorced, I'll bet," grumbled Mom, looking around the cottage as if for a lurking gamekeeper.

On rainy afternoons, Elizabeth and I stayed in the spare bedroom and listened to the aunt's records, Frank Sinatra singing "Autumn Leaves" and other songs of love and loss. Over and over we played them to drown out our laughter and chagrin as we read the unmarried aunt's love letters, which we'd found bundled and shoved behind the records. They had been written by a navy man, a sailor. "I'm polishing my white shoes buck naked on my bunk. You should see me!" he had written. Our eyes widened to take him in, and we giggled.

"I think he's a bit too coy," I suggested, and we exhausted ourselves in a fit of laughter, avoiding what we wouldn't say.

Committed to being virgins, sworn to virtue until we gave ourselves to the "right" man, we couldn't admit that already we touched ourselves in secret, tasting for ourselves a pleasure we weren't supposed to know lay so near at hand. Until you were with a man, it didn't count, it didn't exist.

Thrown together on vacation, Elizabeth and I were without the refuge of separate friends, separate classrooms, separate bedrooms, and we fashioned an alliance of sorts. "I'm ashamed of my fat," she confessed one afternoon as she tried to conceal her body from my view as we changed into our bathing suits. For once I didn't respond with a fact or an observation I'd been harboring to squelch her. I didn't say, "Well, if you hadn't gone and eaten the entire cake on the sly . . ." She had eaten a cake. Just before we left for the beach cousin Sandra, for whose young children Elizabeth had been babysitting, had called to tell Mom just that. I'd waited to hear Mom reprimand my sister, but instead she'd only confided her embarrassment to me. Perhaps Mom wanted peace. She had in April bribed Elizabeth with an early birthday present, saying "I'll give it to you if you'll only stop nagging me." Now, hearing my sister's candid shame, I felt a thrill of sympathy, surprised to feel it, more surprised to be glad to.

"Mom stuffs us," I agreed. Gone was my contempt for my sister's choice of favorite foods—hot dogs, spaghetti, chicken drumsticks, Milky Way candy bars, chocolate-covered cherries, butterscotch almond ice cream, bologna. Gone was my scorn for her plump thighs and calves, her double chin, the soft and pasty white skin of the bulge her belly made, the dimples-in-cream look to the flesh over her ribcage. We had a common goal—to be sleek as movie starlets. And we had a common enemy in our mother, who couldn't help herself— or us—but urged on us fried chicken, mashed potatoes with pan gravy and butter, sausages, batter bread, black-eyed peas and stewed tomatoes with sugar; our mother, who in Richmond on sum- mer nights several times a week would call out, "Daddy, go and get your three girls double-dip ice cream cones." And she'd call out the flavors she wanted for each of us, the chocolate I found hard to resist, her own peaches and cream, and the butterscotch for Elizabeth.

Quietly Elizabeth and I began to help each other hide food, sneak- ing half of a sandwich beneath the table to the complicit cocker spaniel, wadding toast into a napkin or a pocket, stuffing fist-sized lumps under cushions or into dresser drawers, reminding each other to retrieve them and throw them out before the mayonnaise turned rancid and the bread blued. It was an uneasy alliance. Eliza- beth mocked me with dramatic disgust when I'd wiggle a finger down my throat to make myself throw up. And I'd taunt her when she couldn't resist gobbling half a box of saltwater taffy or choco- lates. But momentary slips and stings were ameliorated by our gen- erally united front: we would be *thin.*

Returned to Richmond, I began to sequester more food, and now not simply to support the alliance I'd made with my sister. I was angry at my breasts and at my mother, the source of my inheritance, never mind that she once mournfully suggested that I should be grateful not only for the engineering of the modern bra, but also to have a mother who would buy the bras I needed. As a girl in the country she'd had no money for a bra, and as her breasts lengthened and spread, she had sewn handkerchiefs together to cover them, using ribbons to hoist them higher. Whereas I had earlier responded with sympathy as she described that not quite credible brassiere, now the story only made me angry. She knew what it felt like to be too big. She had felt a similar awkward shame. She too had walked into study hall with her head high and her shoulders tilted forward and ever so slightly rounded, hoping to conceal her breasts. Mrs. Lewis helped Cookie count calories; Mrs. Banning split a turkey sandwich between Melissa and me and gave Melissa, who was diet- ing, the "smaller half." Why couldn't Mom help me? Why couldn't she see me?

In order to see myself, I locked myself into my sister's bathroom and took off all my clothes. Hers was the only interior door in the house that locked. I stood on my toes to see more of me in the small, high mirror. I preened. I struck a pose. I touched myself here and there and down there. I closed my eyes and imagined a man who would see me. That's all I could manage to say: a man. I had no boyfriend, no one specifically in mind. Outside the bathroom window, a spring robin bumped and pecked at the window glass, pecked and fluttered, flew away, flew back, fluttered and pecked rapidly, madly, repeating the nonsense over and over, seeing himself as a rival male, or as his own mate, I couldn't tell. I laughed at the robin. Silly bird that couldn't see itself.

Before cotillions in the winter, I'd sit at the vanity table Mom had bought for Elizabeth's room. She had starched the frilly white skirt, rubbed the glass top to a shine that squeaked. Every southern young lady should have one, she said. Dressed up and wearing the only shade of lipstick Mom allowed—"powder pink"—I studied my face to see what others saw when they looked at me. The vanity table sat where my piano had been moved in my last year of piano lessons. Seated now in my finery, I gazed uncertainly at a face and flesh that were, according to the Preacher in Ecclesiastes, grass: *Vanity, Vanity—All is Vanity*, said the Preacher.

Before the mirror of the vanity table, I tried to see myself through the eyes of my dance partner, whoever he would be. I tried to see myself as Kent Lewis would see me. As Melissa or Carolyn or Corbin, Armistead Merriweather or Meade Davidson would see me. Only when I saw myself as my mother would see me was I beautiful, and that was embarrassing, because she saw—I had to admit it— herself. "It's all uphill until you're seventeen," she had told me. "And it's downhill after that." Her words were dismaying. I didn't think I was beautiful yet, and I only had a few more years, if she were right, to become beautiful before the gradual decline began. My mother had grayed early, and her breasts had obeyed the laws of gravity, childbearing, and nursing. She'd told me that "once upon a time" she had been "raahther beautiful" drawing out the "ah" vowel until it was as velvety as her pride.

"It's harmless," Mrs. Parrish had remarked to Mom, who had mortified me by calling to complain about the strip poker we'd played at the slumber party at Bear Island. "They're just at that age, curious. I'd rather have them explore the gifts and perils of the flesh together and at home than . . ."

"Don't they have sisters?" Mom finally laughed.

"Only some of them do," said the woman who had married the man Aunt Billie once had dated. "Don't worry. They're a lot more prudish than we are. We raised them right."

I put down the receiver on the other phone quietly, hoping they hadn't heard me listening on the line as if my life, or reputation, depended on it.

"Women Rule the World," Mrs. McCue had decreed in an Upper School assembly a few years before. Mrs. McCue had retired, but her words had not. Standing before us now was Miss Abbey Castle, her successor, repeating Miss McCue's words as, late to the morning assembly by twenty minutes, I whispered my excuses to Miss West before I prepared to slink to my seat in shame. I'd been in the bathroom, sick, I told her. Actually I'd been in the library reading in the stacks and had lost track of time.

Miss Castle, head of Upper School, was busy preparing us for St. Catherine's Day at the end of the month. On that day, a senior voted most like Saint Catherine would appear before the entire Upper School in McVey Auditorium, dressed and crowned like the saint the school honored for her faith and for the martyrdom that had elevated her. Miss Castle then repeated Mrs. McCue's famous dictum, affirming the moral preeminence of women in our civilization. Although men might hold the visible positions of power and influence, behind every president, senator, general, and business executive, there was a woman: his mother. Women ruled because, standing behind, like a good wind at your back, women trained the minds and governed the hearts of those children who became the world's leaders. Wives took over where mothers left off. "You are in training to be the 'unacknowledged legislators of the world,'" Mrs. McCue was said to have concluded proudly, quoting an English poet.

In Ellett Hall, I had seen the portrait of Mrs. McCue, a trim woman in good shoe leather and a wool suit, her face as Scottish as those I would, years later, see in restored photographs of women on the island of Harris, fulling the wool that would be sewn into Harris tweed jackets, like those worn by the natty fathers of St. Catherine's girls in Richmond. Miss Castle revived Mrs. McCue's words with a gaiety that proclaimed them gospel. Years later I'd recognize that the gaiety, a mask for defiance and resignation, was intended to offer us comfort as we learned to accept our place in the scheme of things. It also allowed the comforter herself to be comforted. At the time, the boast fell on my ears without any slur of complicity. Hearing, I was simply pleased.

Rigorous in their self-discipline, enthusiastic in their scholarship, their aspirations high, their expectations demanding, many of our teachers were elderly ladies who still wore their fathers' names. Miss West, Miss Castle, Miss McKenney, Miss Fitchett, Miss Walton, Miss Keim, Miss Ruffin, Miss Salley. No one called them old maids. Old Maids was a card game; our teachers were authorities to be reckoned with. The celebrated prank of locking Middle School's Miss Thruston in the lavatory adjacent to her classroom would not be tried in Upper School. In my new studies, whole worlds were opening to me, and the heralds of the unlocked doors were these maiden ladies who had missed their chances to stand each behind a man and rule. But they didn't need that opportunity to exercise their wisdom and authority. They had us.

In rare moments of daydreaming in class, I studied my teachers.

Miss West taught us Latin. Her hair might be too short, her glasses too cat-eyed, her stomach prominent, her breath bad, but she loved the Latin language and Roman civilization so much I forgave her transgressions of appearance. Latin she raised from the dead, tracing our English words to their Latin roots, fulfilling her duty to deliver me spellbound to Miss Fitchett's Julius Caesar, Cicero, and Virgil.

Behind those Roman statesmen in togas stood tiny Miss Fitchett, who embodied her name, swatting away the indecisive as if it were a fly.

Behind the Old Testament stood Miss McKenney.

"What did you girls see when your parents read you about Noah and the Ark," she challenged. I remembered imagining a globe of water, an atlas of flooded plains, a tublike boat rocking on the waves of the South Pole. When no one said anything, I offered these images, and Miss McKenney smiled. "Good, that's good. Your parents taught you to believe *literally* every word." She paused. "You saw doves and rainbows, too, I suppose." We nodded. I watched the corn-gold stubble over her upper lip, a mustache brilliant in the sidelong sunlight coming in the classroom window. "But that was seeing through a glass darkly." Again she paused. "Now you must learn the spirit of the old stories. You must learn to see by *metaphor*," and she began to rework the story. I gasped. We had permission to think for ourselves, even about *The Bible*?

Miss Ruthalia Keim, our French teacher, was given to humming Maurice Chevalier as she made a quick turn on tiny ankles, finishing with a wiggle of her ample body. Her bobbed gray hair and bangs fringed an equine face. Down she'd plop, elbows on the low teacher's desk, standing with her generous rear end jutted out, facing the class with her low neckline and elderly cleavage. From this position, smiling knowingly, she'd quiz us on vocabulary, tossing out whole sentences of complex French to us. We had to be daring enough to return aloud a reply in French. "Je ne sais pas" was heresy.

Mrs. Coleman, my only married teacher, taught as sweetly as a grandmother would, gaining her authority through a humility so evident that she became transparent. Reading aloud passages from Dickens or Shakespeare, she vanished, and in her place stood Sydney Carton. Pip. Puck. Lady Macbeth. Through her we met Silas Marner. Jane Eyre. Becky Sharpe.

"You really like reading books, don't you," Melissa said, close on my elbow as we left Mrs. Coleman's classroom. "I mean, you really *do*, don't you?"

She's right, I thought, amazed that her simple, succinct sentence summed me up. I couldn't have said it myself, even though I knew that in the hours I spent reading I never missed a living human soul. Unwittingly, Melissa Banning had handed me myself. A lover of books. That was who I was. That was me.

"You're what my mother calls a *bluestocking*," she added, but the label—perhaps intended to link me to the fate of an old maid—fluttered away. I knew Melissa well enough by now to recognize her talent for giving a compliment and mocking it with a little sting.

Spending more time at her house now than at Cookie Lewis's, I considered Melissa my best friend in the large group of girls that regularly met on Saturdays to play bridge, four tables of us. We had organized the bridge club as our mothers organized theirs—so I was told. In any attempt to emulate our social mothers, I was at a disadvantage. My parents, I realized, had no social life beyond what they knew at St. Giles, where none of my friends went to church. Mom and Dad participated in choir practice and deacons' meetings, covered dish suppers and study groups. When it came time to organize the bridge club meetings, therefore, I stood back and let the other girls make the arrangements. The locations of our meetings rotated, and the hostess of the day served a lunch of sandwiches, chips, cupcakes, and Coca-Colas. Corbin White brought her older sister's cigarettes, or if we were in Melissa's paneled basement, finding packs of cigarettes behind the bar was a snap. She had older brothers, and both of her parents smoked.

I learned the game of bridge quickly, taking out books from the library and devouring Charles Goren's column in the newspaper. I loved the sly innuendo of bidding, the discipline of counting cards, the triumph of the trump. A giddy pleasure it was to figure out who held the jack, who the king, reserving my queen to cancel the jack when the unsuspecting opposition played it, protecting her from the king, should that more powerful card be lurking. All of us, the "smart" girls, strove for the ideal bridge table—a game played with savvy and acumen, with no table talk or distractions.

Elizabeth mocked us. It was school on Saturday, she said. Had I made an "A" in bridge yet?

So different from my family, the Bannings fascinated me with their worldliness. Mr. and Mrs. Banning were socially engaged every Saturday night. They went to the Country Club, to the Commonwealth Club, to the houses of their friends for drinks and dinner. They also dressed up, black tie and evening gown. Mrs. Banning descended the basement stairs one evening, ostensibly to remind Melissa and me of a minor duty, actually to display her purple satin dress with a daring single shoulder strap.

I gasped, "You look beautiful!"

Mrs. Banning smiled grandly.

Making a face, Melissa turned away from her mother. The spitting image of her plain father, she did not choose to compliment her mother, who worked hard to remain beautiful. Whenever her mother ate an entire box of Sara Lee cupcakes, Melissa told me, she would perform rigorous exercises in the naked privacy of her bedroom. We had all seen Mrs. Banning striding up and down Grove

Avenue's sidewalks grimly, too absorbed to acknowledge the toots of the horn a friend might sound to encourage her onward. Her curious incivility fascinated me, and I gradually realized that Mrs. Banning wanted to be ignored. She was merely "out for a walk." She wasn't "exercising." A lady was effortlessly fit and trim or effortlessly pleasing and plump. Willing herself thin, Mrs. Banning resembled the grim, angry reaper. She also resembled my mother when she was angry at my refusals to eat, frustrated by her failure to persuade or force down me another mouthful. To be thin, my plump mother asserted, was *unnatural*.

At fifteen, my character had largely been untested. Mrs. Coleman, citing Milton, said that our virtues were "cloistered," and that was just fine, she smiled. We were heroines in training. Like everyone else, she seemed to think that a girl's virtue and her virginity were one and the same. If that were true, certainly I could agree that I had not yet been tested, and hardly tempted. My "beaux," as my mother liked to refer to them, hadn't been dangerously appealing. Donald Smith had kissed me before a cotillion, hastily, as if unsure of the sweetness of his breath, or—worse thought—of mine. Lowndes Nelson had phoned to ask me over to Garland Moore's house in the afternoon. They had planned a little music and dancing. Other girls would be there, he said. They were "nice" boys, and so I had bicycled over. Other girls were there; Garland's mother was not. Innocent enough, I thought, and enough *not* that it was interesting. I stayed and tried to do the new dance steps—the chicken, the mashed potato, the tried-and-true jitterbug. Moving toward each other for a slower dance, Lowndes and I were both startled when his hard penis—it had to be that—pushed into my skirt, grazing my pubis. I felt him, he felt me, and we leaped apart as if lightning had struck the floor between us. The shock of contact had been too intimate; unprepared for it, we looked away, pretending nothing had happened, then danced, careful to keep our bodies far apart.

More recently John Page Williams, the son of a minister with a name my mother ranked "as old as Virginia," was escorting me to the movies every other weekend. We weren't "snowed." John Page was licensed to drive, and when we single dated, he would count "pididdles"—cars on the highway with only one headlight on. When he saw a "pididdle," he said I owed him a kiss. "Who made that rule?" I laughed, but when he parked the car in front of my house—with the front porch light on, bright as stage lighting and meant to discourage the devil's temptations, I let him kiss me.

Melissa would write in my yearbook at the year's close, "Be good with J.P." She might have saved her ink. The temptations offered by Satan, said to be a smooth talker, had left me cold. I was content to wait and see who would enter my life and change it. Wasn't that the plot line?

Waiting, I fixed my eyes on the handsome tenor in the First Presbyterian Church choir, concocting romantic encounters. Not as handsome as Cary Grant or William Holden, or as polished and misunderstood as Mr. Darcy in *Pride and Prejudice,* or as doomed as Sydney Carton in *A Tale of Two Cities,* or as wealthy and decadent as many a European in Henry James, he was—the handsome chorister—at least as distant and more malleable. I thought up what he would say to me and what I would reply. I let his words—my words—swell and roll in my head, where I could be as passionate as I dared, as demure as called for.

It would have been far more daring to summon into my fantasies the boys I danced with, or yearned to dance with, at the boy-girl weekend parties I was occasionally invited to attend. With parents upstairs, teenagers gathered in the recreational room of the basement or in the den, with fast music followed by slow music followed by fast music, the lights lowered or turned back on by the chaperoning parent. These parties netted me at best a waltz with tall Seldon Harris or Benjy Winn, during which I had to be careful not to dance too close because the other wallflowers, from whose tight bouquet I was only temporarily released, were watching to see *if* flesh pressed, *where* it pressed, and *how long.*

Once, just once, Seldon's fingers brushed my shoulder carelessly, grazing near my collarbone, or lower, and I felt between my legs a stupendous flash of yearning. It was sudden, unbidden.

"Sexual intercourse is a communion," as my mother described it. It was sacred. It was like the Lord's Supper. Partaken. Holy. Sanctioned only by married love and sacrifice. I wondered if Mom wanted us plump and unattractive so that the boys would stay away. It would be easier then to keep her daughters virginal. Whether I believed these thoughts or not, fat felt like punishment.

I wondered if the many lovers in the movies were punished because their attitudes toward lovemaking were not so devout. In wedlock or out of it, women who were too ambitious or too success-ful—like Eleanor Parker in *Interrupted Melody*—suffered. At the height of her operatic career and married to a good man—Glenn Ford—she was struck down with polio. Or Jane Wyman, struck blind and having her sight restored in a risky operation performed by the man she'd wrongly spurned, Rock Hudson. Or Deborah Kerr, struck by a car as she was running to her tryst with Cary Grant, whom love had reformed from roué to responsible fiancé. They would both have to suffer before they could have each other. In the movies, the suffering gave new meaning to romance. No passion was legitimate without it.

Into a darkened and candlelit McVey auditorium, the Upper School filed quietly, each class sitting together as a class, waiting for the curtain to be raised on the senior most like Saint Catherine. She had been broken on the wheel in Egypt, in Alexandria. The seniors' gold school rings, designed to resemble rings with family crests engraved on them, showed the crown of victory and the wheel of pain that were the proof of her faith and love. The voting for the girl who would be Saint Catherine had been very close, so said the rumors, and there was a sense of suspense. Who would she be?

The curtain rumpled, rippled, then tugged itself into an ogee arch that made an alcove of light. I recognized the standard-bearer, kneeling before Saint Catherine, dressed in choir robes. She repre-sented our devotion to the martyred saint. I did not, however, recog-nize Saint Catherine, perhaps because of her crown or the makeup, or more likely because she was a boarding student. There was whis-pering among a few of the seniors. They clearly knew who she was—a girl like them who took Latin or French, who dissected frogs, who played hockey or tennis, and who beyond any worldly accomplishment was well known for acts of tender self-abnegation, doing what was needful, never for her own sake, but for God's.

I liked not knowing who she was. Now I could see the Saint Catherine before me, dressed in her long silk dress and crown of fulfillment, as the saint herself, or at least as close as wardrobe and makeup allowed in the transformation of an ordinary mortal who had, in all probability, kissed boys. If you believed the backlighting, the saint was shot through with light from the far side of the world's limits. Before the upright, slender, and awkwardly transfigured image of the martyr, before this living icon who had opened up to an inner dimension with clarity and humility, I felt fallen. I was a sprawl of darkness and division. I was the heart's perplexity incarnate. I pressed farther back into my seat in the dark auditorium as the Glee Club and assembled classes began singing "Jerusalem." It was a very strange moment, this one, with Saint Catherine radiantly before me—whole, virginal, and inexplicable.

# 10

## *Faith, Hope, Charity*

"Amma is coming to live in Richmond," Mom announced one night at the dinner table. Elizabeth and I looked at each other quickly. Which of us would have to give up her bedroom? Immediately I began constructing an argument in my mind, listing the reasons Elizabeth's room would be more suitable for Amma—it was farther away, it had an adjoining bathroom, it was larger. And then I realized that if Amma were to move into Elizabeth's room, Elizabeth would move into mine, a smaller room with a double bed.

But Elizabeth wouldn't be asked to move. Because I was the older, I'd be the one chosen to sacrifice. With a forkful of corn pudding halfway to my mouth, I mentally emptied out my closet and moved my desk from my room into my sister's room.

Then Mom added, "She won't live here, of course."

I tried not to show my relief. Elizabeth made good use of the opportunity provided by Mom's self-absorption to whisk a piece of bread from her plate and hide it in her lap. Mom murmured piteously, "As if there wasn't enough to do!"

But she had already found the boardinghouse on Maple Avenue, near St. Catherine's, where Amma could have a nice room, near enough so that Mom might drop in to see her on her way home from school. *Too near! Too near!* I cried out silently, immediately resentful. I didn't want my friends in the ninth grade to know that my grandmother, like a poor relation in a novel, had moved into a boardinghouse just around the corner from St. Catherine's. The house, I imagined, would be dark and shabby, nearly hidden from view by two tall black spruce trees.

Mom said she would do Amma's grocery shopping and laundry, bring her over for dinner now and then, take her to the doctor. Amma was "doing poorly," she said, and no one seemed to know why as yet.

"Why do you have to take care of her?" I asked, edgy because Mom seemed flustered. There were other grown children. Uncle Billy, Uncle Theo, and Aunt Too-Too right in town; Uncle Ashton in Norfolk. Only Uncle Dennis lived two states away.

"I'm the older daughter," Mom replied. "It falls to me."

Dad's face closed in on itself and looked dark, but he said nothing.

"Amma's *yellow.*" Elizabeth sounded shocked. After a half year on Maple Avenue and exploratory surgery, Amma had been diagnosed with cancer. "The cancer's *eating* her, and she's turning yellow," my sister emphasized. She had come into my bedroom and was standing right beside me, hands on her hips. Looking up from the homework on my desk, I considered the possibility that she was trying to frighten me, but Elizabeth's concern for Amma showed in her eyes. Amma's cancer, we'd been told, had spread everywhere, but it had begun in her liver. Mom had told me that Amma was *jaundiced,* and I had looked up the word. Now I turned it over in my mind again. *Jaundiced* was a word whose connotations included *cynical, detached, unconcerned.*

Thinking of Amma's body, wasted from within by cancer, I saw a bowl with worms breeding in it—and then I thought of the science experiment I'd done in fifth grade. I'd put a chunk of raw beef in a glass jar, left it open for a day to the air, then shut it away in the dark of the basement. When I remembered to open the lid and look in, the air filled with a buzz of green bottle flies. Amma hated flies.

I wondered what shade of yellow Amma's skin had turned. I imagined my mother at her bedside in the hospital. I could see her hands push hair back from her forehead, her gray eyes darting here and there. I saw her forehead furrow, her mouth open, nearly speechless, calling "Mother?" softly.

But Amma lay there still as a statue. Buttercup. Mustard. Jonquil. Margarine. Amelia County mud. There she was.

There she was, who once was the source of eight children, all but two still living. There she was, whose favorite tree, the sycamore, raised a rare light of appreciation into her eyes. I marveled at how little I knew about Amma.

Buttercup. Mustard. Mud.

I knew Elizabeth wanted me to talk to her about the distress and fear I preferred to keep to myself. I had not hardened my heart, as pharaoh had, but my feelings did not reveal themselves, even to me, quickly. I needed to think it over first. I needed to see it for myself—to imagine. I had to make it vivid. I needed time to find the right words.

With Amma's illness now diagnosed as cancer, I felt ashamed of my resentment that she'd been moved so near St. Catherine's. But it was hard to call up love for Amma, who had always brought with her a sense of displacement and loss. Now, however, the family seemed to love Amma because she was dying. Mom said the ties of the blood were the strongest, stronger than marriage. She usually said this when Elizabeth and I were at odds, using words to try to shame us back into a harmony we resisted and that felt false, because it was forced.

Did people love because they felt they should?

Did they love in spite of—or because of?—their own unloving feelings?

Did people love because they were afraid not to?

Why did no one else in the family ask questions like this? It was all cloudburst, then sunshine and never you mind, or worse, a verse from the Bible. *Were I to ask them, I'd get nowhere,* I wrote on my grammar assignment on the subjunctive.

Next afternoon, I heard voices in the kitchen when I got home from school, and I put down my books and headed for the kitchen.

"No, no, I'll just run along," a familiar voice was saying to Mom as I approached the kitchen door. I saw Too-Too first, leaning against the icebox. Although her voice was high-pitched and cheery, Too-Too had backed away, so close to the icebox she could have melted into the door and joined the milk in the cool interior. Mom sawed away with a knife at a cold joint of lamb left from Sunday dinner. As the solidified white borders of fat crumpled away, Mom hacked the meat from the bone. Dark brown "au jus" had congealed on the plate and was speckled with bits of the fat. Her thin hair falling out of the side combs, her face clenched, almost savage, Mom looked up and commanded, "Come on in here. I want you to know how to do this when I'm gone."

I came to a halt at the threshold, speechless.

Mom put down the carving knife, took a slice of cold, fatty lamb, and folded it roughly inside a slice of Nolde's bread. She held it out in Too-Too's direction.

"Take it," she insisted. "You must be starved."

"No, no," Too-Too demurred. "We missed lunch so long ago, my appetite's completely gone."

They must have been to see Amma, I thought. Too-Too must have come to give Mom a ride to the nursing home to see their mother. I didn't know exactly where Amma was now, and Elizabeth didn't know either. "Mom thinks she's protecting us," I told Elizabeth.

"I think we should be allowed to visit her," she had objected.

Mother was hungry, and if Too-Too would not eat, if neither of her daughters would eat as much as she wanted them to at the dinner table, if her own mother was dying: well then, she was hungry; she would eat. She took a large mouthful of the sandwich and gestured to me, her free hand picking up the carving knife.

I shook my head. *I should join her, I should do what she wants, I should make her feel less alone,* I thought. But I couldn't eat that cold, fatty lamb. Mom forced a snort of air from her nose in disapproval, then shrugged. What could she do?

"Well, I'd better be running along," Too-Too said. She paused and studied Mom. "I'll call you in the morning. You go on now and take a load off your feet. Get some rest."

Too-Too slipped past me.

"I'll go with her to the door," I murmured to Mom.

Every day Mom looked more weary. No one would say we were waiting for Amma to die, but it felt that way.

"Remember her the way she was," Mom had demanded yesterday, pushing into my hands an old photograph, brownish in its tints and tones. As if someone had died, the lady in the photograph wore a dark silk dress with a high collar, her abundant dark hair parted in the middle and brushed away from her face, fastened so that her hair swelled on each side of the part like the plump breast of a bird. Next to her stood a child of perhaps two years, the lady's hands hidden by the child's white clothing. The child wore a close-fitting white linen bonnet—more chaplet than bonnet—tied beneath her chin with a large bow. Her buttoned linen coat was starched, and from the shoulders there stood out points of lace, like wings. She held her little hands together as she and her mother gazed off in the same direction, the child a study of pensive contentment. Although she smiled, the dark-haired lady's eyes were softly sad. Whatever the source of her grief, she wouldn't be the one to speak about it. Mother and daughter, the pair looked like English history. They looked Victorian.

"Who is it?" I blurted out, meaning the child, recognizing my mother's eyes in the child's face only as I spoke the question. Before Mom could answer, I added quickly, "Is that Amma?" and I pointed to the dark lady. Glancing quickly at her face, moving my eyes across it without pausing, I could detect my sister's features in Amma's face, and that surprised me. Mom always professed not to know whom Elizabeth resembled, but there she was, a shadow in Amma's face.

"It was a long time ago," Mom answered. "Look at her regal bearing."

*Elizabeth looks like Amma.* How could Mom *not* know that?

"I only remember Amma with long white hair," I began, breaking off when Mom abandoned the photograph and rushed into her bedroom. I could hear her blowing her nose. Then she cleared her throat with that choked noise that fell between a skid and high C on the piano. The bed creaked, and she called out, "Get me up in time to put on the potatoes."

I stood where I stood, outside her door, holding the photograph in my hand. Two figures against a blank background. Two figures tucked inside an oval meant to protect them from the unknown, meant to yoke them into an intimacy that would never fail. At the door, Too-Too had said, shaking her head, "I could tell you stories." Then she brightened. "That's for another time!" And she dashed off. Now, outside my mother's door, the stories I did not know pressed around me, their secrets intact. I heard my mother's breath growing deeper and more even.

I remembered her saying, "I want you to know how to do this when I'm gone." I saw again the white kitchen table, the hungry look to her hands, her thin silver hair with its faint blue tint. She looked pale, unsatisfied. But when I tried to imagine her death—the room; the position of her feet; other people dressed in white, in black; the timbre of her breathing—I couldn't. I tried to hear her voice come closer to being able to say, *Ease my death.* But I couldn't see her death. I could only tell myself that were she to look down to the foot of her bed, in that finally unimaginable room, I would be there. "I will be there," I whispered, standing by myself, standing nowhere, unprotected, outside her room, my heart blind and stupefied.

In the open casket, Amma's face was smooth and composed. Her cheeks were rouged. Was it Amma? She wore one of her dark suits, a white frill at the neck. She wore a hat, as if she had just arrived in Richmond from the country. I looked around for her large black pocketbook, trying to keep my balance in my new high-heeled shoes. Red, they were wrong for wake or funeral, but my dress was navy blue. The seams in my stockings, supposed to rise straight up the backs of my legs, were already turning crooked.

Mother appeared at my side, materializing out of a room made unreal by background organ music and dim lights. The funeral parlor was crowded with family I had rarely or never seen, the room so hot I felt queasy. Mother took my arm cozily and said, "Doesn't she look beautiful?"

I will never know what I might have felt or how I might have responded had she, saying nothing at all, simply stood with me as I looked at the first person I'd ever seen dead. Beautiful? No, she wasn't beautiful, but there was room in my mother's question for one answer only.

The hand can be quicker than the eye—is it quicker than the heart, too? Instinctively I shook free of my mother's grip on my arm. I didn't want a dishonest bond, even if it meant I had to see her immediate woundedness, before which I was defenseless, then angry. The feelings just came, and I knew them for what they were. That surprised me. But to show even a fraction of these feelings was not permissible in the etiquette of the funeral parlor.

As I paused, understanding intervened. My mother had seen Amma yellow, and I had not. Perhaps now, by contrast, Amma did look beautiful. By the time I felt contrition and sympathy, Mom had moved away from me and been met by an older lady I didn't know, who hugged her. I was beginning to sink into my own thoughts when Elizabeth came over and whispered that Amma's suit had been stuffed with tissue paper to make her clothes fit. We winced.

All the next day, during the long ride to Concord Presbyterian Church, located somewhere in the country, I was careful to be polite and solicitous around Mom. Then I realized it was too late, she didn't need me. As the chief caregiver to Amma, she was the focus of attention and gratitude. She had sacrificed to take care of her mother and now took a central place in the ceremony of mourning. I felt bad that, as a daughter, mother wouldn't be allowed the family Bible—it would go to one of Amma's sons. Wouldn't Mom want it?

"The estate," I heard Uncle Ashton say, would be "small, if anything," and nothing would be said about it in the obituary.

Representing Dad's family, Mimi and Uncle Allan followed our car to Concord Presbyterian Church, and they left after the service. They had not gone inside the church for the "viewing" Mom had said that people in the country would expect. I didn't know where in the country we were, but we couldn't, I thought, be that far from Richmond, if you counted miles. I was surprised we weren't in Amelia. Wasn't it Amelia Mom called home? We were somewhere south of Petersburg. If one were to use a school compass, putting down the fixed leg with the point—that was Richmond. Turning the mobile leg with the pencil, drawing a circle—that would delineate the edge of the known world. Beyond it—yonder—was outer darkness and anonymity, and over that boundary we had carried Amma's strange remains.

It was dark when, finally, we were back on the road, feeling our way home.

We had attended a Methodist Church on the North side, sung Methodist hymns, and listened to a Methodist sermon. We sang "Onward, Christian Soldiers." The church service didn't seem very different to me from a Presbyterian one.

"You can't beat the Episcopal hymnbook," I teased my mother afterward, and she looked at me as if I'd said tomAto, not tomAHto. Such disloyalty! Such heresy! It wouldn't have done to have pointed out that the Episcopal hymnbook—the one we used at St. Catherine's—was closer to England and to the queen than the Presbyterian hymnbook my mother defended hotly, if mutely.

I asked why Ashton Doyle's family was Methodist and not Presbyterian, like us. Mom laughed. "In our family," she said, "we stick to our guns." When Amma married my grandfather, she was Presbyterian, and Leigh Richmond Doyle was Methodist. As a compromise, when there were children, my grandfather agreed to drive the boys to the Methodist Church, among them Ashton. Amma had gathered up the girls and had taken them in the buggy wagon to Concord Presbyterian Church. Hers was a sure hand on the reins—that was the explanation. But until we'd gone to the Methodist Church with cousin Sandra, Ashton's younger daughter, now married and living in Richmond, I hadn't known about the religious divide. That was the power of asking questions. At least sometimes a question worked like a spade in the garden and churned old dirt up to the surface.

"They're Irish," my father said, as if that explained everything about the Doyles, and Mom glared at him. "*English,*" she said firmly. Castleton, Edmunds—*English.*

On the way to Sandra's after church, Mom assured us that Ashton and Gerry would arrive from Norfolk, just up for a visit. Sandra had said she was making creamed chicken, rice, and tomAHto aspic. It was all perfectly normal, she said.

If it was so perfectly normal, I thought, why say so? Even the menu sounded too perfectly normal.

As we were taking off our coats, I smelled a freshly baking turkey. So much for Mom's assurances. To cook a turkey meant a big occasion. "It won't be ready for another hour," Sandra wailed. I smiled. So we were having a "perfectly normal big occasion," the sort that put grown-ups in a swivet.

Just then Ashton and Gerry came to the door. When Ashton saw Mom, he exclaimed, "Well, I might have known it!"

"Now Ashton," Gerry soothed. She was much taller than he was and wore high heels anyway. Most Doyles were little bantam roosters, Sandra had said once. She'd inherited her mother's length of bone. Tall also, I'd laughed with her, as if our height excused us from being hens in the Doyle chicken yard.

I didn't laugh now, however. Ashton turned on his heel and demanded, "Where's my hat? I'm leaving. You should have told me, Sandra. *Where's my hat!?*"

After Sandra and her husband, Dick, intervened, Ashton calmed down and removed his hat. It had never left his head.

Elizabeth and I sat on the sofa and looked out the picture window that offered us a view of the blank backyard. One skeleton tree, a bare picnic table. I could hear a series of puffs of air from Elizabeth's nose, prelude to a snigger or a snuffle. Neither of us knew whether to laugh or cry. I didn't dare risk looking at her. The grown-ups considered us briefly and motioned each other toward the kitchen. It wouldn't do for the family to argue in front of the children.

From the kitchen then came raised voices, interjections, and interruptions. Then Dad left the kitchen.

"I'm not helping the situation," he muttered.

I looked at his eyes. He was okay. He was calm.

"Doyles," he said to Dick, who had followed him out. There was a football game on the television, and Dick settled Dad down in the chair before it with a sherry.

Should we pretend to watch TV, too? We watched the screen and listened to the kitchen.

"Ashton, you of all people should know I would never . . ." and Mom began to cry.

I wondered why she said *you of all people.* Now Dad pushed up from his seat, then sank back down.

Dick came over to Elizabeth and me. "It's okay," he said. "Let them have it out. This is how the Doyles mourn their loved ones. They have a fight. Once the air is cleared, everything will be fine. You'll see."

Listening, we learned that days after Amma's funeral, Ashton had confronted Mom over the "estate." Where was the insurance policy that named Too-Too as the beneficiary? Ashton had helped Amma take it out when Louise was still a young child with no father to support her. Now Too-Too was owed that money by the insurance policy.

"It's simple," he said. "Either you stole your sister's money, or you didn't."

Mom's voice grew louder and more mournful. There had been so many bills.

More quietly Ashton said, "You had no right." He paused and cleared his throat. "Leastwise without talking to me or to Lou."

"But Ashton . . ." Mom's voice trailed off. All the voices became too soft to hear.

*Let the past be the past,* finally I heard Mom say.

And, right on schedule, Sandra sang out, "Turkey's done!"

It was over.

On the drive home, Mom pouted. "As if I *could* have called on them!"

Dad nodded, his eyes on the road. "That's right," he said.

"No one but . . . well, they didn't offer to lift a finger, not a blessed one of them."

The rift between Mom and Ashton, which I'd thought bridged, apparently wasn't. Or was this just the acrid smell of smoke after the house had burned down? I wondered if in Ashton's car there was also a lingering smoke of resentment and blame. The gulf between the living and the dead seemed small compared to that between the living and the living.

Elizabeth started to say something, and I poked her in the ribs. She nodded. We shouldn't say P-turkey.

"Well, I can forgive," Dad was saying. "But I don't think I can forget."

Mom looked over at him, pleased. "You're so loyal," she murmured.

From the look on Dad's face, she might have well have said, "Rise, Sir John."

Every night after supper, the family settled into the separate rituals that defined each of us. My mother washed dishes. My father dozed and watched the news. My sister listened to records. I sat at my desk trying to think through the assignment Miss Gwathmey had given us in Bible studies. To do this assignment right, she'd warned—but with her warm, crooked, red-lipstick smile—you'll have to think and think hard.

Recently hired, Miss Gwathmey was young. She sparkled with intelligence, wore makeup, and drove a red thunderbird. Engaged to a young man at Washington and Lee, she taught . . . Bible studies? Did she have a Bible in her glove compartment? Did she and her Beloved read the Song of Solomon to each other? *Your eyes are doves behind your veil, your hair is like a flock of goats, moving down the slopes of Gilead.*

At first, Miss Gwathmey had set us to learning the lists of the kings of Israel and Judah. We pored over the prophets, memorized psalms. After some weeks of this, Miss Gwathmey complained that her assignments were too academic. "You have to *live the questions* these stories raise." To help us do just that, she gave us each a story to study. We were to investigate, imagine, inquire. We were to pick a character and become so intimate with him that we could be that person. See with his eyes, hear with his ears, know his heart, live his faith. Clear about his strengths and weaknesses and our own, we were to apply the problem that the biblical hero faced to our own experience—if we could. The essay was due in a week.

*And God tempted Abraham, and said unto him, Take Isaac, thine only son, whom thou lovest, and get thee to the land of Moriah, and offer him there for a burnt offering upon the mountain I will show thee . . .* The story gave me the opportunity of slipping inside Abraham or Isaac, and I reread the story in Genesis in both the Revised Standard Version and the King James, sifting detail, listening for nuance, weighing changes in tone. It was a troubling story. Even when I tried to take raw notes, I was unable to put words down on the expectant and demanding straight blue lines of my composition paper. At school, I talked with other girls about their stories and their progress, but I kept my difficulties to myself. When I thought about Abraham's binding Isaac and drawing the knife, I fled the scene on Mt. Moriah, watching as the heights turned into our basement, the long knife into my father's leather belt.

Nancy Spreen was working with a story in Judges about Jeptha, the son of a harlot, a brigand chosen to be a general, who before battle against the Ammonites promised God that, should he be given the victory, he would offer as burnt offering whoever first came out of his own house to greet him on his return. I could understand praying like that, bargaining in desperation, promising the moon. After his victory in battle, met upon his homecoming by his daughter, Jeptha had to keep his promise and sacrifice what he loved, his daughter. Jeptha's daughter, obedient to the sacrifice, had asked only for two months' time to mourn her coming death as a virgin, for she had not "known" a man. I could imagine composing songs, relishing the sympathy and horror of my friends, and Nancy was going to write as Jeptha's daughter, sorrowful and angry. She would wear purple and sing a lament in the style of the Psalms.

If I could imagine having the courage to be that obedient, I could also imagine running away. Jeptha's daughter, however, didn't run; she obeyed and died. Was obedience at times self-slaughter? That was a question I couldn't yet consider—and didn't until years later. Jeptha kept his promise to God—however he might have felt personally—although I wondered if the weight of his daughter's value to him was as great as that of a son might be. Would he have killed his son? He might have. Jeptha, it seemed to me, valued his reputation as a keeper of his word more than he valued a daughter or a son.

Abraham, however, confounded me. I remembered how he had been praised in Sunday school as the model of faith in God, and how easily I had agreed. When God made demands, one obeyed. But how could Abraham have been willing to kill his own son? That he'd talked to no one about God's orders showed that he was ashamed and fearful. He kept what he would do a secret. If he struggled with his decision to obey, he didn't let on to his wife or to Isaac. He had, at the summit of the mountain, bound his son, and he had raised his own hand—no one made him do it.

What kind of God, I asked myself, would *ask you* to kill your son? How could Abraham say to his son, or to anyone, "God told me to do this?"

Who would believe him?

And how did he know the voice he heard was God's? Even if he proved to God by obedience that he had faith, how did having faith make a planned murder holy?

I knew I wasn't fully able to enter the dark of Abraham's heart. Could I express Isaac's distress and outrage? What could I find in my own life to liken to the experience of "being" Abraham or Isaac? God had not asked me to do anything against my conscience or human law. Except for hiding food, I was mostly obedient. Was Isaac afraid of his father? I could write about that fear . . . but no. To mention my fear of Dad's anger would bring shame on him, on me. That was too risky.

I couldn't talk to Dad, but perhaps I could talk to my mother about her having taken Amma's insurance money without telling anyone. She had broken a code, if not a law, in the name of love, just as Abraham had nearly broken a law—Thou shalt not kill—while in the grip of faith. It wasn't an exact match, but if I knew how she felt, perhaps I could understand Abraham. I imagined Abraham's face

with my mother's features when she was brooding or sad, and I
burst into tears. Why was that?

I didn't want to know and swiftly returned to thinking other
things through.

I remembered Ashton's words—either she had stolen her sister's
money or she hadn't. Clearly it wasn't that simple—or was it? "Either
you killed our son or you didn't," I could hear Sarah saying to Abraham. "It wasn't God's hand that held the knife; it was your own."

Mom was in bed rereading *The Rosary.* It was a book about a love
so noble the heroine could deceive the beloved for his own good. It
was a book about self-sacrifice I'd read at my mother's urging.
"Mom," I asked at her door. "Do you remember when Amma was
sick, you decided to . . ."

"I've wanted to talk to you about that time," Mom said quietly.
She shut her book and looked at me steadily. "You know there's
nothing greater than a mother's love. That's how it is for you and
for most children."

I wondered where this was going. I hated it when she did my
thinking for me. I hadn't even finished my question. About to
protest, I heard in another part of my mind an admonition. *Be quiet,*
said my mind. *Just listen.*

"But it wasn't that way for me." Mom's eyes brimmed. "You may as
well know." And she told me that Amma, for whom she had sacrificed
so much at the end, had, when Mom was only a girl, disowned her.

"Disowned you?"

"Cast me out of her heart," Mom said softly and dramatically. I
didn't then read melodrama as a red flag, and I drew nearer. "My
two oldest brothers, they went to my mother and said that Ashton
was trying to steal the farm from her."

"When was this, Mom?"

"After they came back from the First World War. Those years
were so hard, and we had so little." She cleared her throat. "I said to
Mother, 'Ashton wouldn't do something like that'—and she looked
at me hard. I'll never forget that look. Never. She said, 'Well then,
Miss, if you hold with Ashton, you break with me.'"

"She may as well have killed me then and there," Mom said.

"What happened?" I asked, nearly speechless.

She said she had gone off to college—thanks to Uncle Percy—but
that Amma wouldn't let her have anything to take from her room.

"She said it wasn't my house or Ashton's anymore." At Christmas Mom had gone to Ashton's in Norfolk—he'd moved to Norfolk to better himself. "After I got my diploma and my job in Amelia, after I moved in with Aunt T, I never looked back."

She lifted her chin, then paused. "I've tried to love you better than that. With all my love *and* with all the love I didn't get."

"Oh, Mom," I said, and I hugged her. She needs a mother, I realized suddenly as she clung to me. She needs a mother, and she has only me. The thought made me back gently away. How could I be her mother?

"That should help you to understand," she said, after a few minutes, both of us near tears.

But of course I didn't understand. Mom had answered a question I hadn't asked, and although I now understood why the house had felt so pinched and strained whenever Amma visited, I understood even less why Mom would have cashed in the insurance policy.

"Why did you do so much for Amma when she was dying?" I asked. I wanted to add, *Why did you risk family censure and perhaps even break the law* for a woman who had pitched you out of her heart?

"It was my duty," Mom said simply. "I only did for her what you'd do for me."

"Well, Ashton didn't understand what you did or why."

"But God did. It was God told me what to do. And if you don't obey God, you're nothing."

*How can you know it was God?* I wanted to ask. His ghostly voice inside her mind was as troubling to me as God's voice inside Abraham's.

"With faith, you can do anything," my mother added, but I said none of what I was thinking.

She brightened. "Here I am keeping you from your homework, and it's nearly ten o'clock. You go on back to your room now, my precious." And she opened her book.

Back at my desk, I found that I could make an outline. I began to write—but Abraham, I decided, I'd avoid Abraham. He would kill Isaac because not to be obedient to God was self-murder. He loved himself more than he loved his son. I'd leave him alone with his faith, with his self-love, and with his terrible, or convenient, God. No, I would be Isaac. I would express his sense of betrayal and bewilderment, feelings that may have moved him years later to tell the story, when it was safe to tell it, when he could understand how his father had said "God" and "faith"—an excuse for doing what you do without knowing why you do it.

As for my own experience, I couldn't talk about my mother's having been "disowned" by her mother, nor would I understand for many years the false connections between love and ownership or the injury they combined to construe. If I could not compare my experience with Isaac's, I could, however, inhabit the realm of contrast. I could write about how I had once stolen Hershey bars from the drugstore. I'd been tempted and succumbed. God neither ordered nor sanctioned my theft, my hunger, my greed. My act, unlike Abraham's, wasn't the transgression of a human law for a supposed higher law or higher love. What I did was wrong, but comprehensible.

*Who can understand Abraham?* That would be my final sentence. I'd have to hope Miss Gwathmey would consider the question earned and not judge Isaac's bewilderment, and mine, as failures of the imagination.

## 11

# The King of Spades

"I found the Lord, honey. I found the Lord." It was Dad's voice at the front door of our house on Lexington Road.

"Don't wake the girls, it's the middle of the night. Hush now!"

"I saw angels," Dad insisted.

Again Mom shushed him. I heard the heavy thud of a suitcase, footsteps, their bedroom door closing, muffled voices I couldn't make out behind their closed door. Elizabeth would tell me later she'd slept through Dad's late night arrival, but then her bedroom was at the back of the house.

Dad had been away on business in Atlanta for several days, and we weren't expecting him home until the weekend, certainly not in the middle of the night, in the middle of the week. Why was he home? His voice had been urgent, Mom's alarmed. As I lay awake, wondering if I should go to their door and knock, I realized that I had already been awakened earlier, by the shrill of the telephone. I'd heard Mom's voice—something was wrong, no one called after ten in the evening—but I'd drifted back to sleep.

What had my father meant by *found the Lord*? In the Old Testament, men heard voices, saw angels, or had visions of chariots rising into the clouds. In the New Testament, Saul on the road to Tarsus had fallen, blinded by the sudden light of revelation, and he had struggled to his feet a changed man, a new man. Had anything like that happened to my father? Had anything like that happened to anyone we knew? Such visions seemed to me unlikely, and terrible. But here was Dad, saying he'd found the Lord and offering a glimpse of angels as proof. Although I had watched my father's devoted service to the church for many years, I didn't know much about the state of his soul. I didn't know what being religious felt like for him. He would refer to himself as a *sinner*, and his was the adamant belief that there was a Satan as well as a God. Like my mother, he, too, believed firmly in a literal reading of the Bible. If Satan's name was in the Bible, then the existence of Hell, the probability of punishment, and the certainty of a separate principle of Evil were assured. Whenever I voiced questions, Dad argued me down sternly, his eyes dark with anger. It was impertinent that I would ask such questions. That I would even question the existence of Satan, that alone proved Satan was at work. *Get Thee behind me, Satan,* he would remind me, was Jesus' response in the wilderness. Did I think I could improve on that? I didn't mind sparring with my father verbally, although his simmering anger was unnerving. I did mind his brooding silences. But whatever he thought, I decided, a literal red devil with a cloven foot was far more unreal than one's own red anger, one's own sense of not being good enough.

Next morning only my mother got up to make breakfast and see us off to St. Catherine's. She had called in sick, and she was taking the day off. I looked at her carefully. Mom wasn't someone who could hide her feelings easily. When she moped, she moped. When she sulked, she sulked. When she was angry, she said, "I'll tell you straight out . . ." and she told you. When she watched a romantic movie, her face shone with rapture. When she aimed to please, she pleased. When she wasn't in the mood for nonsense, she could cut you to the quick. Mom was formidable; or as Elizabeth put it, she wore the pants in the family. Now in her blue quilted bathrobe, the tattered one with the worn pockets, and still in her hairnet, she looked sleep-worn, years older. But I didn't think she appeared to be sick. She was calm, her eyes a pale gray, and they met mine steadily. She knew I was looking at her, and she took care to reveal nothing.

"Didn't Dad come in last night from Atlanta?" I asked her. I wanted to ask casually, but Elizabeth heard a catch in my voice, a snag in the silk.

"Dad's home? Already?"

He was, Mom said. Home early, but sleeping late. We should gather our things and take care not to wake him on our way out of the house. "He'll be here this afternoon when you get back from school," she said.

But he wasn't.

By the time I'd finished with classes and a literary magazine meeting, I'd missed the bus and had to walk home in the late light of early November. There were no lights on in the living room. Elizabeth hadn't returned home from hockey practice. Recently she'd been recognized as a fearless, feisty, strong-legged talent, a natural for a field hockey goalie. Pleased to be playing on a varsity team, she'd lost weight and her classmates cheered her at the games as she kicked and swatted and blocked the goal from the opposing team's attempts to score. Her classmates had stopped calling her "Fatterson." She'd had only one poor showing, by misfortune the game Dad had attended. On the way home, he'd tried to advise her about technique, succeeding only in upsetting her. She'd stormed in the front door, tearful. "It's bad enough losing the game," she'd blurted out. "You don't have to rub it in." Through the living room. Slam. Through my room. Slam. Into her bedroom. Slam, bang went two more doors. Dad had appeared hurt, but he said nothing, nor did he defend himself. It wasn't his way to rub things in, and I wanted to say to him that I knew that, but he went to change his clothes and then climbed the attic steps. He was "fixing something" upstairs, he said, and would be down when supper was ready.

I stood in the darkened living room, aware that the house was too quiet, and I went over to my parents' bedroom door, parted slightly, and looked inside. Before Mom spoke, before I could call out to her, I knew she was alone. I knew she needed me. Where was Dad? I drew close to her bed and saw that she was crying. Seeing me, she moaned.

"Your father's not here. They've taken him to Tucker's."

I went cold. Tucker's was the psychiatric hospital we passed on our left on the way down Grove when we went to the library. If you had no money and were crazy, you were put away in the state institution in Williamsburg. If you had money, you went to Tucker's and had private care. Did we have enough money for Tucker's?

"Your father's had a nervous breakdown," Mom continued, raising herself on one elbow. Then she sank back into the pillow, giving up her attempt to be calm. She covered her face with her hands. "The doctor says it probably goes all the way back to his childhood." *Childhood* she drew out into a wail.

I did what I could to comfort her, but I had no more idea than she did what it could mean, to have a wound that "went back to childhood."

"I'll make dinner," I offered hesitantly. In my mother's assessment of her daughters' character traits and proven abilities when she assigned kitchen tasks, I was the dishwasher, Elizabeth was the natural chef. But Mom nodded, and I went into the kitchen to explore the icebox, hoping for leftovers we could heat up. Mom was motionless in her bed, perhaps asleep, perhaps in a despondency too deep for words; my sister still wasn't home. I shut the door to my room quietly and sat at my desk, staring at the list of my homework assignments, wondering why, if I felt such despair, I couldn't cry.

The next day, Mom pulled herself together. She had to. Having taken off one day from work, she now put on her lipstick and with it a public cheerfulness, pulled up her slip so it didn't show below the hem of her skirt, and returned to her second grade classroom, where the most pressing problems were phonics and learning to subtract. In almost no time, Uncle Allan came over to the house to review Dad's financial records, pleased to find them orderly, meticulous. He deposited one thousand dollars into my parents' bank account to tide us over. Heartened by his generosity, Mom encouraged Elizabeth and me to be brave—but not to breathe a word of our troubles to any of our friends at St. Catherine's or at church. "This is strictly a family matter," she said.

Sitting at my desk, I wondered who I'd tell. Fewer and fewer of my friends telephoned me, and so I knew that Melissa was gossiping about me. She'd turned on me; that was her nature. Why had I thought she'd be different with me? Sensing my bewilderment and loneliness, Elizabeth stopped one afternoon on her way through my room to hers. "What's the matter?" she said. "Your friends find out who you *really* are?"

It was, oddly, an interesting question, but not one I'd let myself discuss with Elizabeth, who wanted it to hurt me. I said nothing, and she continued to bait me, concluding bluntly: "You're cold, Margaret."

I said nothing, keeping my eyes on the paper I was trying to outline for American history.

"Look at you. Dad's sick, and what kind of feelings are you showing anyone? You just don't care, do you?"

I wheeled around in my chair, knocking books off the desk, and
told her to keep her mouth shut. What did she know about my feelings? I thrust at her a notebook page on which I'd listed how I could
help the family, how I might make a little extra money. There were
expenses I was sure I could defray, or defer, or cancel altogether.
Immediately the list looked puny and pathetic in my eyes, but I
forced my voice to be firm and steady. "Not everyone shrieks and
cries. There are other ways to have feelings," I said, surprised to see
a faint look of respect on my sister's face, then a glimmer of satisfac-
tion. Her forehead smoothed out.

"Okay, then," she concluded, and handed back the list.

It wasn't the list, I realized, that had swayed her to acknowledge
my way of handling myself as valid. She had gotten my goat, I'd
wheeled around, I'd raised my voice. Violence and volume—she
understood these displays. As she abandoned the room, I imagined
that I could see the shadows of old bruises from Dad's belt on the
backs of her legs. Bruises she suffered. Bruises she understood. For
as long as I could remember I had tried to avoid my father's angry
punishments, but she had baited him and met him in battle. If she
couldn't best him, or save herself, she would not be cowed, and
even now Dad preferred her to me, I thought. He respected her
anger and did not like my distanced dignity, what he called my
"playing the queen."

"We're so different," I whispered to my sister's closed door. "And
it's not my fault." I wasn't ready to say it also wasn't her fault, but I
was beginning to question why in our family there was so much
blaming of others. No one said, "It's my fault." We found someone
else to blame, a way to duck it. I remembered how my mother,
struck down into the ashes like Job on the day Dad was taken to
Tucker's, sobbed about the motive and cue for his distress going
back to childhood. Then she swallowed hard and wiped away her
tears, saying, "At least it's not anything I've done. The doctor
assured me of that." That said, she buried her head in the pillow.

I stared out my bedroom window into the burning bush of the red
dogwood leaves, the fires in those leaves banked, nearly snuffed out
in the fading light. I stared at the daisy blooms on my wallpaper and
wished a wind would rise out of the wall and sweep them away. I

pinched myself, hard, so that it hurt. Who was I to be asking for signs
and miracles. I hardly knew what to think. My mother had her pillow for comfort. It had her confidence; it carried her troubles into its
soft feathery interior and buried them there. My sister had her closed
door and a boyfriend to talk to. Under Melissa's influence, my circle
of friends was no longer phoning me. Melissa's gossip had made me
a pariah. I was alone, fully alone for the first time in my life.

Dad, I realized suddenly, didn't have any friends either. There
were people he talked to at work and at church, but did he have
friends? Ever since we'd been going to St. Catherine's, Mom had
learned to shield Dad from casual pleasantries and exchanges with
the parents of my friends. "You never know what's going to come
out of that man's mouth," Mom would say mournfully. She worried
about grammar. She worried about pronunciation. She worried
about the word *ain't*. Dad said "fo" for *four*, "doh" for *door*. He said
*fambly, chimbly, priddy*. He said *bimeby*, as in *We're going to get there
bimeby*. Mom declared that the family cook in Bon Air had taken care
of Dad while Nanny flounced off into Richmond to go to the
Women's Club, taking the train in the morning and staying away all
day. Dad talked the way he did because of the colored cook. And the
cook, as I had only recently learned, probably spoke as she did
because such expressions and pronunciations were common in
early slave-owning Virginia. Distressed Cavaliers and indentured
servants from southwestern England—from Wessex and Sussex—
used the words Dad's family cook had used in Bon Air. A Sussex
accent, in England extinct by 1860, flourished among poor whites
and blacks of the American South. *Bide where you be*. Mom made it
sound as if Dad grew up next to the family woodstove with the colored people, or back of the woodshed getting whipped. How did
Dad feel about himself? You couldn't be a white man in west-end
Richmond and talk like a colored man and not have somebody look
at you and know something was wrong.

Would I become lonely, like Dad? He had no friends to talk to; and
now I had no one to talk to but myself.

Younger, I'd been given a diary with a lock on it, and I'd written in
it until its pages were full, often writing about my sister and our
daily cold war. Assigned a character sketch in English class recently,
I had written about my sister, stunned to realize, as I wrote, how little I knew her. To cover my embarrassment, wanting a good grade

and worried that I might have to read the sketch aloud in class, I'd invented details—making Elizabeth a stereotyped younger sister who borrowed my clothes and copied me. Cleverly written, it had fooled everyone but my sister. After reading it, Elizabeth was offended. "You don't care enough to know who I really am!" she had charged.

I wondered if now, having felt what it was like to be shut out, I could write in the privacy of a journal and be more honest. Writing in solitude, I might break through the silences that had gathered in my heart. A short story had been assigned in English class, and we had been advised to draw on our experiences, using our imaginations to deepen the innocent experience into higher knowledge. Were I to disguise our family and write about a lonely man gone mad and taken from his family, the story might have readers who would see through my inventions and find at the core of the story my broken father, my sorrowful mother, my rude sister, and a scornful someone so like me that gossip and rumor would flare. I couldn't write anything about my family and show it to others.

And yet, write I must, I decided; write I would. Not for other readers but words for my eyes only. I pulled from my desk a spiral notebook I'd been saving for Latin composition. Instead of a dead language, I'd write words that would fall like seeds into a secret garden. A puff of wind, and the lock and key to that garden would show itself from beneath the long tendrils of ivy. Inside that secret garden, the door carefully closed behind me, I'd be where I could say anything. I could whisper whatever I was afraid to say. I could hear only myself speaking what only I knew. And if I didn't know, if I couldn't speak, I would be alone in a place of solace and possible burgeoning, of turned earth and gentle rain. No one would be looking at me. I wouldn't have to be what anyone else wanted me to be. I could see and say what I saw. And if it turned out I was living in a world too mysterious to understand, or if it happened that I was hopelessly ignorant or blind, then I could pray. I could pray and in that solitude "rectify the heart," as the new minister at St. Giles liked to say. I'd thought it a pompous phrase. Now the words seemed right.

Writing in the spiral notebook, I promised myself the discipline and joy of writing each day—before I began my homework. If not then, before going to bed. *Cross my heart and hope to die,* I whispered to myself, feeling again like a child and liking the feeling. I would start by writing about breakfast with my family around the small kitchen table when Elizabeth and I played forts and moats with our eggs and toast or when Dad took us to the basement, his eyes flashing fire.

In my notebook, I could talk to myself all I wanted. When, however, I wanted to know how Dad was getting along at Tucker's, Mom was evasive. She gave Elizabeth and me provocative but incomplete bits of information. Then she'd say, "No one really knows."

"Mom," I finally said in a stern voice. "I heard Dad when he came home from Atlanta. He said he'd seen angels."

Uneasily Mom began talking, and the more she talked, the more she seemed grateful to talk. Elizabeth looked at me and nodded, as if I'd done a good thing. Then she winked, and I knew she was thinking about her own theory, based as usual on something overheard. Something about Mom and Dad in bed. What Dad wanted Mom to do, what Mom wouldn't.

But Mom was talking angrily about the failure of Dad's company to see in Dad a good man. He'd been passed over for a promotion. "I think he feels ashamed," she concluded. "A man is supposed to succeed." If Mom was angry at the company, she also shared the business world's respect for success, a mix of feelings not unlike the resentment and gratitude she focused on Uncle Allan. I let it all sink in, and next I was asking Mom about the angels.

"They were pink," she replied wryly. *Textbook pink,* she said, and I thought about the pink elephants in a cartoon about drunks. But Dad was a teetotaler, wasn't he? Mom shook her head sadly. He'd been drinking gin on the sly in the attic, and he couldn't just have one drink.

Mom was wearing her red-and-white scarf with New York and Paris and London sketched on it, the scarf fastened by a bar pin. While she talked, she hunched her shoulders forward and pushed her hair out of her face. She has such high hopes for us, I thought, and for Dad. If she'd been a character in a book, I would have pitied her dashed hopes, and I might even have seen the hope for what it more nakedly was. As we sat with her and as she let herself confide in both my sister and me, I loved her so much I ached. I could feel the ache in my body and in hers, and I wanted Elizabeth to go away so that I could share the moment with only my mother.

"You didn't know?" Elizabeth asked her.

How could we have known? Mom replied uneasily. Then, contradicting herself, she said, "Remember the night he came back from playing bridge with Uncle John and Too-Too? I was so embarrassed. It was like a dinner we went to once at the Eastons' house. He drank too much then, too."

"I was on a date with Harry," Elizabeth interrupted. "No one tells me anything."

But I remembered.

Mom and Dad had briefly made an effort to develop a social life. On one Saturday night a month, they'd meet Uncle John and Too-Too to play bridge. They were lightening up. They were practicing how to be social, starting with the family. Elizabeth had gone to the movies with her boyfriend Harry, and I'd been home alone when they came in early, Dad whooping and stumbling, happy as I'd never seen him except when he'd played in the waves with us at Virginia Beach, tumbling about. Uncle John, who had driven our car, came in next, saying, "Whoa there, fella. Slow down." But Dad had only laughed and laughed. Soon after, the bridge games and drinks on Saturday night had ceased.

Childhood. Gin. And what else? I wondered. There had to be more to it. Otherwise, wouldn't Dad be home with us by now, not still at Tucker's talking to doctors, taking pills, and tooling leather in afternoon crafts?

Finally Mom told us about the shock treatments. Each one, she said, cut to the quick and left him in a woozy calm.

I tried to imagine the machine that delivered the shock. Later, in my journal, I wondered if it was like the electric chair for a man given the death sentence, but with the electricity delivered at a lower voltage. Mom had said that the instrument of healing—her words—was a kind of inverted bowl put on top of his head. In my journal, I imagined a wired helmet. I imagined a half moon of a bowl shoved down on Dad's head. I trembled and imagined an old-fashioned haircut, a way to trim ragged edges. At dinner Mom only said, "Don't think about it. If I thought about it I'd go crazy." In a firmer, formal voice, as if reading an advertisement, she added that the shock treatment erased certain memories. "The unpleasant ones."

I wanted to ask if, after the shock treatment, Dad would remember who we were. Would he remember who *he* was? If you took away someone's memories, didn't you take away part of the person? I wanted all of my father back, not part of him. Watching my face, Mom said not to worry. The doctors were the experts. They'd promised her that Dad could come home for dinner soon, for a short visit. He wasn't ready just yet to come home for good.

*Home for good.* The words sounded hopeful, and I clung to them.

Someone from Tucker's was to drive Dad home for dinner. Relieved that she could now *do* something for Dad, Mom was planning a steak dinner with all the trimmings. She wanted to *feed her man,* a phrase Mom often used that, for reasons I didn't entirely understand, made me flinch. I could already hear the open-mouthed chewing and lip-slapping pleasure of eating.

I wandered into Elizabeth's room at five o'clock, having decided not to change from my school clothing, as if an ordinary wool skirt and wool sweater would make the coming evening also ordinary. Normal. Standing before her open closet, Elizabeth was flicking coat hangers from right to left, looking over her clothes.

"I don't think we should dress up," she announced without looking at me.

"I don't think we should either," I answered and watched her let out a deep breath.

We had an hour to kill. We could play double solitaire, or we could help Mom in the kitchen. We could do our homework.

"It'll be a good dinner, like a birthday dinner, but I'll serve the plates in the kitchen," Mom said, mostly to herself, when we asked if we could help. She was browning the meringue on the lemon pie in the oven. My sister and I went into the living room and sat as if expecting a guest.

At the knock on the front door, I whispered to Elizabeth, "We should let Mom open the door. She'll want to see him first."

"Mom, he's here," Elizabeth called, and she came rushing from the kitchen, smoothing her hair, tossing her apron into one of the wing chairs.

That's not Dad knocking, I thought. Dad wouldn't knock. It must be his driver knocking. I imagined Dad on the other side of the closed door, the closed door of his own house, standing back in another man's shadow as this stranger rapped for permission to enter. Dad wouldn't have his wallet or his keys.

When Mom opened the door, I heard a businesslike voice say, "I'll be back at eight o'clock," and the gate to the front porch clicked shut. I couldn't see my father. At first he was hidden in the dark of the porch. Mom hadn't put on the front porch light, perhaps so that the neighbors wouldn't see Dad come home in the hospital's car. Once he was inside the living room, I couldn't see Dad's face because he had lowered it, leaning over to embrace my mother. Finally he lifted his head and looked over at my sister and me as we waited, standing a little stiffly by the sofa. The face that looked over at us smiled, and it was a genuine smile, but he was different. Mom had warned us that he might still be a little woozy, that the shock treatments of the day before might not have worn off. The face I saw was pale. My father, who loved the out-of-doors, had been ruddy. The face I saw had dark circles and uncertain eyes. His lips were wet, slick, a little slack.

In a husky voice Dad called us over to him. As Mom stepped back, we went over to Dad, simultaneously. How odd it felt, doing anything with my sister, even crossing a room and feeling the same split-second joy. *Dad was home. We were all together.* As in the stories I'd heard about his postwar homecoming, Elizabeth sprang into his arms, and I held back. Then he opened one arm and drew me in.

Dad was home, but he had come in a whiter, softer body that wore clothes more loosely. I thought he smelled sweet, like medicine or a new aftershave lotion. His skin was clammy. Mom, who must also have been standing back and looking at the changes in him, said quickly, "Let's go to the table before the steak gets overdone. We all like it rare."

"Here's your old place at the head of the table," she said, standing behind Dad after he sat down, rubbing his shoulders. For the first time, Dad relaxed a little and smiled.

"I haven't forgotten," he said.

I wanted to cry, and I didn't want to.

Elizabeth slipped into her seat nearest him, and I looked over at Mom. "I'll get the plates," she murmured, and I sat down.

The steak was done to a turn, the baked potatoes hot and mealy, running with butter, and there were three green vegetables. Mom had given Dad the choicest pieces of the sirloin and kept up a running commentary on the food: what she'd cooked and how, why she had chosen not to serve beets. She complained that the Safeway didn't have oyster root to fix.

Dad wasn't eating with his customary gusto. His hand shook, and I wondered if he was nervous being home, or if the tremor came from the shock treatments. During a lull in our recounting of news from school, he left the table and retrieved from his coat pocket two leather belts, one for me, one for Elizabeth. He had tooled them at hospital crafts, stamping into the tan leather little leaves and flowers. He said he had thought about us every day he was away.

But the simplicity and dignity of his words and his gesture faded quickly. Dad wasn't coming back from a business trip, handing out the little hotel soaps. Tucker's was no hotel, and these belts weren't little soaps that washed away time and distance. He wanted more from us than we could give him. We thanked him—too polite—and even then I knew we were failing him. I tried to offer more words of thanks, but whatever I said sounded wrong.

When it was safe, Elizabeth glanced my way. She knew I'd lied when I'd said that I'd wear the belt he'd given me. Wanting him to take pride in his work, I'd even invented a skirt to wear it with, blue with belt loops. I knew I'd never wear the belt. I wouldn't dare.

With its oddly shaped buckle, the belt was hopelessly out of fashion, nothing like the cloth and elastic belts with leather trim and heavy brass buckles now for sale at Steve and Anna's. At school someone—Melissa, or a girl to whom Melissa had gossiped—might look at the belt and ask pointedly, "Where did *that* come from?" And what would I say then? And besides, I would think hours later, trying to get to sleep, it was a *belt* Dad had given me, exactly the last gift I would ever want from my father. A belt with the basement and all my fear of his anger buckled into the notches, however loose I wore it, however tight. I couldn't believe that my father wouldn't know how I felt.

Then again, how could he?

How could he know what I wouldn't tell him? And I would never tell him, not now, not ever. Especially not now.

Later into the meal, Dad glanced at me and said, "See how quietly I'm eating?" I nodded and tried to smile easily, then looked back at my plate and trimmed fat away from my next bite of steak, wanting the floor to open and let me sink from sight. He was trying so hard to please. He was trying so hard, and I hated myself for every criticism or cool glance I'd ever directed his way as he slapped his lips at a meal or chewed with his mouth open, making the noises of pleasure and abandon, night noises from across the hall when I'd been a little girl, and we'd all slept with our bedroom doors open.

To calm myself, I put a pat of butter on my potato skin and caught Mom smiling at me approvingly. Here I am also eating carefully, I thought. Here I am eating more than I want to eat. Eating so that Mom will relax, Dad will smack his lips, Elizabeth will sass and fuss. Wanting wanting wanting us to be the family we once had been around the table. I didn't like who we were now, so careful to be careful that I could feel the temperature drop five degrees with each sentence we spoke, our words acting like a draft in the room. We behaved as if someone had left a door ajar or a window open; someone had broken a windowpane, someone had forgotten to give the attic door the extra push that made it latch. It was everyone's and no one's fault.

In the living room after dinner, Dad sat down wearily in his wing chair. He looked heavier, as if the dinner had changed to pounds immediately, lifting up his spirits, weighing down his flesh. Mom pulled the little fireside stool over and sat next to Dad. She leaned over and put her head on his knees. She called Dad, lovingly, "Pop."

"I'm not a Pop, I'm a Daddy," my father roused himself to answer, but Mom, failing to hear, wouldn't take the hint. Lost perhaps in an inchoate remorse or stalled in an unwelcome realization, she repeated firmly, "Pop." I tried to send her a signal—raised eyebrows, a gesture of my hand half hidden behind my skirt—but she didn't, or wouldn't, see me.

Why was she so insistent on this change of name? I wondered. She continued to call Dad "Pop," not just once more but three times more, four, as if the dinner had indeed marked a birth, as if among the balloons at the birthday party the one with my father's name on it had been lanced by a small pin—*pop*. On the floor I saw the shrunken, shriveled skin of the balloon, a lolling, mute red tongue, a tiny shroud of pain.

At eight sharp there came a knock at the door. Dad promised to come home soon, and I nodded, smiling what I hoped was a smile. Mom went to the door with him and, in front of the man waiting in the darkness of the porch, kissed Dad on the cheek.

After a few weeks, on my return from school, winded by a run through the dark from the bus stop, my face red with the cold air and my eyes tearing, I found Dad sitting in one of the wing chairs in the living room reading the newspaper. He was home. I saw his suitcase at the foot of the attic stairs, ready to be taken up. He'd unpacked. He was home to stay. When I said, "Hi, Dad," he lowered the newspaper and replied easily, "Hello there, Mar-Leigh."

And that was that. It was as if he'd never been away. In the weeks and months that followed, when he was so quiet he seemed absent, he was absent in our midst. If during such an absence I wanted to talk to him, I took out my journal and wrote in it.

In the crowded classroom I reread the comments written in red on the last page of my essay, then looked again at the letter grade. It resembled a moon half effaced, a face with half of itself gone missing. A blow dart or a stream of spit was aimed at it. Meant as objective evaluation, not meant to signify punishment or disfigurement, the grade was C-. Below average. A grade I'd never before received on any paper of mine, certainly not in English, not even in math. I was stunned: a C- was unthinkable. Even so, the low grade by itself couldn't quite account for the humiliation, the shame I felt.

I should never have taken the assigned topic for the argumentative essay, I chided myself, sidestepping the shame briefly, angry that no one else in the class had claimed the topic or volunteered for it, especially not after Susan Abbot had with her bold passion claimed the opposing topic. For each topic, Mrs. Woodward had assigned someone to write an argument pro, someone else to write the argument con. "And so who will argue *for* segregation?" she had asked after Susan elected to argue against it. Sensing challenge, I'd risen to the bait. No one could be, should or would be, sanguine about the murderous lynching of, say, Emmett Till in 1955. But who among our set would speak against Orval Faubus and his refusal to integrate the schools in Arkansas? Who would speak for integration in Virginia? Hadn't Carolyn Rawling's father years before argued against integration in the highest court in the land, and he was someone in our midst, a parent, an authority. While it wasn't polite to talk about the necessity of segregation, everyone I knew tacitly favored it. It was what we knew; it was our custom. In Virginia, we weren't killers; we kept to ourselves, and they kept to themselves. I remembered how I'd made a wry face, shrugged, then raised my hand to shoulder the burden of the argument to keep the races separate. And for my reckless courage—was it courage? No, it wasn't courage. For my unwise impulse to be the defender of what I probably thought safe—the majority view—I was now regarded by a cartoon face that stuck out its tongue at me: C-.

For the writing itself, Mrs. Woodward had awarded an A; for my "reasoning," a D. The quotation marks around *reasoning* were hers. I tried to enjoy the A for writing skill, pleased that I knew what Mrs. Woodward valued and demanded, proud that I could rise to her standard, which was uncompromising. Sentences should be focused, balanced, rhythmic; word choice, exact; detail, precise, sufficient. She would compromise neither accuracy nor truth for style and wit. Wit she enjoyed, but wit without substance was ornament affixed to emptiness: a waste of time and material, a distraction that could in fact collapse an argument because it weakened the credibility of the speaker. *Well-written* she put in red ink at the close of the paper, but she advised me to reconsider my "reasoning"—it was unsound. I had *generalized* from personal opinion, and, considering the higher principles involved, ethical and legal principles, the reasons I'd offered for segregation were *irrelevant.* "Consider your sources," she wrote. "Those you consulted, those you neglected to consult."

*Consider my sources.* Well then, I would need to consider my mother; I would have to consider myself, the inheritor of the family's views and values. I had argued only briefly from law, citing the now overturned *Plessy vs. Ferguson,* which had asserted the justice of separate but equal. Much of my argument, now I realized, had judged the Negro in general. *They* are; *they* are not. *They are not like us:* that had been the core of the position I'd taken, narrowing my view to Virginia. What, historically, did Virginia value, I had asked rhetorically,

and answered: a culture based on the work ethic, success, and hierar-
chy, the "ladder of success." Had the Negro been able, he would have
risen. Having written that much, I'd drawn a blank. Searching for
detail or evidence, I'd called across the hall to my mother, asking for
"reasons the Negro shouldn't be integrated into white society." The
spread of disease, illiteracy, poverty, sexual promiscuity, and crime—
my mother had cited these, listing them easily. And so against the elegance of a white man's estate, his grounds, his sentences, his ethics, I
had contrasted the Negro's crudeness, poverty, obscenity, ignorance.
Only now, reviewing my paper, did I see, looking out at me from
between the blue-ruled lines and Mrs. Woodward's red scrawl,
Marie's face. Writing, I had not once remembered Marie's humor, her
humanity, the long hours she worked, her hymn singing, her generosity to my mother, her patience with Betsy and me. I had written as if
stoical and scary Edwin, the killer of chickens, a man I knew only at a
distance, could be generalized into an entire race, itself knowable
only by contrast with whites. *They* were different, not like us, and
therefore a threat were we to commingle. *Commingle* was my mother's
word, offered blithely, lightly—the way adults lilted a word so not to
sink into the deep invisible mire of unsanctioned sexuality. *Commingle* carried with it the shame that unwise daughters might bring to
their families, the fear of humiliation and downfall.

And so I had, I concluded, used my so-called courage to take on a
topic that called for the defense of customs erected on fear. I had
missed the point. Instead of arguing inequality before the law—but
how could one argue that?—I had tried to prove inequality by a
generalized difference based on effect not on cause. Focusing on
false personality, and not on principle, I'd reasoned like a parent
with two children, one bad, one good. Wasn't a bad child required
to change her behavior, rise to the challenge, improve? Without fact,
I had reasoned speciously—without proper evidence, without
heart. I looked over the paper. How cold it was. It was as cold as my
sister said I was.

I was barely breathing now, and so intent I heard little of what went
on in the classroom. But I couldn't ignore what I'd done, what until
now I'd forgotten. *They're like us*—hadn't I realized that, once, much
younger, reading, off by myself in the house, entering by way of
imagination into a Negro family's life? *They're like us*—I'd known that
in my bones, down deep, so deep a knowing that denial couldn't

touch it, nor could fear. *They're like us.* Trying to argue otherwise, I had betrayed my deeper knowing. Arguing otherwise, using someone else's reasons—my mother's—I'd betrayed myself. The reasons I'd given were unreasonable, even if I wanted them to be otherwise. *Unsound,* Mrs. Woodward had said. *Unsound* meant unreasonable, but it was also the unspoken despair, the madness one keeps hidden, hushed up. Elizabeth and I were not to speak of Dad's illness and the shock treatments. If we did, he would be shunned—we might be, too.

The bell rang, and in the rustling of papers stuffed into notebooks, I busied myself gratefully. The next class was algebra. For once in my life I was grateful for algebra, whose obscure equations gradually clarified, whose answers were *right* or *wrong.* Algebra, in whose classroom a *C* in the margin meant *Correct.*

That night I had a dream so vivid I jotted it down in my journal notebook in the morning, my hand shaking as I wrote. In the dream, my father, wearing dirty clothes, was standing in the backyard, in the middle of a garden, holding a spade. He had been digging. All around him was bright light. It was very still in the dream, nothing moved. The light seemed to come from behind or within my father. And then in the stillness and light, my father's skin slowly deepened and turned dark, like a colored man's.

"And yet," I wrote in my journal, puzzled, "he was clearly himself. Even happy."

God was omniscient; only God could see what was predestined, my mother announced as we washed dishes after supper. I rinsed a plate and waited. Usually when Mom began with a pronouncement about God, she was worried. This was prologue. She cleared her throat, nodding her head for emphasis: *only God* could see.

But God, I thought to myself, however much He knew, kept quiet. God was a deep silence who spoke only to those He would test by sending them out to prophesy when his people were confused and corrupted. No coal had kissed my mouth. Or my mother's, even if she thought so. Her unquestioning faith was annoying. I did not understand why things happened as they did, why my father suffered his breakdown, or why I was experiencing the treachery and betrayal of a friend.

Mom scraped the roasting pan free of bits of skin and the congealed chicken grease she called "essence." Clearing her throat, she said she had bad news from only three houses up the street. Mr. Easton, Dad's boss, had died . . . *by his own hand.* I held a plate suspended over the soapy water, a long pause. How was Dad taking what Mom went on to call *a tragedy*? I wondered if my father would be considered for the vacancy, if he'd be promoted. If he wasn't offered the position, how would he handle the disappointment? I dipped the plate into the water and watched it sink below the surface of the soap bubbles, curious that, after my concern for my father, a single word had floated into my mind. *Ophelia.* As so often happened, Mom replied to my silence as if I'd spoken aloud.

"Our lives unfold like a book already written by the Almighty," she said.

"Or a play," I added. We were reading *Hamlet* in English class. Whether or not she heard me, Mom warmed to her theme. God was the author of the story, she continued confidently, and Mr. Easton had sinned terribly, ending his life in the upstairs guest bedroom with a shotgun, taking the story into his own hands, without waiting to see how God would work things out.

But who knew what Mr. Easton was going through? Certainly, I thought, we didn't know what he'd felt or what he'd thought. How could we judge him?

"God is the author of the story," Mom repeated, "and Mr. Easton should have thought of his wife." Leaving her a note downstairs, to keep her from stumbling on his dead body in shocked surprise— wasn't that just like a man? He'd tried, he'd made a gesture, but it just wasn't thoughtful enough. "Ah-men!" she concluded ruefully and shook her head, folding into God's mysterious silence Mr. Easton, my father, and all men.

Mom frequently made general assertions about social customs that gave them the force of a universal physical law, and her pronouncements were linked to her mood. Whatever it might be, that mood had a depth like a quarry—one didn't know how far it was to the bottom. I had given up trying to fathom or to measure Mom's moods. I would roll my eyes when, in matters of fashion, she'd exclaim, "Why, *everyone's* wearing them!" Now as she dumped all men into the garbage, I wondered why. She must have been hurt more than I'd realized by Dad's illness—or was it another, earlier man? Or was it simply her way of speaking, a way to clinch her argument?

Perhaps, I mused, everyone needed an inner voice, an omniscient narrator who could clarify what was in someone else's mind and heart—and in one's own. If not the voice of an omniscient narrator, at least everyone needed an inner director to help you play your role in the play.

Mom opened the icebox door and looked in. What she was thinking I couldn't discern. She tapped the edge of the door impatiently. She might have been looking for a dessert to offer me or for the ingredients for tomorrow's dinner. She might have been thinking about sinful Mr. Easton. She might have been thinking about Dad. I knew she wasn't thinking about God. God made her confident, not impatient. If Mom didn't want to tell you her thoughts, there was no getting her to. If she wanted to, there was no stopping her. I turned back to rinsing the dishes and putting away the dried silverware. We were probably the only family in the West End that used what had many years before been a baby's diaper—now freshly laundered and bleached—as a dish towel. Whenever any of my former friends had come to spend the night, I'd tucked the kitchen diapers out of sight.

In our house, each of us brooded silently. There weren't any extended soliloquies to overhear. I'd learned to keep my anger to myself, even if it meant smoldering. When Mom and Dad and Elizabeth were angry, they spoke loud words, but they later said they hadn't meant what they'd said. Since their anger was mostly hot air, I considered their loud outbursts as opaque as any silence would be. Was it like that in the other houses on our street? Did anyone *talk about* what they were going through? Within our Stonewall Court neighborhood, was there anyone who knew what Dad suffered when he was sick? Did anyone understand about Mr. Easton and his despair or fear? What really happened behind all the closed front doors? From behind these closed doors, emerged into public view upright adults with impenetrably cheerful, polite faces.

By contrast, the heroic in literature happened in public view. I liked to think about tragic heroes, men whose lives were far outside the ordinary, men who showed themselves for what they grandly were. I was awed by the power of each hero and by his downfall, each man brought low by a flaw, a single tragic error from which all sorrow and devastation flowed. The flaw became the fate each man suffered.

Since I hadn't read *Antony and Cleopatra,* it appeared that women ruled the world only from behind the scenes, as Mrs. McCue had said. Women seldom faced the choices and trials of a Macbeth or a Hamlet. Perhaps that explained why diminutive if cheerfully bossy Miss Salley, the drama coach, never chose to produce tragedies. She preferred Shakespeare's comedies, *A Midsummer Night's Dream* or *Twelfth Night.* She chose liberally from Gilbert and Sullivan's musicals, or she selected romantic comedies set in the drawing rooms of well-to-do families whose mores were Victorian, whose rivalries and mismatched matchmakings were comically sorted out, "missunderstanding" and chaos followed by resolution and delight. A lighthearted soul—her first name, Alma, meant *soul* in Spanish—Miss Salley put on plays by A. A. Milne, J. M. Barrie, and Cornelia Otis Skinner.

In our all-girls school, Miss Alma Salley had no choice but to cast girls in the male roles. Necessity, however, was for her the source of keen pleasure. Girls in trousers or plus fours, girls with their chests wrapped tightly by a towel to flatten their breasts—to cast girls as men was Miss Salley's revenge on the Elizabethan stage, which allowed only male actors. About acting, she liked to say mysteriously, "There are more ways than one to skin a cat."

Like Miss Salley, I also cast my classmates into Shakespeare's plays, mentally assigning them to the male or female roles that suited them. Melissa, who was ambitious, wasn't she Macbeth at heart? Virginia Willard might be Cordelia; Susan Abbot, Portia. Whose part might I play? Neither Caesar nor Brutus—I wasn't inclined to try to rule or to rebel. I didn't want to be Ophelia and go mad. I was more like Hamlet, brooding at my desk, daydreaming over the dishes or in the church pew or on the sidelines of an athletic event. If I had a cause and a cue for action, I didn't know what it would be. *To thine own self be true?* But that was Polonius, full of high sentence and moral advice, then hiding behind the arras to eavesdrop. Polonius, like my mother, knew by rote the social and moral commandments. Hamlet's dilemma was to figure out what was true, what was his own self, not another's. His omniscient narrator was, curse the luck, the ghost of his father—and who could trust a ghost?

"Clap your hands and twirl about on one leg—try it," Mr. Knox directed. He wanted me to let my body show the delight that filled the young Irish girl I was supposed to portray, a delight I'd been reaching for with my voice alone, straining at it. When I followed his instructions, I was met with a baffled look and a voice inflected with disappointment. "Not like that. Can't you be less . . . less deliberate? Joy isn't so *diligent*," he said.

Try as I might, I couldn't clap and twirl, twirl and clap my way into the embodiment of youth and high spirits. Unused to receiving instruction from a teacher who was a man, I had fallen into a fatal self-consciousness. Fifteen minutes later, however, no longer the focus of Mr. Knox's scrutiny, and with the cast of *The Wayward Saint* in stitches, diverted by the moment's spontaneous revelry, I clapped my hands and did a quick twirl. Mr. Knox looked at me in swift surprise. "That's it! That's it!" he called, jumping out of his seat and waving his arms. "When you forget yourself, you can do it!"

I looked away shyly.

"Where is feeling found," Mr. Knox had asked softly, "if not *within yourself?*"

After two years of trying out for a part—any part—in a play put on by the St. Kit's Players, which took its actors and actresses from the students of St. Christopher's and St. Catherine's schools, I had been given the female lead in *The Wayward Saint*. Before this, my experience on stage had been confined to wordless roles, my first in sixth grade when, because I was tall, I was selected to stand ceremoniously on stage, a guard in *The Mikado*. I'd been easily cast. Miss Salley had come looking not for talent but for height. As a guard in the Mikado's court, I had little to do but what came natural to me: study the scene from the sidelines. Spellbound, I watched the grand illusion of the play evolving, a magical transformation. Older, I'd worked backstage on other productions, and as a freshman in Upper School I'd played a shepherd in *A Midsummer Night's Dream*. Again a walk-on, I observed as others took the lead, saying their lines, becoming who they were not, masking and unmasking according to the twists and turns of a plot they didn't have to live off stage.

Now, in my junior year, Mr. Knox had judged that I was right for the role of the ostracized Irish lass who entrusts a priest, the so-called wayward saint, with the story of her romantic longing for the Protestant boy, surprised to find that the priest would befriend her. There was a "big" scene for the lass. Mr. Knox had said he sensed "something" in me that would rise to meet the depth of grief in that scene when the Irish girl tells the priest about the tragic death of her sweetheart on a lonely country road.

Of the two female parts in the play, clearly I had the better one. I would have the "big" scene, and Corbin White, who would be the priest's housekeeper, would have the on-stage kiss—a kiss that would likely make some of our classmates in the audience snicker, others whisper, and still others (had I been the one kissed) spread rumors. Angry at myself for caring what Melissa or anyone else "thought," I was relieved not to be the housekeeper who got kissed.

The role as the so-called romantic lead set me challenges. Unsure that I was pretty enough, I had to make myself more than pretty. I had to be beautiful, and that meant I had to keep thin. I steeled myself for more skirmishes with Mom at the dining table. In the "big" scene, the Irish girl had to recount what she'd undergone to the Irish priest, a long narrative. I had to remember the lines, of course, and also Mr. Knox's instructions about pace and modulation—but I had to keep these instructions from obstructing my feeling. Not only did I have to feel my feelings, I had to cry.

At home, as I rehearsed my lines, I listened to Beethoven on our record player, especially to adagio movements in the symphonies. Elizabeth thought I was daydreaming about a boyfriend, and I didn't bother to tell her I was doing something far more difficult, trying to find my way back to the music that was, Mom had promised, always inside me. That was where my deep feelings were. If I sat in the living room with no one else and listened to it as I said my lines, the words of the script sank into the music, the music into my mind, and from nowhere, from a depth I didn't know existed, I felt a tremor.

Rehearsals drew closer to opening night. One night I found that if I stood by myself, backstage, out of the sight of anyone in the cast, if I stood hidden in the darkness waiting for my entrance cue, and breathed once deeply, and then forced my breathing to turn ragged and quick, my body gradually took charge and re-created the feelings I would need for the lines I would say once I was on stage. Once my breath was at the right pitch, I could not only feel the grief and wonder, I could remember the music. Not only that, once on stage I could "see" the scene I had to describe to the priest. Seeing it, I felt it more sharply; feeling it, I was both the boy who died and the frightened girl who mourned and who would later see his spirit or ghost on a lonely road at night. When the words were done and I flung myself on my knees, my head in the priest's lap; when finally I felt his hand smoothing my hair, I knew myself to be a child soothed by the father she didn't have, and my silent sobs deepened, my body shuddered.

By dress rehearsal, when I looked in the mirror, even though I was looking at my own face with a greasepaint "widow's peak"—said to intensify beauty under the stage lights—and even though I was wearing the spring dress I'd bought with my own allowance, I saw only the Irish lass. Her story had become my own; mine had disappeared into hers. At the very least, she was my inner companion, someone to whom, like a real friend or a child's imaginary companion, I could talk. Didn't I know how her loneliness felt?

"You're talking to yourself again," Elizabeth would tease me, but I wasn't. I was practicing my lines. The more intimate I became with the girl's life, the less I felt the slings and arrows of misfortune in my own. Given what the Irish girl had lost, my own losses seemed slight. To lose a friend wasn't the end of the world. Had Mr. Easton only found a way into another role, another life, perhaps he might have discovered his own despair healed. And my father . . . well, I couldn't really allow myself to feel what I felt for my father except when I was saying the Irish girl's lines and could sob, my face hidden from view.

Acting on stage allowed me to be simultaneously visible and invisible. Before everyone, there I was; and yet I was *other*. In acting, I had discovered the redemptive power of the imagination and a circuitous way back to the music inside me. I had discovered a way to put aside my own pain by taking on someone else's. That pain I would release in words. The words were set by the script, but the music I listened to as I learned the words made the words mine. It was a curious, mysterious process.

In church I might still sing "Faith of our fathers, holy faith / We will be true to you 'til death"—but I was putting my faith in make-believe.

After the academic day at St. Catherine's, after rehearsals, at home I was alone in my room, with my books and thoughts as once I had been solitary in the plum tree in our backyard, quietly letting the dark come on and melt the outline of the swings into the dogwood canopy, the tree branches into the evening air. The sound of car tires bit into the gravel of a neighbor's driveway. A car door thudded, a screen door banged shut. A mockingbird's song lifted from the dim clematis on the fence, and I listened to it intently, sorting out each set of repeated notes which the mockingbird mimicked from another bird's song and made its own. One by one the stars appeared, the boundless and brilliant wheel of the stars, incarnate in the motionless tumult I still called *the heavens*. At my desk, I learned the assigned French vocabulary and idioms; I said the Latin passages aloud until I could almost hear Roman Cicero declaim and Virgil grandly brood. I puzzled out problems in algebra until what was a chaos of possibility reduced to the elegance of a solved equation.

In biology Miss Walton had written on the board what she called a "stunning" truth: *Ontogeny recapitulates phylogeny*. She had shown us how the developing human fetus passed through stages of life in the lower phyla: zygote, then a multicelled cluster; then frog, bird, lower mammal, human mammal—to become human was to be in this procession of otherness; *to be* was to become other. I could see how growth was a process of construction and rejection—intricate, but also simple. Each new form modified an earlier form, increasing it without erasing it entirely. With each alteration and revision, the final form emerged, more distinct, more fully *itself* and more *other*. As I closed the biology text, the spring night wind in the plum tree rose internally as I turned to reading "Ode to a Nightingale" and "Lines Composed a Few Miles above Tintern Abbey." I looked around my room. The glow-in-the-dark stars had been painted over, but the wallpaper bower of petite daisies on a pink background remained the meadow I'd picked out as a child. It surrounded my bed, whose tall posts I'd once called "trees." Every night my mother came to the door and called "Good night" promptly at ten o'clock. At times I saw myself from such a distance, I could think of my self as *A Girl at her Desk*—and ask, as if I were someone else, *What is she turning into?* The hours of study passed quietly, page by page, night by night-wind night, and I was alone in the company of English poets, historians, scientists, and Latin bards.

By late autumn of my junior year at St. Catherine's I no longer missed my old friends, the girls within the circle of power, the girls who decided who among them would take on the most prominent and responsible offices as seniors. Forget them, I reminded myself. Some months before the tryouts for *The Wayward Saint*, I had vowed not to accept the role Melissa had written for me. She might have tarnished my reputation and cost me friendships, but I was not, in my own mind, tarnished. With each boy I dated, a new facet of myself emerged. With Bill Cardin, who jilted me, I was surprisingly calm and judicious. He had been too old, I too innocent. With Bob Parker, I was happy to learn to kiss. Even to date him—he went to a public high school—was a quiet protest against the snobbery that had hurt my father. I watched my mother's distress as I went out the door with this unremarkable suitor—I knew how to quell her anxieties by praying with her and then, the perfect hypocrite, doing as I liked discreetly. For Bob I was "the golden girl," or so he said when we broke up. With feckless Jack Parkinson of an old Virginia family, I was the girl he, a junior at the University of Virginia, had "robbed" from the cradle—but "so mature you'd never know she was sixteen," said the girls his friends dated. What another person saw in me, I turned on myself as a question. Was I "golden"? Was I "mature?" I didn't always agree.

"What's *this one* like?" I heard Melissa ask Kathy Parrish, who lived near the Parkinsons and knew the family. Only minutes before the morning study hall bell would ring, I was closed into a bathroom stall, still adjusting my clothes, when Melissa rushed into the bathroom to interrogate Kathy. Neither knew I was in the bathroom.

"He's a nice boy," Kathy said into the running water at the sink.

Before she could continue, I flushed the toilet and opened the door of the stall.

Melissa looked blankly at me; I looked blankly at her.

Kathy looked at us both in the mirror and turned red.

No one said a word.

Melissa suddenly turned and left in the little puff of wind provided by the hinged door. I smiled at Kathy, who was still so embarrassed that now she left the room without drying her hands, even though she hadn't said a single harmful syllable.

*There,* I thought. *I saw them, I heard them—it hasn't been my imagination.* For months and months I had watched my friends withdraw. None had offered a word of explanation. And while I had known that Melissa must be gossiping and turning my friends against me, while I'd imagined what she might say, now I'd witnessed the "offstage" scene unfold. You couldn't get more offstage than the bathroom. Hidden from her view, I had heard her tone of voice when she said *this one.* She was still snooping and trying to collect "dirt."

Instead of feeling hurt, I now felt vindicated. Wasn't it all too small-minded, too tawdry? *Merde,* I said to myself, armored by the sophistication of French. It was a scene fit to be played out in a bathroom, the scent of whose chemical cleaners overpowered both clean air and foul. I washed my hands of them and walked to my desk in the study hall, just under the bell.

By early winter, I was editor of the literary magazine, a position earned by ability, not gained by election. I was also working as a volunteer aide at the Veteran's Administration Hospital. Everyone in the junior class was required to participate in this volunteer program, but only a few of us continued to visit beyond the mandated period. Among these volunteers I found new friends, Ellen Gordon and Lynn Murphy, girls who like me studied hard and "dated." We had about us the unmistakable aura of being outside the circle of power and outside the other cliques that had been in existence since the sixth grade. The three of us continued to visit the paraplegic wards, wearing our candy-striped aprons and best smiles. I didn't understand why it was satisfying to feed a man who stank of urine or whose baby food dinner dribbled down into a crease in his chin until I heard myself coax, "Eat another bite, there you go: that'll stick to your ribs," sounding, I was appalled to admit, like my mother. To treat a man as a child was to feel powerful, I was discovering, and my hand shook. I looked away as the injured man I spoon-fed slurped the food.

Most of the men we ministered to in small ways had been injured while in the armed services, or in car or motorcycle or surfing accidents. Their helplessness wasn't entirely discouraging as long as I could sense a vestige of the earlier person, the one before the accident, still there despite his crippled body. I tended the two of them, the injured man and the earlier self stranded in the body I fed. Often I was assigned to a man called Stuart, whose earlier wholeness was clear to me. I watched the light rise in his eyes when his fiancée of thirty years entered the room, a woman now in her midforties who continued her fidelity to the man who was injured before they could marry.

"I hope they had sex," whispered Ellen. "At least once," she added, her quick laughter retreating into the prim tone of voice most girls effected. By April, Lynn and Ellen and I were going out with boys in the senior class at St. Christopher's. We called ourselves the T.U.V.—the three unholy virgins, an acronym we refused to translate should anyone overhear our private joke and inquire. "We may be unholy," we confided among ourselves, "but we're still virgins."

The inner drawer of the slant-top desk, where Dad had once locked his army pistol, was unlocked and empty. In the top drawer of the desk I found Dad's accounts of household finances, and I thumbed through them without interest even though Mom and Dad considered finances hush-hush. Having worked for two summers at an insurance company, tallying debits and credits, I was bored by columns of figures. Somewhere in the desk, I fancied, I might find my mother's love letters, the ones she had either hidden or destroyed after Elizabeth and I had, as children, found them in an attic trunk. Surely she wouldn't throw them away! In the middle drawers, however, I found only the linens for the dining room table, cloth considered too fine for us, just right for the company we never invited for dinner.

In the bottom drawer I uncovered a stack of formal studio portraits of my mother, dressed up and smiling for the camera. One by one I removed the photographs from their tissue-paper sleeves and matting paper folders, lining them up against the sofa cushions beneath the tinted photographs of Betsy and me in our pink organdy dresses. These tinted photographs embarrassed me, displayed so prominently above the sofa, the family icons any date of mine would have to encounter upon entering the living room.

"Of course not!" my mother had retorted when I asked if we could hang the Audubon birds in place of my sister and me. "It's how I want to remember you and your sister," she insisted. "These are for posterity, and besides, you two are, as long as you live, *the center of our lives.*" Her words spoke for Dad, too.

Propped against the cushions of the sofa where Elizabeth and I sat to make small talk with our dates and our parents before we were allowed to leave the house—it was only proper for our parents to have a moment or two to look over the young men who were taking their girls off into the dark of the night—I lined up a row of smiling mothers. Stepping back to review them, I gasped. How lovely she had been! And how much she was changed, I thought, feeling guilty. When these portraits were made, my mother hadn't been a mother. I called to mind her gray hair, her lined face shadowed by concern. What had we done to her?

In the earliest portrait, the one with the border of a green design I would years later recognize as Art Deco, my mother wears a sleeveless, V-necked chiffon as she regards the camera serenely, a corsage on her left shoulder, a necklace of pearls and crystal beads around her slender neck, her cropped hair parted low on one side and swept to the other side in waves and ripples. Swept *seductively*—that was the word. On the lower border in Amma's handwriting were these words, "This was dear little M.L." If the inscription meant anything, the photograph was taken to mark Mom's graduation or prom night, before she had been "disowned" by Amma. In three of the later photographs, all from a studio in Richmond and dated 1939, Mom would have been approaching her marriage. In one she smiles, and her dimples flash. In the other two, her face angles to the side, and she gazes off to a distant ideal. These two were studies in womanly purity and hopefulness, the virtues she admired in the heroines of Florence Barclay novels.

Where, in these portraits, was the hopeful, desperate girl with crooked front teeth, the girl who had used "an orange stick" to put pressure on her teeth, one by one, and straighten them? Where was the girl who had covered her breasts in shame? The girl who, fearful and courageous, had traveled farther than her mother or her sisters ever had, taking a degree at Farmville Normal School—where was that fiercely determined girl? Gone away with the country girl who had an A only in nature studies and in glee club; the girl with the D in physical education, the student who'd been made to repeat composition and grammar. Where was the one who, even now, slipped and said "can't hardly," and then flinched when her older daughter corrected her?

The more I looked, the more I gradually understood that behind this pink heroine, blushing with piety and romance, was my determined and careworn mother, underlining the words she didn't know as she read, writing the dictionary definitions in the margin, marking the short and long vowels and the stresses so that she could say them correctly. Words like *aviary, acquiescent, shrewd, misogynist*. This same girl wrote "June 24" beside the casual description "a June day," turning the heroine's ordinary day into her own wedding day and "summer's morn." The same woman wrote "Come Holy Spirit" in the margin near the printed words "Veni, Creator Spiritus." And she was certainly every inch my mother, the reader who underlined every religiously tinged or romantic sentiment uttered in the book, writing in bold script on the concluding page: *They only live who love!*

Obedient to God, Love, and Necessity, here was the young woman who had married, risked the childbirth that had killed her beloved older sister, risked it twice, suffered it, and now championed it. Like Jane in *The Rosary*, who ministered to a husband she called "Boy," my mother cared for my father with what she called "maternal tenderness." The highest love was maternal—was that what the hopeful girl in these photographs believed she was aiming for as she struck a pose and acted the part?

Looking at the photographs, I didn't see the mother I struggled with at the dining room table. Discontented, frustrated, I put the photographs back into the bottom drawer of the desk without realizing that as hard as I would struggle with my mother and resent her power, loving her was the secret I would come to hide from myself for years—I would have to.

As sure as the moon reflected the sun, waxing and waning in its prescribed cycle, a good daughter, according to the Bible, would leave her parents and cleave to her husband, daughter turning into wife, exchanging one source of authority for another in her governance.

Liz and I had only recently met and begun to date the boys we would come to marry, but we had already begun to cleave to their families, as much as propriety would permit. Mom and Dad might caution, set boundaries and curfews, but they didn't attempt to make 37 Lexington Road the center of our expanding social lives. They didn't have the money to offer the hospitality other families could, but they didn't seem to mind. They had walked off the fields of competition to look on from the sidelines. From now on, not they, but their daughters would fly the family colors, and it didn't matter if they flew from someone else's flagpole. By our closing the front door behind us, heading more or less in the "right direction," we were each fulfilling a part of what had to be Mom's mission for her daughters.

For Liz, who struggled each year to earn a grade average that would allow her to pass into the next grade, going to college was not an option. Secure now with her boyfriend, she put pounds back on luxuriously. She would attend Pan American Business School, as had Mom's younger sister. Like Mom, I would go to college—one in Virginia, of course, whichever college offered me the most scholarship money. Any college in New England was too far, too expensive. When I went for college counseling with the intent of convincing Mrs. Coolidge to let me apply to a northern school and try for a scholarship, she held with my mother, more swayed by my mother than by my SATs, achievement scores, and grades. When I pressed Mom at home to change her mind, Dad interrupted us. "Who do you think you are," he demanded heatedly. "You can go right up the road here to Westhampton College and live at home."

Fear made my stomach feel hollow, and then outrage followed fear. I went to my room, closed the door, banged my fist down on my desk. Why did my father have the power to limit me? I fumed. Calmer, I knew his was an empty threat. He would retreat to the background, and Mom would support my going away to a better college as long as I agreed to stay in Virginia.

Dutifully I dropped the Seven Sisters, bowed to the Mason-Dixon line, interviewed at Hollins and Mary Baldwin, and was given the scholarships I would need. With deeper pockets, Hollins offered me more than half of the expenses for tuition, room, and board. I would continue to work summers at the insurance company where I'd been employed summers and then at Liggett and Myers Tobacco Company as a tour guide. My wages would pay for my clothes and social expenses. On campus I'd have a weekend job. It was settled now. If I felt borne along on a river whose currents were taking me to a well-earned destination, my mother didn't doubt that Old Man River was none other than the God of our Fathers. Not that she didn't have ideas of her own as well.

"Do you want to make your debut?" she asked me, slipping into my room one afternoon and lowering her voice.

"Isn't it a little early for that decision?" I grumbled. I wasn't yet graduated; my classmates would be coming out during the summer that followed the first year in college. To be presented to Richmond society by their fathers, to be a debutante, took a lot of money from savings and a lot of planning. Perhaps, then, it wasn't too early for Mom to ask. But for me it was an idle question at best.

Quietly Mom repeated the question.

I was on the floor on my knees, looking around for the mate to a shoe hidden in the jumble of my closet, debating whether or not to knuckle under to my sister's taunts and actually clean the closet. Liz had already started a "hope chest." She neatly organized all her things in her drawers and closet. She could tell me the exact number of her dresses.

Mom would not make this offer to Elizabeth. Of her daughters, I had the better chance of being the embodiment of social graces. I could act the part. On my knees in the closet mess, however, I could feel a truthful retort forming. But when I looked up from my disordered closet and saw the light of shy eagerness in my mother's eyes, I held back my sharp reply.

My mother needed to make this offer.

She needed to extend it, and, I guessed quickly, she needed me to regard it as a serious question, even though she and I both knew I would have to reject the offer. My mother was trying to balance her love and her mission for her gifted daughter with her empty checkbook.

"I don't think I want to do that, Mom," I said evenly. "But thanks anyway."

Mom smiled at me gratefully. We both understood the moment and what it required of us. Understanding our roles, we forgave the necessary question, the required answer, the dance of illusion and fiscal reality. *Do you want* was the question Mom asked; *you're good enough to have* was the unspoken compliment she extended with the inquiry.

In June, as my senior year ended, I was named June Scholar, tying for the honor of first in the class with Nancy Spreen, who would go to Vassar in September. At the Commencement services in McVey Theater, Nancy and I sat next to each other on stage, alongside the June Queen and other prize winners, and we heard ourselves described to the audience by Miss Susanna Turner, the headmistress. That's me she's talking about, I thought. Rather, that's I. There I was, center stage, no longer playing the Irish lass or the male lead in the senior play, *The Romantic Age*. I was the tall girl, a June Scholar with special prizes in history and Latin—but not in English. Ellen had taken that prize, which I'd been expected to garner, and I had clapped hard for my best friend. In the audience, Mimi and Nanny sat with Mom and Dad and heard me described as imaginative and independent.

"Independent" surprised me. All of us looked like brides, lacking only veils and bridegrooms. Like St. Catherine, we had our gold rings, we had our books and our victory palms. If any one of us feared the wheel of pain that might lie ahead, our faces didn't show it. So what if my hand-me-down dress had fit its previous owner better than it now fit me, the bodice a little too tight, the dress a bit "too off the shoulder." Sitting with the daisy chain we'd carried into the auditorium at our feet, on stage we glowed. We were the completion and perfection of the promises our parents had made; we were new promises we ourselves might make for the future.

I watched from the stage as my mother and father, small faces in the assembled audience, smiled at me proudly.

My childhood was now concluded, wasn't it?

As if to mourn its passing, my parents went off home for a sandwich on the back porch, while I accompanied Lynn and her family, as their guest, to the Commonwealth Club for roast beef and baked Alaska. Why hadn't Mom invited Mimi and Nanny for a special lunch, I wondered as I waited on the grass with Nancy Spreen. The photographer from the *Richmond Times-Dispatch* rummaged in his bag for the right lens. I could see Mom and Dad heading for Dad's Chevrolet, parked in the Lower School lot, withdrawing into the background, becoming smaller and smaller figures in the field.

Lynn and her parents waited for the photographer to finish with the picture. Mr. Murphy tapped the face of his watch. He'd made a reservation at the club, and that needed to be respected. Various other parents were milling around in the crush of family and friends, a litter of daisy petals and commencement programs on the lawn. Lynn slipped away from her parents and whispered to me, "My mother overheard someone say that you're *the pearl in the oyster.*" As she returned to her waiting parents, I wished my mother had said the words, then I was glad she hadn't. I turned quickly away from the camera to shake off the tears, turning back with the right broad smile.

Why should I want to hear my mother call me the pearl in the oyster? I chided myself. What else had she been saying for years?

*Margaret*, at root, meant *pearl*.

*Pearl* was my role, my root, my road. My road, at whose beginning and at whose horizon point—as far as I could now see—stood my mother, ready and oh so willing to direct my path.

I could imagine her, dressed like the women of old and crying out in a loud voice, *"Who shall ascend the hill of the Lord? And who shall stand in his holy place?"*

Again crying out, *"Take delight in the Lord! And he will give you the desires of his heart."*

And again, within the shadows of palm branches on the noon road: *"Selah!"*

We had turned off the Chula Road in Amelia, jouncing on the hard, rutted lane that curved between the July cornfields, heading toward Aunt T's farmhouse, when around a blind corner in the field of high corn we were met nearly head-on by a black Model-T Ford. I maneuvered Dad's car alongside the Model-T, thinking *I'm in a time warp. This is 1966, another year of the Civil Rights movement and the illegal war in Vietnam, and I'm looking at a Model-T Ford make its way through a cornfield?*

The old man who peered out the open window wore a city hat and country overalls. His shirt, white with a button-down collar, could have been worn with a suit. The old man scowled at us, his mouth a sunken crescent, his chin a raw-boned thrust at the world—*take that.* He looked like a cross between a Snopes and a Compson in Faulkner's Yoknapatawpha; or he might have stepped from the pages of Flannery O'Connor's rural South, a Bible thumper with a thing about salvation. It dawned on me that I was looking at the first live person I'd ever seen without teeth, without even false teeth.

The old man shrilled, "Who in God's name are *you*?" He squinted at us. We could have been city politicians, snake-oil salesmen, or snakes.

"Why, Unc, you know who I am," my mother called out gaily. "And this is Margaret Leigh, you remember my older daughter. This is Margaret." When he said nothing, she added, "She's just graduated with honors from college. She's engaged to be married."

Unc—he was Aunt T's brother Gordon Harvie—continued to look at us as if we were part of the rutted road he had to get over. Riding in the passenger seat, Mom leaned my way, pressing her body so near that I pulled back into the seat and away from the wheel, making myself small. Why had she said I was getting married? And I wished she wouldn't brag about college. If Unc was to recognize either of us, he'd recognize my mother. He hadn't seen me since I was a child.

Still brusque and cranky, his voice had the sharp edge of a hawk's whistle. We were welcome to drive on back to the house, he announced, but he was headed to Chula to buy groceries. He released the throttle, and the Model T, like Virginia politics, inched forward in little quivers, a horse stalled in the starting gate.

*I was right to come here,* I thought. And right to insist that my mother come with me. The world I remembered from my childhood summers, the same southern world I'd rediscovered in the pages of southern short stories and novels in college, was her world, too. We didn't share much of the same world anymore. Since college, we couldn't talk about religion or politics or a woman's role in or out of marriage. I was questioning everything, and at the same time going ahead with the plans for my marriage to a boy of good family from Richmond. I was of two minds about most things.

In Richmond, I'd bought a copy of *Childbirth without Fear,* and I was reading it and also trying to help my mother with the wedding and all the social details neither of us was any good at. The wedding reception would be on the lawn at Mimi's home, at Alandale, under the oak trees and before the white columns of the dignified house, and my mother was glad to have such an elegant southern setting, especially since I was having to marry in a Catholic church which didn't allow the wedding march to be played, the music having originated in an opera at a high-toned moment of illicit passion. "I won't consider you married unless I hear the wedding march," my mother complained and shut her bedroom door on the pope and her difficult daughter, who thought the origin of the wedding march was funny.

Dad stayed clear of the preparations, but my sister, envious that I was marrying before she did, was anxious and testy. Liz now worked as a legal secretary, drove her own car, and had been wearing a diamond engagement ring since she'd graduated from St. Catherine's three years before. Unable to persuade Mike to set a date for the marriage, she had banked the fires of her frustration by adding more and more items to her hope chest and "dowry." She'd loaned me a dining room table she'd bought, allowing it to be used to display gifts, but when the first gift arrived she blew up. She said there was a scratch on the table where I'd put down a silver bowl. Her mood worsened as more gifts arrived. With me home and the wedding preparations under way, she felt eclipsed. "Look," I said to her, exasperated, tired of trying to exhibit a compassion I really didn't feel, "I wish it *were* your wedding."

When I said that, we both just looked at each other. What had I said?

Whenever I took my copy of *The Duel* from my desk—a slim chapbook with a textured gray paper cover, the poems hand-set, the title in green—I smoothed my hand over it as if a stranger, not I, had written the poems. My professor and mentor Louis Rubin had printed the poems handsomely on a letterpress in the basement of his campus house a few months before I graduated. I had given an inscribed copy of my poems to Mom and Dad. I didn't expect Dad to read them, but I thought Mom might. When I asked her if she'd read them, she shook her head. "They're too dark," she said. As far as I knew, my fiancé hadn't read them either.

With a summer grant to write poems, a scholarship for graduate school, and the coming marriage, I should have been—shouldn't I have been?—happy, but I was home-stalled in the sultry summer heat, neither bride, homemaker, graduate student, writer—nor wanderer. I wanted to go back to London to study; I wanted to move deeper South and next door to Faulkner's scuppernong arbor. I wanted to marry Ross, we wanted to march against the Vietnam war, we wanted to move to California, I wanted to slip the nets of family, race, and religion. I wanted to write *Portrait of the Artist as a Young Girl*. I wanted to make love.

Thus far, however, I had spent much of the summer in the backyard on an old reclining chair that imprinted my skin with the hatch marks of its meshed fiber as I lay in the sun and worked on my tan. I watched the red splotches glow and turn green behind my closed eyelids; then I watched them change back from green to red. Sweat stippled my skin, sweat ran between my breasts, sweat pooled between them. *Men sweat, women perspire, ladies glow*—I pulled down my bathing suit an inch or two to measure the contrast between the white skin that didn't see the sun and the darker tan I was achieving on my arms and shoulders. I let myself go wordless in the stunning noon humidity, ignoring my mother's admonitions as she called from the kitchen window. I listened to the bees hum in the clover.

Suddenly I leaped from the chair. How could I change my name?

How could I change my last name when—I said aloud—*you don't even know who Margaret Ferguson is.*

Dizzy, I stood in the sun, getting my bearings. Dogwoods. The swings. Lilac. Back porch and screen door. As soon as I was steady on my feet, I went into the house and asked Mom if we could go back to Amelia, back to Aunt T's. We had to go back there together, I said, and before I married. Given my intensity, Mom was hesitant, but she agreed. She didn't know why I wanted to go back there, and for the life of me neither did I. I was glad she didn't question me closely. I just knew I had to go back—*to our home place,* I'd said to Mom, who had looked both pleased and puzzled.

We sat silently side by side as Unc pulled away slowly in the Model T. He fluttered his hand—"G'wan now"—out the window.

Even so, I felt as if I had come home. In Amelia, the fields and stables, barns, big houses, and shacks slipped seamlessly right out of the pages of southern fiction. Here the land itself fit the land of my literary imagination. In both, trumpet vine ran wild on the fences, a chicken hawk circled over the fields of corn and wheat, the dust of the road sifted like a fine red flour onto the windshields of cars. In Richmond, my imagination floundered under the weight of social custom and family expectations.

Unc had told us that his wife, French, was back at the farmhouse. "She's pretty old," he'd said, as if he weren't. "Marie's there, too," he scowled. "She comes to look after things."

Marie! I smelled the old woodstove, chicken pieces sizzling in bacon grease, the yeasty biscuits. I smelled them as surely as I smelled the hot dirt of the red road.

The farmhouse was still painted milk white, but the barn roof sagged lower and the screens on the back door were popped outward. I haven't been here since I was nine, I thought. I remembered chickens. The chicken yard was bare.

"Lawd, look who's here. Lawd a mercy, look here," trilled a high voice from inside the screen door to the kitchen. I watched, pleased and shy, as my mother and Marie hugged on the steps. "Goodness gracious, sakes alive!"

Mom linked her arm through Marie's, and they turned together to go into the house, leaving me behind them. I remembered how, many years before, Mom would say that Marie had a lot of white blood in her, a remark that, remembered now, made me wince.

Unlike Unc, Marie had known right away who I was, and that pleased me. Now I heard her asking Mom, "Where's Betsy?" Her voice rose, sharp and highly treble, as she asked, "Your younger one, she still fat?" The word *fat* shimmered, with high-pitched amusement more than with criticism. In a moment that was as full of the unchanged past as it was with changes evident in the present, it wasn't a rude question. She might have expected a response that gave her my sister grown up and without baby fat. She had no way of knowing that Liz had added on so many pounds that now even Mom worried. I remembered Marie's tone of voice—direct, familiar, self-assured, with that edge to her amusement. But, no longer a child, I heard it with a difference. The tone chafed a bit at the boundaries between white woman and black. She would say what she pleased, but her tone protected her. For a moment, between us fell the shadow of Virginia's rigid codes of decorum and racial injustice.

As they turned to go into the kitchen, I lagged behind, stalled in a chaos of feelings, the joy of seeing Marie again mixed with anger at long injustice. I was also feeling sorry for Elizabeth. *I should have asked Liz to come with us,* I thought. Of course she had to be at work, but I should have asked.

Turning away from the house, I looked for old landmarks—anything familiar. In a way I couldn't explain, I felt troubled. The woodshed where Edwin had killed chickens had been torn down—or had it fallen? The orchard trees—had they been pear trees? Or apple? The trees had been cut, the orchard left to broom straw, burdock, red clay. I remembered Edwin in his overalls, then remembered seeing in a civil rights march a black man who had carried a hand-lettered sign that had asserted his equality and manhood with such simplicity and dignity and truth that I'd been left speechless. Where was Edwin now, and who had he been in those years of my childhood when I didn't see any more of him than his bare arm and the bright hatchet as he beheaded chickens in front of the woodshed? I'd been taught, and I had learned, to think of him as *different*.

Looking at the yard where the woodshed wasn't, I remembered how my sister—we'd called her Betsy—had cried out, "Do it again!"

when Edwin had cut off the head of a hen, and for the briefest flicker of a moment I wanted to be a child again with Betsy—to see Edwin differently, to see her differently. To "do it again." As a girl I'd kept a list of my sister's sins, her shortcomings, saying in private whatever I wanted to, if only because I could fold the paper or close the diary, concealing what I must have considered evidence I could use in justifying my indifference to her. I could go my way without her, I could look down on her because we were different, too. I'd built the foundation of my life, I realized suddenly, on that sense of difference.

"You can look around," I heard Marie say, "but it's not like it was when Miss T was here. Miss French, she failing bad."

Quickly, I followed Mom and Marie into the kitchen. The old-fashioned telephone—two shorts and a long—no longer hung in the hallway. Where there had been the hulking woodstove, I saw a white electric stove. "May I look upstairs?" I asked Marie. "I used to sleep in Aunt T's room."

Marie nodded, looking me over more closely. "My, my, you're tall. You takes after your daddy," she mused. "But your face look like your Mama's, that's plain as day." Her tone was warm, and Mom beamed with pleasure.

As I left the room, I heard Mom and Marie telling each other how they looked exactly the same as they had years before, little affectionate lies that meant to say they still felt the same way about each other. Marie had grown more stout, I thought, and she now had gray wires in her hair. She still wore the rimless dime-store glasses that made her eyes look enormously brown. She still wore a faded and clean apron over a faded, clean print dress with a flat, white collar.

But how small the rooms had become! Had I slid down that gentle curve of railing? I remembered a steep descent, a long, daring avalanche of speed. Upstairs, I cracked open Aunt T's bedroom door. The room smelled sour and sharp like the den of an animal. No face powder smell, no scent of clean cotton sheets. The walnut-post bed with the imposing headboard—that was there, and also the walnut wardrobe with the mirror on the door. The fire grate was littered with newspaper. The pull shades were pulled down on the door to the sunporch, and the room had the dull glow of old parchment, of brown paper oiled by fried chicken grease. I didn't go inside, even though I wanted to look out to the sunporch, and beyond the sunporch windows into the field where at night I had watched the moon rise behind the clump of holly bushes and the one tall pine tree, singing myself to sleep in a borrowed room where I slept without my sister.

Downstairs, as I passed the kitchen where my mother sat at the table with Marie drinking buttermilk, I heard Marie say that French was so gone in the head she sometimes used the bedroom fireplace for a toilet. "I can't get angry with her. I feel right sorry for her, I do. Gone to jail in her own body, and she used to be so lovely. You remember. Gordon couldn't keep her here in Amelia, she had to go to Richmond to mingle with her set. She used to be so lovely—that's what I think about when I clean up her business."

Wasn't it curious, I thought, how much at home Mom was with Marie? Never mind what she said about keeping "the coloreds" separate, with Marie she was at home, more so than with anyone I'd seen her with in Richmond. I paused, then kept walking, trying to remember French. As a child, I'd rarely seen her. I remembered a tailored elegance that seemed odd at the farm she only visited, even though it was her husband's. After the fire at Harvie Hall, she must have been relieved when Aunt T moved into the smaller farmhouse she and Gordon owned. Aunt T had simply taken the little she had left down the farm road, past the lush garden, around the barn, past the springhouse and the chicken yard, in through the back door that banged and let in flies. After the fire, French could stay in social Richmond, and she did. No, French was not an intimate part of my Amelia childhood, although she was part of what my mother called *family*. Of Aunt T, Mom had always said, "She was like a mother to me."

Even as a child I had always wanted to see Harvie Hall, the house my mother left the day she married. Of course, I couldn't see Aunt T now either; she had died when I was ten, or eleven.

There isn't much left to see, I thought sadly. Again the silhouette of the holly bushes and the tall pine tree flickered into mind. Perhaps they were still there, east of the house. Perhaps if I saw them again, even in the full glare of the sun, I could bring back that long-ago child who depended on the presence of her mother and father for well-being and love, who said her prayers at night and ran freely into the open fields in the morning. What had that felt like? Or was I only imagining an innocence to my childhood, an innocence that was nostalgic and not at all as real as my earlier dismay at the way I regarded my sister—the way I still regarded her, if I could admit that to myself. I almost could.

Crossing around the house, just past the east porch, I heard a shrill cry, a sudden voice calling, "Hey, girl. Hey, girlie-girl. Hey, girl."

I turned in the direction of the voice, which came from just behind me on the porch beneath the sleeping porches and Aunt T's bedroom.

An old woman with long white hair, uncombed and unkempt, chanted at me. She wore a loose, red kimono, and it hung open, exposing clay-yellow skin, low-slung breasts, and a bald pubis, the slit clearly visible. On her pubis only a few white hairs remained, and they shone like wires. Her body had gone backward in time, passing womanhood and girlhood, back to a second childhood. I kept my gaze on her—she was careless, defiant. She flipped her kimono wider open. She lifted it by the edges of the shimmering red material, and her feet shuffled in what I suppose was a dance step. Her eyes never left mine. She wanted me to see. She wanted to be seen.

"Hey, girl. Hey, girl girl girl girl girl."

I backed off slowly and rounded the corner of the house, making for the kitchen. Hearing Mom's laughter float out the screen door, I turned and struck off, walking fast, as if I had somewhere to get to. My breath was ragged, my mouth dry.

The old woman had to be French, but why had French spoken to me like that? Flirtatious, contemptuous. *Girl, girl, girl, girl, girl.*

Against the white house, her red kimono had been bright as blood, the east porch bare as a stage once the play has run and the set's been struck. Again I saw the kimono flash open. She was Crazy Jane. She was the flip side of Joanna Burden in *Light in August*—she was Hecate, I mused. And then I tossed aside the literary references. Here was an old woman gone mad, a foolish mind in a carnival of fleshy collapse. And yet, with the sun filtering through it, the red-as-fire kimono had shaded her white, white skin a sensual pink.

Out of breath, I stopped and looked around. I'd arrived at the old barn, looking down the road in the direction of the tall oaks and black gum trees that marked the foundation of old Harvie Hall. The house had burned when I was a baby. When I was a child, it had stood sentinel in the ashes and wood's earth. When I was a child, little trees had begun to grow where once there had been rooms. Old Harvie Hall, the house my mother yearned back to when she talked of "the olden days," was a brick foundation, one chimney of the original four left standing. This was what was left of the house whose luster, like a ruby, lit up the dark corners of my mother's mind.

The sun hurt my eyes. I pulled a sprig of white clematis off the rusted barbed wire fence and touched the wire thorn lightly with my index finger, pressing down steadily, denting the flesh, stopping short of bringing through the skin a bead of blood. I watched myself, as if I were someone else, finger against barbed wire. Why did I want to hurt myself? I let the moment of standing in the sun with my finger pressed against the barbed wire expand until, like the encounter with French, it had the force of dream. But it wasn't a dream. Seeing French or standing here in the red dirt road—what could feel more starkly real?

I ran my tongue around my lips and swallowed. My mouth was dry, but my hands no longer shook.

What had happened? I had turned the corner of the house, I had heard all the name I really had—*girl, girlie-girl*—and I had seen, as if in a sunstruck mirror, myself: time-warped, time-wived, willful.

Is that what had happened?

I looked at the film of dust on my sandal straps, on my feet. Wearing the road, I walked on until I reached the stand of oaks and black gum trees. Looking at the ruined foundation of the old house and at the trees that had taken root where once there had been floors, I was looking at memory itself, the past and the present fused together.

When I was a child—the phrase shadowed my mind like a refrain—I had hunted the foundations and wood's earth here and found one china cup, white, intact. I remember thinking then, *my mother drank milk from this cup as a child.* This would also have been the house where my mother's wedding photographs had been taken, where she posed in the gauzy dress with the long train around her feet in a swirl.

I let the shade of the oaks and the dapple of light draw me in, imagining a banister, stairs, and a railing. I heard footsteps coming up behind me on the stair—either it would be my grandmother with her long white bolt of hair brushed out silk to her knees, or it was my mother as a young girl, my mother in a cotton nightgown quietly cupping a day-old rabbit, dead.

Now I wanted to make the imagined house real, to dig beneath the leaves and fallen branches, to find another cup, still whole—but I couldn't bring myself to kneel down. Overhead the oaks swayed. Over the field, a cawing; above the cawing, a billow of clouds, towers of white.

Writing a poem in my head, I heard women in long white dresses with puffed sleeves reading aloud from books with blank pages. Quietly their voices crossed over each other like braids, telling the arts of dust and milk, larder and closet. I imagined my mother staring off into space, where she could see—lined up into sentences— her grandchildren, her future, mute cups she must fill with milk, with advice.

*I will never have children,* I whispered to the pied earth beneath the oaks. *I will never have children.*

I spoke with pain and recognition, as if a coal had kissed my mouth.

*What else can you tell me, old house,* I asked. But why should it answer? This house—it wasn't really a home place. Could I admit that?

Although I had imagined that my mother had been raised here, she hadn't been. She'd been raised in McKenney, a girl whose father had died when she was eleven, a girl who would come to be disowned by her mother. With one mind, my own mind, I could see this now. In her stories of the olden days she had combined her memories of her father's house in McKenney and her memories of the house where she'd lived with Aunt T in Amelia, the house that burned. She had constructed a home where there had been none.

And when Mom told her stories—when she told me about her brother Ashton hunting squirrels for Brunswick stew, when she told me about Uncle Billy and Uncle Theo mowing the fields at harvest in circles, when she'd told me about going to bed in the winter with a hot brick at the foot of her bed—I'd seen in my imagination only the smaller farmhouse I had visited and called Aunt T's—the same farmhouse on whose porch a short while ago I'd seen the mad old woman open her red kimono, show me her body, call me girl.

*That's your home place, girl,* I murmured. A place you saw in your mind as your mother told her stories.

When Mom told her stories, I had nested one farmhouse inside another until they fused, or at least lived together uneasily in an illusion of unity. I thought of the Russian matrushka dolls with their identical faces, dolls nested one inside the other. Inside the mother, a daughter; inside the daughter, her daughter; and on down until at the end there was a tiny doll that wouldn't open, a bit of painted wood as hard as a seed.

My mother's romance of the olden days, of country life and fine family, was one story; the pain she didn't like to speak of directly— that was another story, and it was my inheritance as surely as the family Bible had a cover brimstone black. *Oh, everything was simpler then,* my mother's stories had seemed to imply, forgetting to include what had hurt. When my mother told her stories, there was no dark side, no disobedience, no willfulness, lust, or adultery; no questions, no pitfalls; no ambition, no greater knowledge, no greater love.

I would have to tell a different story.

I would have to learn in my own life and away from home what the heart is.

I would have a life that would not be like my mother's—that is what the old house had said.

*She will be wondering where I am,* I thought suddenly, touching my face with surprise. My face was wet with tears. I would have to go back to her. I would have to enter the kitchen as if nothing had happened. Neither my mother nor Marie would see it, the cup of memory I carried in my hands, the broken pieces of an earth-stained, porcelain cup into which my life did not fit.

## August 2006

Late-afternoon shadows slowly lengthen and take the nearby field into dusk and nightfall. Summer or winter outside our house in Connecticut, on a clear night the sky is lit by an endless field of night-blooming stars. A barred owl calls in the woods outside. In summer the frogs croak in the pond; in winter an attic rafter will creak as the house settles beneath the snow that stiffens on the roof.

Whatever the season, or reason, it is good to be unable to sleep at night. Put it another way, I am unwilling to resist wakefulness, a *coming to* in which attention and deep concentration lead the prodigal I am beyond separation and resistance, until I arrive, by way of surrender, closer to home, closer to a relatedness, a *withness*. The wind rises, and I move at rest into the night, listening in the rising wind to the lilt of the pine boughs as they lift and let go, lift and let go. Within the wind, the moon rises and rivers in the shining shadow night is. I try to touch the night within me to the night outside. I try to close the distance. It is the only way suffering is cleared.

And at night, I am with my family.

No one has to be born just once; but change can come late, or too late, or not at all. Sometimes there is no time to define afresh oneself—or another—no matter how events, dramatic or not, expose the old social and psychological flaws and hierarchies, no matter how urgently body and mind send signals of breakdown, clues for renewal.

At night I am with my father, his death mercifully quick, a heart attack at daybreak. He was ninety-two, a man who in his last years knew himself to be loving and loved. "Well," he said, looking down, "I can't help it." He had just agreed to my request that he give Liz the money she would need in order to be moved from Angel House and placed under full nursing care—first, as it turned out, in Farmville where Mom had gone to college; then in private care in Amelia, where, young and beautiful, our mother had gone out to meet her life, her fate. Talking it over with my father, I didn't know the road map for Liz's care—how could I know that her decline would mirror the rising line of my mother's life? I did know that caring for her would be hard and expensive. My parents' frugality and careful investments had left them comfortable, and then some, in their old age, and Uncle Allan had been generous to them in his will. For the first time in their lives, they were well off, but it was too late for my mother, whose habits of mind were fearful and frugal. My sister's dependence on getting and profligate spending had left her needy; the stroke had taken her from her family and from their family printing company, which without her weakened, floundered, and was failing. I was relieved when Dad said he'd help to support Liz. "We won't tell Mom," he said, pausing. "She won't understand."

And so began our partnership in taking care of Liz and Mom. The new bond between my father and me released us into enjoying each other. Dad began to make frequent long-distance phone calls, and we talked and talked until the years of our silences vanished in a simple honesty. In his own room, Dad lived his own life, made his own choices. He visited Mom in the adjoining nursing wing each day, and they would nap together on the double bed the nurses had asked me to buy for them, worried that my parents would tumble out of the narrow single.

After moving into the nursing wing, for some years my mother recovered a measure of her verbal skills. With my parents one night after supper, I wheeled them closer for a good-night kiss before Dad would roll his wheelchair off to his bedroom and I wheel Mom to hers. After a long kiss, Mom said to my father, "Do you want me? Do you want me all night?" Dad rubbed his knees, as he does when he's either embarrassed or delighted by the improbable.

Another night as I sat with Mom, she looked over at the bed and complained, "You know, your father doesn't *do* anything anymore."

"Mom," I replied, "you know, Dad's pretty old now."

"Is he?" she said. "How old is he?"

At the time, my mother was ninety-one, three years older than my father. "He's, let's see, eighty-eight," I replied.

My mother looked at me with that fierce gray-eyed look she gets when she suspects someone's pulling a fast one.

"Well then," she said emphatically, "he's passed me."

After my sister's stroke, Liz was, I think, too much reality for my mother to bear. "I live in the movies," she said, waving away from her everything that might disturb her peace. "Hello, dear," she'd say when I'd bring Liz to see her and Dad, and then she'd retreat into sleepiness. Once I heard her murmur, "To think that a small baby. . . ."

Just after Dad's death, and only months before her own, Liz came finally to live in the room with my mother in the nursing wing of The Chesterfield. Mom lived in periods of confusion and briefer intervals of clarity, and it didn't seem to me that she knew who Liz was, no matter how I coached her in private, reminding her that now she'd have family nearby, a daughter right in the room with her. My mother turned on me a skeptical eye. She still wanted her family around her, I knew that. But the invalid in the next bed, who would shriek with melancholy, who would tease her, or who told dirty jokes to the hilarity of the aides—this was not her daughter.

"It's hard to be kind to mother," Liz announced to me baldly over the phone. "You ought to hear her growl at the aides when they go into her dresser drawers or touch her things."

"Mother has lost her manners," she said decisively.

But wasn't our mother—I tried to reason with her—too old to understand much of what went on? Mom could respond only to a smile, a compliment, an *I love you.* "She just wants to be loved," I said, "and she can't really love us back." This was a fact I accepted, and the acceptance made it easier to offer my mother the love she needed.

In the pause, I could imagine my sister squinting one eye and screwing up her mouth. Then she said, "She's not my mother anymore."

After all our phone calls and talks, after my long visits with Liz, I had to admit to myself that in dark or daylight I wasn't sure I knew her. Her accounts of her marriage differed dramatically from her husband's. I didn't know if she was being finally truthful, or if the stroke was talking. For most of her adult life, she had resisted losing weight. She had been diagnosed with Stein-Leventhal syndrome, whose fateful progression led from ovarian cyst to possible infertility, from obesity to diabetes, heart attack, or stroke.

After her stroke, she watched soap operas or videos of movies from the 1950s. Daily she watched the Food Channel. She overate whenever she could. She indulged self-protectively in romantic illusions about another man in the nursing home; she indulged in despair; she indulged in wild plans for the future. She would live in an apartment by herself; she'd find a job.

*She needs a future, she needs hope,* I'd tell David, my second husband, who was taken aback by her delusions. It wouldn't be compassionate to challenge her, I thought; it wouldn't be compassionate, I thought, not to.

At night, when my thoughts are with my sister, I remember our mother's youthful ambition, her dreams for our success, the force of her will to live through us. Those dreams—it took both my sister and me to live them, to try to, fail to, or, thinking better of it, decide not to.

Talking with my sister at the end of her life often felt like talking to my mother in earlier years. She couldn't be budged from an opinion, especially one rooted in illusion, social custom, or a child's faith in God. She might weep or hang up the phone abruptly if she didn't like what she heard. She never apologized. Perhaps my sister's stroke magnified whatever similarities there were between herself and our mother. Perhaps they both responded to confinement and discomfort similarly. Certainly the faulty reasoning my sister suffered bore some similarity to the mental detours we excuse because of senility. When I found myself comparing them, I'd pull myself up short and ask what gave me the right to judge. I'd remember my own flaws—my stubbornness, my ability to keep judgmental lists of someone else's flaws, to name just two. After I left home, I had missed years of knowing both my mother and my sister. Now my sister's stroke and my mother's aphasia put up opaque screens. Nonetheless, I couldn't stop thinking that both my mother and my sister were *orphans*—that is, they both felt themselves to have been disowned; they felt poor. There were times I couldn't get over how alike they seemed.

"How else do you hold on to your mother if she doesn't love you—or if you *think* she doesn't," my husband asked, reasoning with my dismay. "You become her."

In time, instead of challenging my sister's fantasies—they were her buffers against despair, after all—I cooked up projects for us to do together. We would write a book, *The Prodigal Daughter*. I would write the text, and she said she would illustrate it. *Do you remember the time when.* . . . These words fit easily into our phone conversations, and they brought us closer. At first enthusiastic about the partnership, over time Liz became dispirited, beaten down by the uncompromising reality of her immobility and physical loneliness. No project, no recipe, no menu, no plan for the future diverted her. I knew she wanted to die. She told me many times she wasn't afraid of dying.

When her death came, I had to think of it as the only way change could come to her. Kept comfortable, she slipped away in a day and a half. "Hello, Margaret," she said as her husband held the phone to her ear so that she could hear my voice. After her funeral, an aide from the nursing home took me aside. "Your sister, she tell me many times she knew you were there for her." I swallowed hard and for the first time understood: my sister's last words to me were a greeting, a welcoming home—not a good-bye.

And at night I am with my mother—with the mother I remember loving, with the mother who was too much with me for my own good, with the mother I never had. There are many versions of one's mother. But as a stain fades when water is poured through it, gradually, over the years, my anger and churlish resistance to my mother also faded. How it did so remains, in a way, a mystery—as mysterious as grace, some might say. More than physical distance, for years I needed detachment, tolerance, a sense of humor, a generosity of spirit—and they were hard to come by. One morning, however, well into my forties, I woke up and said to myself, as if I were someone else, *Where did they go?* Where were they, my angers and resentments? I almost missed them, I complained with a puzzled smile, then took back the complaint. Years of hard work—the disciplines of writing, remarriage, counseling, meditation, sobriety—I had these to thank for the ease of being I felt, a lightness of spirit that comes about only after long grieving. I remembered what Alice Miller's book had said about the gifted child, loved for complicated reasons by a self-focused mother, sent out into life to achieve and accomplish and succeed, always hungry for praise, confusing it with love. Reading *Prisoners of Childhood*, I had put the book and my head down on my knees—I was sitting in my study, in an old armchair much like one in my parents' living room in the house on Lexington Road—and I had wrapped my arms around my knees and sobbed with recognition and relief. Someone had named what I felt—it was *loss*. In the midst of having, there was loss; in the midst of abundance, loss; in my mother's arms, loss. And there was no replacing this particular loss: "The former child no longer exists nor do the parents," Miller had written. There was no way to disguise or change the loss; "only mourning for what has been missed, missed at the crucial time, can lead to real healing."

After my father died, my mother's frayed memory protected her from holding on to grief, and it continues to shield her. She doesn't mention my sister. She lives in the nursing wing of The Chesterfield, calling it *a big house*, taken care of by nurses and aides, many of whom live in nearby Amelia County just down the road from Aunt T's old farmhouse. That "family" house has been regentrified. Down the red clay lane, on the footprint of Harvie Hall, there is a new house, still in the Harvie family, with a big summer porch under the tall oaks that have grown up since I was a girl. Now when my mother's younger sister, my aunt Too-Too, phones me, she often talks about the days when my mother brought her from McKenney to live with her in Amelia. It's a new story for me to hear, one that suggests how much it must have meant for my mother to unite with a part of her fractured family, sister and sister.

My mother and I are all that remain of the original family now, just as earlier in my life, with my father overseas in England and with my sister as yet a stitch in my mother's side, we lived, my mother and I, with only each other. Those are days and nights for which, all through the night now, no matter how wakeful I am, I have no memory—unless the memory of being held in her arms survives as this ache to hold her, an ache that feels bred in the bone. Now that I am more her mother than she mine, mine is the hunger to know the child she has irrevocably become, drawn now so far inside herself that I can't touch the hem of her cotton nightdress as she rises out of her body and rambles beyond the spreading fields of wheat and stars, back through the night orchard of pear trees, across the moon-flooded, wild meadow—slowly, oh so slowly, going home.

Margaret Gibson is the author of nine books of poetry, most recently *Icon and Evidence, Autumn Grasses,* and *One Body.* She is Professor Emeritus of English at the University of Connecticut and lives in Preston, Connecticut.